Working for the State

Employment Relations in the Public Services

Edited by

Susan Corby

and

Graham Symon

First published 2011 by
PALGRAVE MACMILLAN

Palgrave Macmillan in the UK is an imprint of Macmillan Publishers
Limited, registered in England, company number 785998, of Houndmills,
Basingstoke, Hampshire RG21 6XS.

Palgrave Macmillan in the US is a division of St Martin's Press LLC,
175 Fifth Avenue, New York, NY 10010.

Palgrave Macmillan is the global academic imprint of the above companies
and has companies and representatives throughout the world.

Palgrave® and Macmillan® are registered trademarks in the United States,
the United Kingdom, Europe and other countries.

ISBN 978–0–230–27863–9

This book is printed on paper suitable for recycling and made from fully
managed and sustained forest sources. Logging, pulping and manufacturing
processes are expected to conform to the environmental regulations of the
country of origin.

A catalogue record for this book is available from the British Library.

Library of Congress Cataloging-in-Publication Data
Working for the state : employment relations in the public services /
edited by Susan Corby and Graham Symon.
p. cm.
Includes index.
ISBN 978–0–230–27863–9 (hardback)
1. Great Britain—Officials and employees. 2. Industrial relations—Great
Britain. I. Corby, Susan, 1941– II. Symon, Graham.
JN425.W67 2011
352.60941—dc23   2011021096

10   9   8   7   6   5   4   3   2   1
20   19 18 17 16 15 14 13 12 11

Printed and bound in Great Britain by
CPI Antony Rowe, Chippenham and Eastbourne

Contents

List of Tables and Figures

Tables

Figures

Notes on Contributors

Stephen Bach is Professor of Employment Relations at the Department of Management, King's College, London. His research focuses on new ways of working in public services, international migration of health professionals and comparative public service HRM. His books include *Employment Relations and the Health Service* (Routledge, 2004) and he is editor of *Managing Human Resources* (Blackwell, 2005).

Susan Corby is Professor of Employment Relations at the University of Greenwich Business School. Before becoming an academic, she was a senior trade union official in two public sector trade unions and has published widely on public sector employment relations and equality. She is currently a member of the Central Arbitration Committee and is carrying out a research project into employment tribunals funded by the Economic and Social Research Council.

Ian Cunningham is Reader in Employment Relations in the Department of Human Resource Management, University of Strathclyde. His research interests include employment issues in non-profit/voluntary organisations, absence management and employee involvement and participation. He has recently published in the journals *Work, Employment and Society*, *The International Journal of Human Resource Management* and *Economic and Industrial Democracy*; he is also currently treasurer of the British Universities Industrial Relations Association (BUIRA).

Michael Gold is Professor of Comparative Employment Relations at Royal Holloway University of London. His principal research interests focus on EU social and employment policy and employee involvement and participation. He recently edited *Employment Policy in the European Union: Origins, Themes and Prospects* (Palgrave Macmillan, 2009) and co-edited *The European Company Statute: A New Approach to Corporate Governance* (Peter Lang, 2009).

Peter Graham is Senior Lecturer in Human Resources and Organisational Behaviour at the University of Greenwich's Business School. He has previously served as an officer in the Royal Navy and has worked as a management consultant. In his academic career he has worked at the Universities of Bath and Cranfield.

Jane Lethbridge is Principal Lecturer at the Public Services International Research Unit (PSIRU) at the University of Greenwich. Her main research interests are the commercialisation of health and social care worldwide, social dialogue and trade union responses to liberalisation and privatisation; topics on which she has published widely. She is currently developing research on the changing nature of professionalisation for teachers, nurses and social workers.

Patrick McGurk is Principal Lecturer in Human Resources and Organisational Behaviour at the University of Greenwich Business School. His research concerns management and leadership development in the public services, and he has published in the *International Journal of Public Sector Management* and the *Journal of Management Development*.

Jean Shaoul is Professor of Public Accountability at Manchester Business School where she focuses on public accountability and social distributional issues in the context of business and public policy. She has written widely in both academic and more popular forums on privatisation – especially water and rail transport – and the use of private finance in public infrastructure in transport and health care in the UK and internationally. She also takes an interest in international regulatory reform and public expenditure and is a regular contributor to the *World Socialist Web Site* (www.wsws.org).

Graham Symon is Senior Lecturer in Human Resources and Organisational Behaviour at the University of Greenwich Business School where he has been since 2008, having previously held posts at other institutions in Scotland and England. His research interests are in the areas of industrial relations and policy analysis. He has published articles and contributed to books on the topics of post-compulsory education policy, trade unions and local governance.

Ulke Veersma is Senior Lecturer in International Human Resource Management at the University of Greenwich Business School. His research specialism is employee participation, particularly in the context of the European social agenda. He has published widely in journals and books. His most recent book – co-edited with Leisink and Steijn – is *Industrial Relations in the New Europe* (Edward Elgar, 2007).

Geoff White is Professor of Human Resource Management and previously Director of Research at the University of Greenwich Business School. After ten years at Incomes Data Services he became an academic specialising and publishing widely in the field of reward management, especially public sector pay. He is currently researching the introduction of a minimum wage in Hong Kong. He has advised the Low Pay Commission, the Local Government Pay Commission, the Universities and Colleges Employers Association, the Booth Inquiry on Police Pay and the Hutton Fair Pay Review. His books include *Employee Reward* (CIPD, 2008) with Perkins and *Reward Management: A Critical Text* (Routledge, 2009) with Druker.

List of Acronyms

ASHE	Annual Survey of Hours and Earnings
BSF	Building Schools for the Future
CCT	Compulsory Competitive Tendering
CEMR-EP	Council of European Municipalities and Regions
COHSE	Confederation of Health Service Employees
DfES	Department for Education and Skills
DM	Diploma in Management
EIS	Educational Institute of Scotland
EMU	European Monetary Union
EPSU	European Federation of Public Service Unions
EUPAN	European Public Administration Network
GCHQ	Government Communications Headquarters
GDP	Gross Domestic Profit
GGE	General Government Expenditure
GMB	General, Municipal and Boilermakers' Union
HCAs	Health care assistants
HLTAs	Higher level teaching assistants
HMIC	Her Majesty's Inspectorate of Constabulary
HMRC	Her Majesty's Revenue and Customs
HR	Human Resources
HRM	Human Resource Management
IMF	International Monetary Fund
IPDS	Integrated Personal Development System
LIFT	Local Investment Finance Trust
NALGO	National Association of Local Government Officers
NAO	National Audit Office
NCVO	National Council for Voluntary Organisations
NHS	National Health Service
NPM	New Public Management
NSPCC	National Society for the Prevention of Cruelty to Children
NUPE	National Union of Public Employees
NUT	National Union of Teachers
OECD	Organisation for Economic Co-operation and Development

PFI	Private Finance Initiative
PIU	Performance and Innovation Unit
PPP	Public Private Partnerships
PSOs	Public Service Organisations
RCN	Royal College of Nursing
SSDCs	Sectoral Social Dialogue Committees
TAs	Teaching Assistants
TUC	Trades Union Congress
TUNED	Trade Unions' National and European Administration Network
TUPE	Transfer of Undertakings (Protection of Employment)
UK	United Kingdom
USA	United States of America

Part I
Introduction

1
From New Labour to a New Era?

Susan Corby and Graham Symon

Introduction

Like Zeus, the ancient Greek King of the Gods, the public sector changes its shape. Thirty-five years ago, the United Kingdom's public sector included, for instance, water, telecommunications and transport services, but they are all now in the private sector. The trajectory is not, however, one way. Thus at the time of writing, some banks – Northern Rock and Royal Bank of Scotland Group – and rail infrastructure – Network Rail – are in the public sector, having previously been in the private sector. Moreover, central and local governments and the National Health Service (NHS) commission private sector organisations to provide some of their services. Also, just as Zeus's lovers may not always have appreciated who he was, it is sometimes difficult to appreciate what is in the public sector. For instance universities are classified by the Office for National Statistics as private sector organisations, although many a bystander – and even university employees – would consider that they are part of the public sector.[1]

European Union law denotes even wider boundaries. It uses the term 'emanation of the state'. This is defined as a body which provides a public service under the control of government and has for that purpose special powers beyond that which result from the normal rules applicable to relations between individuals. This definition, therefore, covers not only what are commonly regarded as public sector organisations, it also covers privatised industries, transport and some services – for instance, prisons – run by the private sector.

Although the composition of the public sector may change over time and its boundaries are contestable and blurred by contracting out, this book argues that the public sector and its employment relations are distinctive and thus merit separate study. This distinctiveness does not relate to the absence of profit, as not-for-profit organisations can be found in the private sector. Nor does it relate to the law. The UK, in contrast to most European countries, is unusual in never having subjected public employees as a whole to a separate legal regime (Bach and Winchester, 2003; *see also* Chapter 2), although certain categories of workers, such as the police have long been subject to distinctive statutory rules and procedures (Morris, 2004).

So to what does the distinction relate? Partly it relates to the greater strength of trade unions in the public sector in terms of membership, density and union recognition, in comparison to the private sector (Barratt, 2009), though even here there are exceptions. For instance there are no recognised trade unions in the police and the armed forces. Partly it relates to the reward systems in the public sector, in comparison to the private sector – for instance pay review bodies operate only in the public sector (Corby and Lindop, 2009). Partly it relates to the fact that the public sector workforce is distinguishable from the private sector: more feminised, older, more highly educated and professionalised and with longer job tenure (Matthews, 2010). Principally, however, it relates to the fact that those working in the public sector are directly or indirectly working for the state and thus public sector employment relations is suffused with the important dimension of political power. This dimension of political power has various and complex sources: ministers, parliament, local government councillors, school governors and ultimately the electorate. Also, the state exercises considerable economic might in most industrialised societies as distributor and custodian of common goods and regulator of economic activity. So the public sector is 'enveloped in a much more complex web of relationships than simple customer-provider' (Storey, 1992: 56).

This chapter first explores these distinctions. Next it provides historical background to public sector employment relations, starting from the mid-nineteenth century, discussing 'Whitleyism' after World War I, followed by the burgeoning of the welfare state post 1945 and the financial crises of the late 1960s and 1970s with their high levels of inflation and the consequent resort to wage restraint by successive governments, particularly for public sector employees. It then focuses on the Conservative governments of 1979–97 looking both at the governments' actions and the widely documented ideological shift from social democracy to neoliberalism, with associated debates of public choice and notions of producer capture and crowding out, considering how and to what extent such tendencies impact upon employment strategies and practices.

Following this scene setting, the chapter turns to New Labour and its so-called Third Way, 'modernising' agenda, examining its rationale and its differences from and similarities to neoliberalism. It also considers the contradictions between New Labour's belief in market mechanisms, with the individual as an informed consumer and the penchant for diri-giste control and the tension between fiscal discipline and the espoused aim of social justice. The chapter then makes some preliminary points about the new government's approach, looking both at the changes being envisaged for the public sector, the continuities with the past and the tensions that remain. It finally outlines the book's structure and the forthcoming chapters.

Distinguishing the public sector

The main organisations comprising the UK public sector are in the following sub-sectors: central and local government, health care, education, the police, armed forces and the fire services. As we have already said, the defining characteristic of the public sector is the political dimension. Nevertheless the degree of political control varies. Civil servants are directly subject to the wishes of the government, and employment relations changes can be made by decree, such as the ending of national bargaining in the civil service. In other parts of the public sector, however, there are mediating forces, ranging from the relatively powerful – as in the devolved administrations and local government where the controlling political party may differ from that in government – to the relatively weak, such as the boards of quangos (non-departmental public bodies) and NHS trusts.

Fredman and Morris (1989:6) and Morris (2004) argue that there are a number of features relating to the political power of the State, which distinguishes employment in the public sector from private sector employment. First, the government has the power to initiate legislation and to take executive action, which impacts directly on employment relations. For instance it legislated to ban the Prison Officers' Association from inducing industrial action in 1994 (Corby, 2002). Second, the State derives the revenue to pay public sector employees primarily from taxation and not primarily from the output of employees. This allows the government when dealing with its employees to give priority to political or macro-economic factors, rather than commercial ones. For instance, where industrial action has a financial impact, public sector employers – unlike most private sector employers – have the resources to make a political decision not to accede to the demands of employees, whatever the financial cost.

Third, the government, unlike private sector employers, can justify employment relations decisions on grounds of national or public interest. For instance a minister may overturn arbitration decisions in respect of Government Communications Headquarters (GCHQ) on grounds of 'public interest'. Fourth, the State as employer, unlike private sector employers, is subject to the constraints of parliament and both central and local governments are ultimately accountable to their electorates. One concomitant is that there are more formal reporting rules and procedures relating to recruitment and promotion in the public sector than in the private sector. Fifth, public sector employers may be subjected to judicial review and more recently to cases brought under the Human Rights Act 1998.

Beaumont (1992:10) essentially confirms these points, observing that 'public sector organisations' goals are more numerous, intangible and conflicting than is the case for the private sector'. Whereas the private sector employer is concerned with profit and loss, the state has no such relatively simple objective and its role as direct or indirect employer of one-fifth of the workforce is co-mingled with its role as macro-economic manager and political master.

Historical background 1850–1979

We have already argued that the nature of public sector employment relations is distinguishable from private sector employment relations and thus separate description and analysis is justified. Now we briefly summarise the historical background, before looking in more detail at New Labour.

Farnham and Horton (1996) categorise the history of employment relations in the UK public sector up until 1979 into three phases: the public sector's emergence in Victorian Britain; its development in the twentieth century between the two world wars and its expansion and widening scope after World War II (1939–45).

The first phase essentially started with the introduction of regularised employment in the civil service as a result of the Northcote–Trevelyan Report (1853), which recommended open recruitment conducted by independent boards and appointment and promotion based on merit. Organisational structures and relationships of this emerging model ostensibly aspired to classic Weberian notions of the bureaucracy (*see* Du Gay, 2000). Indeed, emanating from the Napoleonic Wars at the turn of the nineteenth century, state apparatus had to expand to administer new models of tax collection to fund warfare. In turn, due to the necessities of the embryonic creep of democratic accountability and the demands of administering an expanding British Empire this state apparatus developed into the archetypal civil service bureaucracy of hierarchy, regulation, process and career (Ferguson, 2001). This is not to say that all arms of the state exuded ethics and propriety; around the time of Northcote–Trevelyan the rather piecemeal Metropolitan Boards of Works that delivered local services were notorious for corruption and inefficiencies among their poorly paid and ill-treated workforce and managers, a scenario resolved ultimately by the formalisation of local government structures and duties and, perhaps, the judicious intervention of righteous 'city fathers' (*see* Hunt, 2004).

The second half of the nineteenth century witnessed the further formalisation and expansion of the state at central and local levels and with it the development of collective employee representation in the public sector. This occurred with both specific public sector unions, as well as by the craft unions within the Royal Ordnance factories, Royal Dockyards and the Her Majesty's Stationery Office (Corby and White, 1999). The former included a teachers' union – the National Union of Elementary Teachers (with a parallel Educational Institute of Scotland), whose members were employed by local school-governing bodies but paid from government grants, and civil service departmental associations such as in the Post Office (then part of the civil service) in 1854 and in Taxes and Excise in 1858 (Beaumont, 1992; Clegg et al., 1964).

The second phase saw both the growth of public sector unions and the development of collective bargaining. For instance, union density in national government rose spectacularly from 18.8 per cent in 1910 to 84 per cent in 1933. Union density in local government and education rose from 33 per cent in 1910 to 52 per cent in 1933 and the equivalent figures for posts/telecoms were 53 per cent and 64 per cent (Clegg, 1985: 545).

This union growth was largely as a result of the government's adoption of a system of collective bargaining and joint consultation. In 1917 such a system had been recommended by J. H. Whitley for British industry and, to give a lead, the government introduced a so-called Whitley system for its own employees – first for those working in government industrial establishments and then from 1919 for non-industrial civil servants at national and departmental level. Also on Whitley lines, in 1919 the government set up the Burnham Committee, a joint national level employer/union committee but with an independent chair, to determine school teachers' pay and conditions. In local government, regional joint councils were established for white-collar staff and a national joint council for local authority manuals, while local authority employers joined with private employers to establish joint councils for gas, electricity, water supply and tramways (Clegg, 1985).

The third phase, from 1945 to 1979, witnessed the expansion of the welfare state and the growth in public sector employment. In 1948 the NHS was established and its employment relations were institutionalised on Whitley lines, while the education sector expanded both because of the raising of the school leaving age and the setting up of new universities and polytechnics. Also after World War II, many industries, including coal, electricity, gas and the railways, were nationalised.

The post-1945 era has been associated – however problematically – with the production paradigm of Fordism (Kirkpatrick, 2006). An ambitious and self-consciously interventionist and expansionist social democratic welfare settlement had been developed based on the blueprint of Beveridge (1942). This was combined with a similarly interventionist industrial policy and a production strategy based on mass-production, central co-ordination and the Keynesian aspiration of sustaining growth and consumption by maintaining full employment in the industrial and public sectors. As a result, national collective agreements became the norm albeit concurrent with vigorous shop-floor industrial relations. It has also been suggested that the technologies and labour process associated with Fordism had an isomorphic impact on the configuration of structures, processes and employment practices in the public sector, with the consequence that the labour process in the public sector has been positioned as part of the general 'politics of production' (Cousins, 1986; Kirkpatrick, 2006). As such, characteristics of Fordism have been associated with branches of the public services such as the NHS and even the education system (Kirkpatrick, 2006).

Not only did the period 1945–79 witness a growth in public sector employment, it also witnessed a growth of public sector professionals and the feminisation of the workforce. For instance professionals in the NHS included doctors, dentists, pharmacists, biochemists, occupational therapists, chiropodists and radiographers. By 1960 a third of the civil service non-industrial workforce were women and over half in local authorities (Farnham and Horton, 1996).

This expansion of the public sector was underpinned by favourable economic conditions from the 1950s to the late 1960s and a political consensus. In this benign context, it is argued that the state was a good or model employer. This model-employer stance included the encouragement of trade unionism, national-level structures for collective bargaining and joint consultation and – for many public sector employees – pay determination based on fair comparisons with the private sector, de facto job security with pensions and sick pay, transparent and detailed procedures for recruitment and promotion and effective grievance machinery (Hepple, 1982).

Nonetheless, this view of the state as a model employer has not gone unchallenged. Coffey and Thornley (2009), for instance, distinguish between procedures and pay outcomes, pointing to areas of low pay and its correspondence with women's employment, while Winchester and Bach (1995) maintain that the idea of the State as a good employer was an aspiration, but the aspiration was not always fully translated into practice. Irrespective of the views of current academics, however, it should be noted that at the time the State was widely regarded as having unproblematic employment relations. For instance the Donovan Commission on employers' associations and trade unions (Royal Commission, 1968) virtually ignored the public sector.

From the late 1960s, however, public sector employment relations began to become less harmonious when the rate of economic growth fell back and unemployment and the rate of inflation rose, exacerbated by the oil crisis of 1973. Indeed the oil crisis is seen – particularly by the Marxian and regulation schools (*see* Kirkpatrick, 2006) – as just one aspect of the 'perfect storm' that was a cyclical crisis of the Fordist mode of production, which had serious implications for industrial production, the viability of the 'overloaded' state apparatus of the day and the cohesiveness and stability of society, illustrated by alarming levels of industrial unrest. As is the way with such crises, it is incumbent upon the State to intervene and attempt to mitigate the shock to the system of production (Harvey, 2007). The response was for successive governments to seek to contain public expenditure by limiting the pay increases of those who worked directly or indirectly for the State through a series of incomes policies and in 1976, after intervention by the International Monetary Fund, the Treasury replaced demand-led expenditure for the civil service and the NHS with cash limits. This resulted in trade unions taking industrial action and banishing 'their traditionally moderate image' (Winchester and Bach, 1995), culminating in 1978–79 in the 'Winter of Discontent' when there was substantial disruption by public sector unions. This resulted in widespread anti-union sentiment and the replacement of a Labour government by what turned out to be four Conservative administrations lasting 18 years.

The Conservative governments 1979–97

When Margaret Thatcher was elected as the prime minister of a Conservative government in 1979, she embarked on a series of radical reforms intended to make the public sector more efficient, reforms which were continued by her successor, John Major. Essentially she was of the view that competition encouraged organisations to become efficient and so the public sector should be opened up to the market. A key exponent of this theory, often termed 'neoliberalism' or 'marketisation', was Hayek, 'the prime minister's [Mrs Thatcher's] own favourite political thinker' (Young, 1990: 200). Interestingly, Hayek had been a vocal critic of the post-1945 Beveridge–Keynes social democratic settlement, explaining how collectivisation and the expansion of state control would compromise social and economic development (Hayek, 1944). Although the New Right (as Thatcher and her neoliberal colleagues were termed) are often portrayed as an ideological insurgency, neoliberalism was an idea whose time had come in the history of capitalism and should be seen as part of the series of measures by the state to mitigate the 1970s crisis of capitalism discussed earlier (Harvey, 2007).

Translating theory into practice, key parts of the public sector were privatised: British Telecom, British Airways, public utilities (gas, water, electricity), steel, coal, the railways and parts of the civil service, such as government research laboratories. Bach and Winchester (2003) maintain that the scale of the privatisation programme was much greater than that adopted by governments in other European countries.

The Conservative governments also reduced the size of the public sector by requiring compulsory competitive tendering, under which there are rival bids from in-house teams and the private sector, with contracts being awarded essentially on the basis of the lowest cost. From 1980 central government required local authorities to put out to tender certain services, such as building repair and highways. Similarly, in 1983 it required the NHS to put out to tender some of its services: catering, cleaning and laundry; and under the Local Government Acts of 1988 and 1992 it required yet more local authority services to be put out to tender, including refuse collection, street cleaning, ground maintenance, sports facility management, security, car parking and housing management.

Privatisations and contracting out, however, were not the only mechanisms the government used to reduce the public sector. From the early 1990s, it adopted the Private Finance Initiative (PFI). Under PFI the private sector is both a provider of services (as with contracting out) and also capital. For instance the private sector both build and run prisons or hospitals, with a contract often lasting many years (20 plus), unlike the shorter contracts (five years or less) under tendering (Corby and White, 1999).

Where it was not possible to privatise parts of the public sector, Conservative governments introduced proxies for market mechanisms. Thus in the civil service it introduced executive agencies, separated structurally and financially from their parent departments and with framework agreements specifying their objectives. By 1 April 1997 there were 110 agencies in the home civil service including bodies as diverse as the Meteorological Office, Vehicle Inspectorate and Ordnance Survey (Government Statistical Service, 1998). In the NHS as a result of the National Health Service and Community Care Act 1990, the government created what it called an internal market with purchasers (so-called GP fundholders and health authorities) and providers (NHS hospitals which were renamed trusts) (Corby, 1992).

In education, the government legislated to wrest further-education colleges and polytechnics (renamed universities) from local authority control and to establish them as independent corporations managed by boards of governors, albeit retaining substantial central government funding, and giving boards of governors significant control over staffing and expenditure. The result was local management of schools, or full control if schools opted for grant-maintained status (Farnham and Giles, 1996).

The Conservative governments' reforms also included reducing the power of the trade unions through a series of legislative measures, notably restricting unions' freedom to take industrial action and outlawing union membership as a condition of employment. These trade union restrictions applied across the private and public sectors, but in addition the government adopted specific anti-union measures in the public sector: for instance, it banned trade union membership at GCHQ, the electronic intelligence gathering centre, and outlawed industrial action by prison officers (Smith and Morton, 1993, 1994).

All the changes summarised above had profound effects on the shape and texture of public sector employment and the experiences of public sector employees. Furthermore, given the belief in the superior efficiency of the private sector, public sector managers were exhorted to emulate private sector practices. For instance, in 1996 the Cabinet Office introduced a benchmarking exercise into the civil service derived from the private sector (Horton, 2000). Also, private sector managers were encouraged to join the public sector, with promotion from within being replaced by open competition. As a result, 13 per cent of those appointed to be chief executives of civil service agencies between 1988 and 1996 came from the private sector (Horton and Jones, 1996). This approach of the public sector emulating the private sector was termed the 'new public management' (Dunleavy and Hood, 1994) and was prevalent not only in the UK but also in many other developed countries (Bach and Della Rocca, 2000; Organisation for Economic Co-operation and Development, 1995).

Another policy consequence of a belief in the superiority of the market was a perception of the citizen as consumer, wielding power in the market place. The Conservatives could, therefore, adopt the language of choice and individual freedom 'with the public no longer being viewed, or viewing themselves, as passive clients to be treated at best with benevolent paternalism and at worst authoritarian resentment' (Thompson, 2007: 20). A key example is the 1991 Citizen's Charter.

Other theoretical dimensions of marketisation include the theories of crowding out and producer capture. Crowding out posits that not only does the State do what it is doing less efficiently than the private sector, it appropriates resources otherwise available for the private sector and requires taxes from those who produce marketed goods and services, which reduces profitability and adversely affects national economic performance. This theory justified the privatisations, described above, as well as tax reductions (*see* Thompson, 2007, for a full discussion).

As to producer capture, the notion is that those working in the public sector, and the trade unions and professional bodies which represent them, act in their own self-interest, rather than that of their clients and seek status by maximising their budgets. This resulted in various policies to reduce producer autonomy including capping local government rates (White and Hutchinson, 1996), introducing general managers in hospitals to curtail the power of doctors (Griffiths, 1983) and introducing a national curriculum and standardised assessments in schools (Farnham and Giles, 1996).

The policies of the Conservative governments were not only derived from and closely aligned with New Right theories, they were also politically convenient. For instance, privatisations helped to bolster the public coffers, while initiatives such as rate capping and the Citizen's Charter were popular. Nevertheless, there were sub-sectoral differences. For instance the government imposed considerable change on the civil service, but little change on the police. Moreover, occasionally political and ideological considerations did not coincide, with the former trumping the latter: for instance the creation of a pay review body for nurses and paramedics in 1983 and for teachers a decade later rather than letting the pay of these groups to be determined by collective bargaining (*see* White, Chapter 5, in this volume).

New Labour 1997–2010

When Labour came to power in 1997, its underpinning philosophy was termed the Third Way and its chief proponent was Anthony Giddens. According to Giddens (1998:70), '[T]he third way argues that what is necessary is ... to go beyond those on the right "who say government is the enemy" and those on the left "who say government is the answer"'. Thus, according to Giddens, the Third Way rejects both neoliberalism and the shrinking of the state and social democracy and the expansion of the state. State legitimacy has to be gained by transparency, openness, efficiency, devolution and the fostering of an active civil society. 'Where government withdraws from direct involvement, its resources might well be necessary to support activities that local groups take over or introduce – above all in poorer areas' (Giddens, 1998:80).

Fredman (2004) has argued that the Third Way envisages a market economy, but with market regulation, albeit not to such an extent that wealth creation is stymied. She also argues that the Third Way puts individual autonomy centre stage, thus rejecting state action to ensure equality of outcome, yet rejecting the neoliberal concept of the individual as a free market agent requiring only formal equal treatment before the law. Further, she submits that the Third Way recognises that unequal outcomes are often the result of a lack of choices and so it seeks to expand individuals' choice, for instance choice in education and childcare and income support. Third Way theorists also argue for accommodation, so that there is partnership, not conflict, at work and so that work/life balance enables accommodation between domestic and employment demands.

This Third Way discourse was translated into a policy framework for the public sector by the White Paper Modernising Government (Cabinet Office, 1999). In summary, New Labour argued that the public services had been neglected and undervalued by the Conservatives, who had assumed that the private sector was best. The bedrock of New Labour's policy, therefore, was an increase in spending on the public sector and, as the public sector is people-intensive, not capital-intensive, this led to an increase in the number of public sector employees. The increase, however, was not immediate as the government initially stuck to its predecessor's spending plans and the increase was halted by the financial crisis starting at the end of 2008 (*see* Shaoul, Chapter 3, in this volume). Also, as part of valuing the public sector, the government sought to treat its public servants fairly, for instance reforming pay systems (*see* White, Chapter 5, in this volume) and acting as a model employer in respect of diversity and family-friendly provisions (*see* Corby, Chapter 6, in this volume).

Arguably the New Labour policy initiative that is likely to endure in the history books is the administrative devolution of powers to Scotland, Wales, Northern Ireland and – to a more limited extent – London (*see* Adams and Robinson, 2002). Although New Labour's wider, more ambitious programme of 'regionalisation' within England did not take off to the desired extent, the capacity of the devolved administrations to make policy decisions divergent from the Westminster/Whitehall agenda has been real and profound. Scotland's modus operandi in particular towards the running of the public sector – with inevitable consequences for employment matters – has taken a markedly different path both under the successive Labour–Liberal Democrat and Scottish National Party regimes. This has courted considerable controversy and has brought Scotland's (and to a lesser extent Wales's) public spending settlement into UK public consciousness, as their spending per capita is higher than in England and their approach to service delivery more corporatist and comprehensive.

As part of an ongoing effort to make the public services more efficient, New Labour adopted a number of initiatives. Chief among these was the setting of targets and the monitoring of performance; the introduction of 'joined up government' for example one-stop shops for those seeking work; the matching of services to people's lives by longer opening hours, for example NHS Direct and electronic delivery, available at any time of the day or night; giving users information so that informed choices could be made (e.g. league tables for hospitals); 'partnership' agreements with the public sector trade unions; and replacing the Conservatives' obligation on local authorities to accept tenders for outsourcing on the basis of price with 'Best Value', a more complex system enabling quality to be taken into account (Bach, 2010; Morris, 2004).

Other initiatives in accordance with this public sector policy framework, included new arrangements for developing public sector leaders as 'key players' (Cabinet Office, 1999) (*see* McGurk, Chapter 9, in this volume); acting in partnership with the public sector trade unions, recognising 'the contribution they can and do make' (ibid.) (*see* Symon, Chapter 10, in this volume); bringing in private sector consultants with the aim of improving public sector efficiency (*see* Graham, Chapter 11, in this volume); and changing labour processes with the aim of improving public sector workers' efficiency. This has included introducing assistants to professionals, such as classroom, health care, social care assistants and Taylorising labour processes by demarcating the work of professionals from the work of assistants (*see* Bach, Chapter 7, in this volume).

There have been many criticisms of New Labour's approach. Chief among them was a criticism that despite its emphasis on expanding opportunities, it showed little or no concern about the unequal distribution of wealth and power both nationally and also in the public sector where there are gendered pockets of low pay (Coffey and Thornley, 2009). Other criticisms of Labour's approach centred on the fact that its emphasis on individual choice, for instance a parent's choice of school, assumed equality of access to knowledge; and, importantly, that despite its rhetoric, in practice New Labour's industrial relations policy amounted 'to little more than acceptance of employer dominance inherited from the Thatcherite era, albeit leavened by measured amounts of European "partnership" rhetoric' (Bain and Taylor, 2007: 57).

Allied with this was the continuance of neoliberalism and marketisation (Wood, 2010). In particular, Labour extended the scope of the private sector in providing public sector services through the private finance initiative, renamed public/private partnership (PPP) used, for example, in London underground and for the building of schools and hospital, a 'book-keeping trick that would allow capital expenditure off the government's balance sheet' (Wood, 2010). New Labour also brought in the private and/or not-for-profit sector, under contract, to run public services, for example educational establishments, hospital operations and general practitioner and social services. Cunningham discusses this at length in Chapter 8. According to Julius (2008) cited in Bach (2010), the UK spends a larger share of its gross domestic product on outsourced services than any OECD country except Sweden and Australia. These developments, among others, have significant ramifications for any notion of 'public sector ethos', which Lethbridge considers in some depth in Chapter 4.

A further criticism is that New Labour not only continued with, but indeed extended Conservative policies as regards target setting and monitoring. This often had perverse consequences. For instance Rose (2009) reported ploys adopted by health service professionals to beat a four-hour deadline on NHS accident and emergency waiting times. In short, there were contradictions in New Labour's approach to the public sector with its belief in market mechanisms, with the individual as an informed consumer, and dirigiste controls to prevent producer capture and the contradiction between cost pressures and New Labour's espoused aim of fairness.

The Coalition

In some respects 2010 marked a watershed. Politically there was a change in government, from New Labour to a Conservative/Liberal Democrat coalition, and economically there was a change from an age of expansion in the role of the state to an age of retrenchment with repercussions for the public sector. First, the shape and size of the public sector is to be reduced. Royal Mail will be privatised and certain so-called quangos (non-departmental public bodies) will be abolished (Cabinet Office, 2010). Furthermore, as the Government has said that the deficit reduction programme takes precedence over any other measures and as there is a commitment to reducing the public sector, this will inevitably have repercussions for the number of public sector jobs.

Second, according to the Coalition agreement, the Government will review the terms and conditions of public servants, particularly in respect of the police (Cabinet Office, 2010: 13); reform the 'rigid national pay and conditions rules' of teachers (Cabinet Office, 2010: 29); and introduce public sector pay restraint, 'while anyone paid more than the Prime Minister in the centrally funded public sector [will have] to have their salary signed off by the Treasury' (Cabinet Office, 2010) (*see* White, Chapter 5, in this volume, for more details). In addition, the Government will establish an 'independent commission to review the long-term affordability of public sector pensions' (Cabinet Office, 2010: 26) and reform the redundancy arrangements for civil servants (Cabinet Office, 2010: 27).

Yet despite these changes, there are continuities. Both New Labour and the Coalition remain wedded to a neoliberal approach, encapsulated in the Coalition's plans to increase competition through greater private sector provision of public services, for instance ensuring new providers can enter the state school system and the criminal justice system.

A number of tensions are explored in greater detail in the forthcoming chapters: the tension between the Government's espoused desire to promote equal pay and its need to control public sector pay; the tension between the Government's espoused desire to promote flexibility in labour processes and the wooing of professionals who will insist on preserving demarcations with non-professionals (Williams and Scott, 2010). Moreover, the new age of austerity increases the existing tension between making public servants dependable and making public servants disposable, with on the one hand the cutting of jobs and, on the other hand, the rhetoric of improving the civil service and making it easier to reward the best civil servants (Cabinet Office, 2010). These tensions will be played out differently in the different sub-sectors.

Ultimately, policymakers find themselves in a plethora of dilemmas over how to design and deliver public services, and how effectively to engage and deploy the associated vast force of labour with its complex institutional and social dynamics. This is within a context of apparently unprecedented fiscal restraint as the Coalition pursues its espoused aim of 'getting the deficit down'. Commentators from both right and left have complained that current models of welfare and public service delivery are obsolete and unsustainable. In seeking to mitigate these factors, policymakers must overcome and/or accommodate not merely fiscal obstacles, but also entrenched vested interests, and at the same time win the support of the electorate and the co-operation of over six million employees.

The forthcoming chapters

The book is structured as follows: after this introductory section, the second section looks at context of the UK public sector – the European context, the economic and financial context and public sector ethos. The third section looks at particular issues: public sector reward policy and practice and equal opportunities. The fourth section looks at actors: sub-professionals, third sector providers of public services, the leaders of public service organisations, organised labour and consultants in the public sector. In the final section we pick out the main themes so far and look forward. Ultimately the concluding chapter seeks to draw from the complex, multifaceted and often seemingly contradictory analyses, key themes and trajectories in public sector employment that will enable enhanced understanding of this most important of phenomena.

Note

1. At the time of writing there is only one university that receives no direct government grant and is therefore not subject to the same level of regulation as all the other universities.

References

Adams, J. and Robinson, P. (eds) (2002) *Devolution in Practice: Public Policy Differences within the UK* (London: IPPR).

Bach, S. (2010) 'Public sector industrial relations: the challenge of modernisation', in T. Colling and M. Terry (eds), *Industrial Relations: Theory and Practice*, 3rd edn (Chichester: Wiley).

Bach, S. and Della Rocca, G. (2000) 'The management strategies of public service employers in Europe', *Industrial Relations Journal*, 31:2, 82–96.

Bach, S. and Winchester, D. (2003) 'Industrial relations in the public sector', in P. Edwards (ed.), *Industrial Relations: Theory and Practice*, 2nd edn (Oxford: Blackwell).

Bain, P. and Taylor, P. (2007) 'A "Third Way"? Industrial relations under New Labour', in G. Mooney and A. Law (eds) *New Labour/Hard Labour? Restructuring and Resistance inside the Welfare Industry* (Bristol: Policy Press).

Barratt, C. (2009) *Trade Union Membership 2008* (London: Dept for Business, Enterprise and Regulatory Reform).

Beaumont, P. (1992) *Public Sector Industrial Relations* (London: Routledge).

Beveridge, W. (1942) *Social Insurance and Allied Services*, Cmd 6404 (London: HMSO).

Cabinet Office (1999) *Modernising Government*, Cm 4310 (London: Cabinet Office).

Cabinet Office (2010) *The Coalition: Our Programme for Government* (London: Cabinet Office).

Clegg, H. A. (1985) *A History of British Trade Unions since 1889*, vol II, 1911–1933 (Oxford: Oxford University Press).

Clegg, H. A., Fox, A. and Thompson, A. F. (1964) *A History of British Trade Unions since 1889*, vol I, 1889–1910 (Oxford: Oxford University Press).

Coffey, D. and Thornley, C. (2009) *Globalization and Varieties of Capitalism* (Basingstoke: Palgrave Macmillan).

Corby, S. (1992) 'Prospects for industrial relations in NHS trusts', *Industrial Relations Journal*, 22:3, 170–180.

Corby, S. (2002) 'On parole: prison service industrial relations', *Industrial Relations Journal*, 33:4, 286–297.

Corby, S. and Lindop, E. (2009) 'Drawing the threads together', in S. Corby, S. Palmer and E. Lindop (eds) *Rethinking Reward* (Basingstoke: Palgrave Macmillan).

Corby, S. and White, G. (1999) 'From the New Right to New Labour', in S. Corby and G. White (eds) *Employee Relations in the Public Services* (London: Routledge).

Cousins, C. (1986) 'The labour process in the state welfare sector', in D. Knights and H. Willmott (eds) *Managing the Labour Process* (Aldershot: Gower).

Du Gay, P. (2000) *In Praise of Bureaucracy: Weber – Organization – Ethics* (London: Sage).

Dunleavy, P. and Hood, C. (1994) 'From old public administration to new public management', *Public Money and Management*, 14 (3), 34–43.

Farnham, D. and Giles, L. (1996) 'Education', in D. Farnham and S. Horton (eds) *Managing People in the Public Services* (Basingstoke: Macmillan).

Farnham, D. and Horton, S. (1996) 'Traditional people management', in D. Farnham and S. Horton (eds), *Managing People in the Public Services* (Basingstoke: Macmillan).

Ferguson, N. (2001) *The Cash Nexus: Money and Power in the Modern World 1700–2000* (London: Allen Lane).

Fredman, S. (2004) 'The ideology of New Labour law', in C. Barnard, S. Deakin and G. Morris (eds), *The Future of Labour Law* (Oxford: Hart).

Fredman, S. and Morris, G. (1989) *The State as Employer* (London: Mansell).

Giddens, A. (1998) *The Third Way* (Cambridge: Polity Press).

Government Statistical Service (1998) *Civil Service Statistics* (London: Cabinet Office).

Griffiths, R. (1983) *NHS Management Inquiry* (London: Dept of Health and Social Security).

Harvey, D. (2007) *Spaces of Global Capitalism: Towards and Theory of Uneven Geographical Development* (London: Verso).

Hayek, F. (1944) *The Road to Serfdom* (London: Routledge and Keegan Paul).

Hepple, B. (1982) 'Labour law and public employees', in Lord Wedderburn of Charlton and W. Murphy (eds) *Labour Law and the Community* (London: Institute of Advanced Legal Studies).

Horton, S. (2000) 'Competency management in the British civil service', *International Journal of Public Sector Management*, 13:4, 354–368.

Horton, S. and Jones, J. (1996) 'Who are the new public managers? An initial analysis of 'Next Steps' chief executives and their managerial role', *Public Policy and Administration*, 11:4, 18–44.

Hunt, T. (2004) *Building Jerusalem: The Rise and Fall of the Victorian City* (London: Weidenfield & Nicolson).

Julius, D. (2008) *Public Services Industry Review* (London: Dept of Business, Enterprise and Regulatory Reform).

Kirkpatrick, I. (2006) 'Post-Fordism and organizational change in state administration', in L. Enrique-Alonso and M. Martinez Lucio (eds) *Employment Relations in a Changing Society: Assessing the Post-Fordist Paradigm* (Basingstoke: Palgrave Macmillan).

Matthews, D. (2010) 'The changing face of public sector employment 1999–2009', *Economic and Labour Market Review*, 4:57, 28–35.

Morris, G. (2004) 'The future of the public/private law divide' in C. Barnard, S. Deakin and G. Morris (eds), *The Future of Labour Law* (Oxford: Hart).

Organisation for Economic Co-operation and Development (1995) *Governance in Transition: Public Management Reforms in OECD Countries* (Paris: OECD).

Rose, D. (2009) 'Hospitals "use ploys" to beat 4-hour deadline on A & E waiting times', *The Times*, 18 November.

Royal Commission on Trade Unions and Employers' Associations (1968) *Report*, Cmnd 3623 (London: HMSO).

Smith, P. and Morton, G. (1993) 'Union exclusion and the decollectivisation of industrial relations in contemporary Britain', *British Journal of Industrial Relations*, 31:1, 97–114.

Smith, P. and Morton, G. (1994) 'Union exclusion: next steps', *Industrial Relations Journal*, 25:1, 222–233.

Storey, J. (1992) 'Human resource management in the public sector' in G. Salaman (ed.), *Human Resource Strategies* (London: Sage).

Thompson, N. (2007) 'From Hayek to New Labour: The changing ideology of public sector provision' in P. Dibben, P. James, I. Roper and G. Wood (eds) *Modernising Work in Public Services* (Basingstoke: Palgrave Macmillan).

White, G. and Hutchinson, B. (1996) 'Local government' in D. Farnham and S. Horton (eds) *Managing People in the Public Services* (Basingstoke: Macmillan).

Winchester, D. and Bach, S. (1995) 'The State: the public sector' in P. Edwards (ed.), *Industrial Relations: Theory and Practice* (Oxford: Blackwell).

Williams, S. and Scott, P. (2010) 'Shooting the past? The modernisation of Conservative Party employment relations policy under David Cameron', *Industrial Relations Journal*, 41:1, 4–18.

Wood, T. (2010) 'Editorial: Good riddance to New Labour', *New Left Review*, 62: March/April, 5–28.

Young, H. (1990) *One of Us* (London: Pan).

Part II
The Context

2
Public Sector Reform and Employment Relations in Europe

Michael Gold and Ulke Veersma

Introduction

The structure and management of public sector activities across Europe have been subject to an onslaught of reform over recent years (Pollitt and Bouckaert, 2004; Proeller and Schedler, 2005). In the UK, the country where public sector reform has arguably been most far-reaching, the Conservative government of Margaret Thatcher began the process in the 1980s through the introduction of supply-side economic policies designed to dismantle alleged rigidities in the operation of the 'free market' (Minford, 1991). These policies included cutting tax rates, deregulating financial markets and – most conspicuously for this chapter – opening up the public sector to competition through privatisation, compulsory competitive tendering and the introduction of internal markets ('marketisation') (*see* Chapter 1, in this volume). The effect on public sector employment in the UK has been dramatic: numbers employed in the civil service, local government and the NHS together fell from 7.4m in 1979 to 5.8m in 2005, even though there was a rise in NHS employment between 1997 and 2005 (Horton, 2009) (*see* Chapter 3, in this volume for a fuller discussion).

Similar reforms have since affected public sector activity across most European Union (EU) member states, to a greater or lesser degree. Though 'it is a well-known fact that Continental Europe has been much less enthusiastic about the idea of public management as marketisation than the Anglo-Saxon countries' (Lane, 2009: 156), it is nevertheless true that other EU member states have come under a range of pressures to reform their public sector, willingly or not. Many such states have, for example, attempted to reduce public expenditure as a proportion of Gross Domestic Product (GDP) and cut budgetary deficits in order to meet the convergence criteria to qualify for Economic and Monetary Union in Europe (EMU), or they have responded to concerns over levels of taxation, the quality of public service and the wish to improve cost-effectiveness by adopting private sector concepts of performance (James, 2004). Demographic changes, with an increasingly large number of pensioners across Europe being supported by decreasing numbers of employees contributing to pension funds, have also played their part in shifting attitudes towards what can and cannot be provided by the public sector.

The significance of these reforms is considerable as they mark a fundamental shift away from the consensus underpinning the post-1945 social settlement, not just in the UK but across swathes of Western Europe. Shared dimensions of this consensus had included a commitment to full employment – supported by the intervention of Keynesian government policies in the free market – the creation of modern welfare states and comprehensive systems of education, and a belief in the need to plan economic and social policy within central and local government and other public agencies. Employers and unions were generally involved at all levels of such policy formulation through formal channels of consultation. The consensus had also reflected an understanding that – in the national interest – certain key sectors of the economy had to be brought under some form of public ownership and/or control.

Though the contours of ownership and control varied greatly from country to country, such sectors included banking and finance, civil aviation, education, iron and steel production, health, mining, postal services, railways and waterways, shipbuilding and utilities like electricity, gas and water.

It was generally believed that these sectors should be operated in the collective interest as they were too important, from a social point of view, to be left to the vagaries and inequalities of the free market. For some 30 years after the end of World War II, these assumptions about the role of the public sector dominated thinking across the political spectrum in the Federal Republic of Germany, Italy and the UK (Harrop, 1999), as well as Benelux and the Nordic countries.

Clearly, these points must not be oversimplified. The notion of a 'consensus', for example, may have been more a matter for political elites than rank-and-file levels of political activity and does not, in any case, account for the occasional U-turn (such as that of Edward Heath, the UK Prime Minister, who confronted the unions over his period of office in the early 1970s). Furthermore, the division between 'private' and 'public' sectors is acknowledged to be blurred and highly interrelated:

Hybrid forms of organisation, such as state-owned enterprises, government corporations, and heavily regulated business firms, mix government auspices and control, with features usually conceived as private economic activity, such as sale of goods or services for a price.
(Rainey and Chun, 2005: 73)

Distinctions between agencies and enterprises, forms of ownership and funding, operating environments and goals and performance criteria have all been used in an attempt to clarify the distinction between private and public, though there is little agreement on the matter (Rainey and Chun, 2005). Nevertheless, this chapter makes an assumption that the basic distinction 'essentially revolves around differences of ownership (collective ownership, in the name of all citizens, versus individual ownership) and motive (social purpose versus profit)' (Bovaird and Löffler, 2009: 5).

Along these two dimensions – ownership and motive – striking shifts in the 'accumulating expectations' of public sector activity have taken place across the industrialised world, evolving from a focus on equal access and equal treatment in the 1950s and 1960s, to concerns over public sector responsiveness to political priorities in the 1970s and to an emphasis on its performance as measured by a wide range of social indicators by the 1990s (Blum and Manning, 2009: 42). The 2008 financial crisis and the prevention of a total collapse of the banking sector only through massive bailouts and subsidies from governments all over Europe will exert still further pressure to slash public expenditure and reform public services. In response, public sector employment relations since the crisis have been marked by waves of protests and demonstrations as workers and students took to the streets, notably in Greece, Ireland, France, Spain and the UK, to condemn the cuts.

It is important also to recognise the role of the EU in moves to reform the public sector. The EU has adopted privatisation as a strand in its policy to deregulate and promote open competition across the member states. Indeed, economic integration within the EU is based primarily on the operation of the Single European Market (SEM), as well as on a degree of market correction undertaken through welfare systems and consultation – or 'social dialogue' – which recognise the need to involve the social partners in the processes generated (Gold, 2009).

This chapter will analyse the impact of reform on public sector employment across Europe. Following an overview of the nature of the pressures on public sector employment practices, it contrasts the principles of employment relations and human resource management (HRM) in the public and private sectors. It then examines the varieties of New Public Management (NPM) that have emerged across certain individual member states before evaluating the role of European integration and EU social dialogue in the introduction of new forms of public sector management. The chapter concludes that, while major variations exist between member states in the pace and nature of reform, considerable repercussions will continue to affect public sector workers into the long term across Europe, though these might best be channelled through appropriate forms of consultation.

Nature of the pressures on public sector employment

A variety of pressures have, then, been increasingly exerted on governments to improve efficiency, performance levels and the quality of services. They have resulted in techniques known as NPM that alter basic understandings of public service to the degree that privatisation and marketisation introduce principles of private sector management into their provision. The transfer of such principles into the public sector may take place merely through the imitation of management ideas, or else through legislation and pressure from higher levels of government. Restructuring the regulatory and structural framework of public services is the main objective of neoliberal policies, advocated by such supranational agencies like the OECD and the IMF. They argue that the cost of public sector bodies places an unacceptable burden on economies in global competition with countries and regions that are less regulated, such as the USA, Eastern Europe and emerging nations in Asia, South America and elsewhere. Open markets created under the flag of neoliberal policies have therefore become a major objective for European countries and governments.

Target setting is one of the key components of NPM (Bouckaert and Van Dooren, 2009). A standardised approach to providing public services is replaced by their marketisation. The underlying assumption is that exposure to market forces will provide more efficient and higher quality services. Large-scale bureaucracy is replaced by decentralised organisations that enshrine the principles of budgeting and market orientation and hence, allegedly, a more efficient public sector apparatus. Public services may not even necessarily form part of this apparatus, but may be outsourced. Research has demonstrated how such reforms have led to changes in working conditions and the marginalisation of certain workers, as well as how outsourced organisations are now providing public services under less favourable conditions (Bordogna,

2003; Pollert, 2007) (*see also* Chapter 8, in this volume.) In these ways, governments have aimed to establish lean public management – basically by cutting the overheads and support functions across the apparatus of public sector bodies.

The transfer of principles of private sector management into the public sector is also accompanied by the introduction of performance-related payment systems. At the same time, lifetime employment becomes less common for public sector workers and their representatives, while managerialism, in terms of output-oriented and arm's length management, is now the dominant style of management. The introduction of more flexible work patterns also advances across areas of the public sector (Martínez Lucio, 2007).

Pressures for reform of public sector management can be found too at the European level where EMU and the introduction of new monetary rules sets limits on maximum levels of inflation, levels of public spending and the state deficit, whilst the basis of the SEM, as noted above, is the notion that deregulation needs to underpin market mechanisms like open competition and the prevention of state subsidies (Hemerijck and Huiskamp, 2002). The question then arises as to the impact of these changes on the public sector, including the provision of services themselves and the nature of employment conditions. Before addressing the changes in public sector employment relations across individual European countries, the specific elements of HRM in the public sector must first be analysed.

Employment relations and HRM in the European public sector

Employment in the public sector has been characterised by specific rules and traditions that date back to the development of the state as the monopolist of power (Elias, 1939) and its role in protecting citizens and guaranteeing a minimum level of welfare. Employees in the public sector, representing this body of national interest, would therefore be privileged with better working conditions and greater job security than workers in the private sector. In exchange, employees would be expected to show more loyalty to their employer and to move up internal career ladders rather than between different organisations. Employment in the public sector used accordingly to follow more standardised practices with rigid job demarcation in line with the ideal type of bureaucracy identified by Max Weber, with a salary instead of a wage and a career structure through which the employee is promoted (Allen, 2004: 112).

Reward systems are based on the various job roles and are negotiated by trade unions within the setting of collectivised industrial relations rather than based on individual performance.

HRM in the public sector has been predominantly based on the principle of a paternalistic style of management with little discretion for employees. Public organisations would furthermore aspire to be 'model employers' providing the best public services with highly motivated employees (Farnham and Horton, 1996). The question has then been raised whether, with the introduction of NPM, there would be a convergence between private and public sectors in practice. As the next section of this chapter will show, some trends, such as decentralisation and the introduction of greater flexibility in employment relations, will indeed lead to increasing similarities between public and private sectors.

Up until now, however, contrasts can be observed in the employment relations and status of workers in the public and private sectors across Europe. The status of employees in specifically central government remains – at least formally – different from the status of employees in the private sector. This applies to reward systems, rules on dismissal and pension entitlements. It should be noted that these differences vary across European countries and that implementation may vary according to the country involved.

Table 2.1 reveals that special status for public servants in central government is quite common across all European countries. There are, however, differences regarding the proportion of employment falling

Table 2.1 Special employment status in central government

State	Special status	Central Government employment (%)
Austria	Beamter	60–6
Belgium	Statutory civil servant	70–5
Germany	Beamter	40–3
Denmark	Statutory civil servant	35
Finland	Career civil servant	83
France	Fonctionnaire publique de l'Etat (titulaire)	100
Ireland	Career civil servant	n.a.
Italy	None	–
Netherlands	Career civil servant	n.a.
Norway	Embetsmann or embetskvinne	n.a.
Portugal	Public servant	74
Sweden	Virtually none	5
UK	None	–

Source: Adapted from Bourgon (2008) and EIRO (2008b).

under special status. Sweden, for example, has less than 5 per cent on life-long employment (mainly judges), with the rest employed on a permanent contract basis in line with all other employees (Bourgon, 2008). In central government in Sweden there is strong management prerogative. Collective bargaining is also strongly decentralised to the agency level and, since the abolition of a century-old system of nation-wide pay scales related to job titles in 1989–1990, pay has become more individualised. These changes have been implemented through consultation with the trade unions, which have collaborated with, rather than opposed developments (Bordogna, 2003). Table 2.1 also reveals that Italy and the UK appear to be the only countries without special status at all for public servants in central government.

A further key distinction with the private sector is that traditionally employment relations in the public sector have been predominantly collectivised across Europe. Trade union membership has accordingly been usually much higher than in the private sector. In the UK, while the national system of employment relations can generally be construed as decentralised, there are actually rather more indicators of a centralised system in the public sector. One such example is the collective agreements for teachers and nurses who have their pay determined by the system of pay-review bodies (*see* Chapter 5, in this volume).

Although the density of unionisation is high in the public sector, and usually higher than in the private sectors, there is still wide variation across European countries. The pattern of trade union membership in the public sector reflects the variation of trade union density across Europe as a whole, though at a higher level of membership, with some exceptions like Belgium. The unionisation rates for a selection of European countries are set out in Table 2.2.

The trade union density rates for most of the former Communist countries of Central and Eastern Europe are lower than in most Western

Table 2.2   Public sector union density across Europe

Over 70 (%)	Also high, but precise figures unavailable	55–70 (%)	40–54 (%)	25–39 (%)	15–24 (%)	Below 15 (%)
Denmark Finland Norway	Greece Luxembourg Malta	Austria Ireland Romania UK	Belgium Germany Italy	Bulgaria Hungary Netherlands Portugal	France	Czech Rep. Estonia Latvia Lithuania Poland Slovakia

Source: Adapted from EIRO (2008a).

European countries; in some of these countries trade unions are almost absent. Only in Bulgaria and Hungary and, even more so, in Romania do trade unions have a higher membership rate. In Romania, for example, 55%–70% of all central government employees are a member of a trade union (EIRO, 2008a). Unions generally reflect the occupational structure of their employees, such as teachers, doctors and nurses.

The public sector therefore remains the most highly unionised sector of the economy across European countries, as in most other parts of the world. Unionisation reflects a high level of organisation in terms of bureaucratic structure and lines of control, which implies a more collective command structure than in the private sectors. Unionisation is also closely related to the motivation of the workforce and loyalty to both the organisation and, as a consequence of the nature of public services, to the public too in the form of a customer service relationship. A high density of unionisation, however, not only reflects the motivation and traditions on the side of the employees when combined with other factors like militancy and activism – witness, for example, the action in France against the raising of the retirement age – but also it reflects the attitudes and style of management. In many cases there is a direct relationship between trade unions and management, as trade unions are involved with internal labour market functions, like recruitment, promotion and the organisation of work (Keller et al., 2001). This involvement may benefit the trade unions in terms of growth in membership and, at the same time, management may also act in a more positive way towards them as management is itself also often unionised.

Partnership between trade unions and employers in the private sector is now a more common feature of UK employment relations, driven not only by an economic agenda of employment and the prevention of job losses, but also by the agenda of training and organisational and employee development (Stuart and Martínez Lucio, 2007). In public sector organisations there is, however, sometimes an almost natural inclination towards partnership. This concept in the public sector is, however, not a recent innovation but a more widespread feature based on the more privileged status of employees. Privileges with regard to pension schemes and, in most European countries, a better regulation of employment such as redundancy procedures, are arguably compensated by employees through their long-term commitment and loyalty to the organisation.

Public sector employment is also different because of the duties of the state and public sector organisations. The means for achieving trade union aims are also different from the private sector. The very nature of public service requires a different regulation of the right to strike as strikes directly affect the public. Employees, because of their main responsibilities at work and the impact they may have on the public, dispose of greater opportunity to disrupt the daily lives of citizens. Their strike action may be very effective, even without the involvement of large numbers of workers and over a shorter period of time. Furthermore, when strikes develop into long-term disputes disrupting essential services, they may be broken by other employees in the public sector who are often themselves members of a trade union. Strikes are, if only for this reason, subject to special regulation, and some areas of the public sector are covered by more specific restrictions than others, depending on the degree to which they may affect the country's national interests of security and stability. In many countries, public sector employees, such as the Beamten in Germany, are not only deprived of the right to strike but also to negotiate their employment relationship collectively – although they have the right to organise and to have their own union or association (Bordogna, 2003). In the case of Germany, Beamten now form one section within Ver.di, the Vereinte Dienstleistungsgewerkschaft (United Services Union). However, the high level of loyalty and the close relationship between management and employees make trade unions in the public sector usually rather reluctant to go on strike.

Marketisation and individualisation of employment relations, as implemented across European countries, may affect loyalty and the hitherto high-trust relationships between management and employees. Some of the specific traits of employment relations in the public sector, such as the limited right to strike and possible (self-) restrictions on collective bargaining, may hence become less typical for public sector employment relations as changes in the sector affect the status of employees. The next section explores further the changes in the public sector and the variety of models of NPM, with their different emphases on policies, means of implementation and impacts on employment relations.

Varieties of New Public Management across Europe

Management principles

Management principles, including target setting and the decentralisation of public services, have had a major impact on public sector organisations, while outsourcing may imply a loss of entitlements regarding redundancy or pension provision. The proportion of career civil servants falls as they lose their public sector status even while occupying a public sector position. As a result, their special prerogatives, such as job security and generous pension entitlements, are gradually abolished. With the adoption of private sector management principles, it becomes easier and less costly to dismiss employees, and redundancy procedures are simplified. In other aspects of employment relations too there is an increase in flexibility, including the adoption of more flexible recruitment practices.

In career structures, decreasing importance may be attached to length of service in favour of merit and performance as criteria for promotion. Often the objective behind these changes in human resource instruments is to introduce greater mobility within the organisation and between the public and private sectors. Mobility is promoted where public sector organisations are increasingly managed like private organisations and where they operate in a partnership with private companies. For the operation of non-profit sector organisations, contractual principal–agent relationships with governments are introduced, which may lead to further marketisation and competition between non-profit organisations. Reform of public sector organisations and employment relationships as described here are not, however, even across all European countries and a wide variety of impacts of marketisation and adoption of NPM principles can be found.

Diversity

Although, as noted above, reforms are widespread across Europe, the diversity of response and outcome is reflected in policies and practices of national governments and public sector organisations (full details may be found in EIRO, 2005; Pollitt and Bouckaert, 2004: Appendix B). National economies and state bodies across Europe have different ways of dealing with economic pressures and demands, dependent not only on the political composition of the government, but also on national cultures and the type of capitalism in specific countries. A helpful distinction may be made in this respect between 'liberal market economies' on the one hand, which include Ireland and the UK, and 'co-ordinated market economies' on the other, which include certain economies of northern continental Europe, such as Germany and Scandinavia (Hall and Soskice, 2001). The former economies are characterised by a limited role for the state, generally weak unions and an ethos of free market capitalism, while the latter retain a more central role for the state in economic regulation, greater influence for unions particularly in pay bargaining and less trade in company shares.

Another factor that impinges on the scope for public sector reform is the administrative structure of the state and the financing of public administration. Analysts distinguish between types of administrative culture: the 'public interest' or 'civic culture' on the one hand of a jurisdiction like that of the UK, and the 'rule of law', or legal state (Rechtsstaat), on the other hand of France and Germany. The former are characterised by high levels of pragmatism and flexibility, while the latter reflect a culture of greater legal control and rigidity (Blum and Manning, 2009). Yet a further factor that affects the scope of reform is the nature of the executive and the state: it is generally easier to introduce reform in unitary systems (France, the Netherlands and the UK) than federal systems (Belgium and Germany). It then becomes possible to group countries according to their receptivity to managerialist policies and practices, with unitary, 'civic culture' liberal market economies at one extreme (notably the UK) and federal, 'rule of law' co-ordinated market economies at the other (notably Germany) – with others, such as France, the Netherlands and Scandinavian countries occupying a range of intermediate positions.

(a) United Kingdom

Indeed, the UK has witnessed the deepest changes in employment relations as an effect of public sector reform (Bach and Della Rocca, 2000). In the UK, this reform was also part of a strategy to reduce the power of trade unions (*see* Chapter 10, in this volume). Other countries in Europe, like Denmark and the Netherlands, followed a similar path, although restricted to specific sectors. The UK, which after the Thatcher period reflected the most explicitly neoliberal philosophy in Europe, has focussed more on private sector incentives and the decentralisation of pay than the co-ordinated market economies. In the UK, job security – even for senior staff – is, more than in any other economy, seriously threatened by the introduction of new recruitment methods (Bordogna, 2003). However, differences in the implementation of NPM principles are not only determined by the degree of co-ordination within the economy and the role of the state, but also by the level of centralisation of collective bargaining. The UK is in this respect a rather special case: though decentralised bargaining is the norm across most sectors of the economy, in areas of the public sector a more centralised system can be found, such as in education and nursing, where pay-review bodies govern nationally determined pay (Bordogna, 2003) (*see* Chapter 5, in this volume).

(b) Germany

Governments in other countries have adhered to more restrained policies, especially co-ordinated market economies characterised by 'rule of law' cultures, such as Germany and France. Although NPM has made inroads into these countries, a 'maintenance strategy' can be identified there: NPM has been introduced in a more restricted way, directed mainly at increasing the efficiency of the existing public sector (Pollitt and Bouckaert, 2004). In both France and Germany a limited use is made of fixed-term contracts, and more centralised collective bargaining remains in place.

With respect to Germany, these comments apply only to that area of the public sector where employees do not benefit from the status of Beamten, who continue to experience lifelong job security though without the right to negotiate collective agreements or go on strike (Dribbusch and Schulten, 2007: 157). While the system of employment relations has been modified to consolidate marketisation and liberalisation, collective bargaining has been reformed in sectors like public transport, utilities and refuse disposal as they have been privatised. Generally, privatisation at both national and local level, with its accompanying decentralisation of collective bargaining, has entailed the negotiation of new collective agreements with, at least for existing staff, the same pay and conditions as before. The outsourcing of services by employers in the formerly publicly owned companies has led, however, to cost reductions achieved through job cuts and pressure on labour costs. For areas of the public sector with a majority of white-collar workers in particular, this has meant a considerable shift in power to the disadvantage of the trade unions. As these workers were usually less inclined to resort to confrontation to defend the status quo, they increasingly dropped out of the scope of centralised collective bargaining. However, collective bargaining for the public sector remains quite centralised when compared with other countries across Europe.

For the Beamten, government decides on pay and working conditions following consultation with the trade unions and professional organisations. Social partnership in Germany has always been a strong tradition in the public sector. It is not uncommon for trade unionists to switch careers and become managers in public administration. Reforms to public management aim not only to achieve cost savings and efficiency, but also the volume of employment. After a short period of growth in the public sector directly following unification of East and West Germany, employment fell between 1991 and 2003 by more than 28 per cent (Dribbusch and Schulten, 2007: 161). Privatisation of the postal services (Bundespost) and the railways (Deutsche Bundesbahn) counted for more than a half of this reduction, but restructuring in the former German Democratic Republic also contributed extensively to the decline.

(c) France

While the introduction of NPM in Germany may have led to a shift in power in employment relations – and the serious questioning of the principles of loyalty and bureaucratic structure – in France, the framework of traditional employment relations in the public sector seems less affected and the system of collective bargaining remains more centralised than in Germany. This is mainly owing to the deeply embedded dirigiste tradition of the state and its civil servants. The status of public servants, inherited from this tradition of the strong interventionist state, remains dominant in France. Administrative law continues to prescribe and regulate most crucial aspects of public employment, such as recruitment, promotion, discipline, remuneration and other aspects of working conditions. Although status in itself is not an obstacle to the reform of employment conditions, the social partners take a very rigid approach to HRM where equal treatment of all civil servants, irrespective of their responsibilities and effectiveness, remains the main principle (Mériaux, 2007: 186).

The system of pay determination in France is also the most centralised in Europe. Government negotiates at the central, national level with the representative trade union confederations covering the three subsectors of the state: central government, local authorities and public hospitals. These negotiations directly determine the employment conditions of around 4.5 m public sector employees and indirectly one million further employees, as agreed levels of pay are implemented through the pay scale and job-classification system (Bordogna, 2003: 49–50). Nevertheless, changing approaches to HRM and public sector performance have led to a slight increase in flexibility in both pay and in the system of job classification itself (Mossé and Tchobanian, 1999). The strong tradition of the state in France and the impact on the role of public servants seems to create major resistance to reform in this sector.

(d) Denmark

Other countries have witnessed more profound changes in public sector employment relations. Denmark, for example, has undergone a process of decentralisation of collective bargaining, which may be labelled as 'co-ordinated decentralisation' (Traxler, 1995). Greater flexibility and adaptability to the needs of individual administrative units and local labour market conditions have been achieved in response to the demands placed on the sectors. More enterprise bargaining has been introduced with increased scope for market incentives (Bordogna, 2003: 51). The minister of finance negotiates on the side of the employers with a coalition of trade union federations; however, a certain percentage of the total pay bill is left to the local level, where the remaining proportion is determined by local collective bargaining.

(e) Italy

A similar type of co-ordinated decentralisation of collective bargaining has taken place in Italy, where collective bargaining is divided between various rounds. The first consists of national negotiations, divided between subsectors of the public services (central government, local government, public education, national health and so on). The second round covers decentralised agreements at the local and unit level of public services. The percentage of total pay that is determined centrally remains, however, very high and job classification systems and pay scales are, for example, fixed in national agreements with low pay differentials between grades, especially in education (Bordogna, 2003: 52).

(f) The Netherlands

Although the introduction of NPM and changes in employment relations reflect certain concepts in the 'varieties of capitalism' literature, it does not hold for all countries. According to the OECD (2010), the Netherlands, for example, was one of Europe's early starters in the development of NPM and the implementation of so-called 'better regulation' policies, and has made steady progress in consolidating and expanding them since the 1990s. A range of policies is now in place, alongside the flagship programme to reduce regulatory burdens on business. Indeed, the Netherlands was at the forefront of privatisation, beginning with the postal services and, later in the 1990s, the railways. It falls, therefore, within a 'moderniser' category (Pollitt and Bouckaert, 2004), rather than a category of 'maintenance-strategy', which implies only marginal reforms, as in Germany and France. All three countries would, however, be generally regarded as coordinated market economies in the varieties of capitalism literature.

That said, although the variation in NPM is as much determined by the type of administrative culture as by economic system, the degree and type of co-ordination in the economy does remain significant. Some of the co-ordinated market economies have long traditions of social partnership, which also affect public sector reform. The Netherlands seems now to be at the cross-roads between, on the one hand, long-standing traditions of structured consultation and, on the other, the development of new approaches that reach out to stakeholders in a very different fashion, for example through the Internet (OECD, 2010). However, new approaches to consultation do not necessarily imply the abandonment of traditional approaches, as they aim rather to improve transparency and the effectiveness of consultation, which are regarded as integral to the development of government policies and the process of introducing new regulations.

In summary, it may be concluded that there are clear differences in the degree of reform implied by the introduction of NPM and changes in employment relations. By its very nature, NPM aims to increase efficiency and cost savings and accordingly has an impact on the decentralisation of collective bargaining and the introduction of HRM, including greater pay flexibility and, most importantly, job security. Outsourcing and privatisation have a detrimental effect on the employment conditions of public sector employees and former employees in that sector. Substantial variations in the public sector remain across Europe, which is another indication of the persistence of national diversity against the trend to convergence under the influence of NPM.

European integration and NPM

At this point the question arises whether – if the introduction of NPM principles do not themselves necessarily lead to a fundamental convergence of public service policy and practice across Europe – the process of European integration may itself have such an effect. European integration has, as a process of policymaking determined by the European institutions, a direct impact on public policies and the provision of public services. However, integration takes various forms and may influence national policies in different ways. Europeanisation and the introduction of NPM are, first of all, affected by EMU, notably the introduction of the euro, and the need to meet the convergence criteria. More recently, the bail-out of the Greek and the Irish economies in 2010 had a direct impact on employment levels and conditions in, above all, the public sector.

Europeanisation does not, however, necessarily have to be prescriptive, but may also take the form of 'framing domestic beliefs', that is, by promoting domestic adjustments to EU objectives through altering the beliefs and expectations of the actors involved (Knill and Lehmkuhl, 2002). This form of Europeanisation applies when there is a broad consensus among the dominant actors over the process of reform at national level. The concept of the European welfare state is closely connected with the notion of employee consultation (or social dialogue) over regulation of the labour market, and so the concept of 'framing domestic beliefs' is a relevant concept as actors are involved in processes of bottom-up policymaking. Social dialogue with the social partners is a common feature of industrial relations systems in most EU member states, and arguably forms part of a European identity.

This process of bottom-up policymaking has also been promoted through the introduction of the Open Method of Co-ordination, an EU policy mechanism that relies on 'soft' forms of regulation to achieve objectives across the European employment strategy (Casey, 2009). Such collective employment relations, in which social dialogue is embedded, are enshrined particularly in the European co-ordinated market economies. The co-ordination of these economies takes place through the trade-off between the interests of the social partners and the state for which purpose social dialogue plays a pivotal role at different levels, both national and European.

EU-level social dialogue in the public sector

'Social dialogue' more technically is also a general term used to describe a variety of arrangements involving discussions between employers, unions and sometimes public authorities at EU level (Carley, 2009). In this section, the term is applied specifically to bipartite consultation at EU sectoral levels, a process dating back to the 1950s. The European Commission (EC) set up various joint committees – with equal representation of employers and unions – in sectors affected by common Community policies, including a number in the public sector (such as inland waterways, 1967; rail transport, 1971; civil aviation, 1990; telecommunications, 1990; and postal services, 1994). In 1998, all joint committees were replaced by sectoral social dialogue committees (SSDCs) designed to harmonise their operation – by 2008 there were 35, and some 25 'joint texts' had been agreed in railways, postal services and telecommunications, with a further 20 in civil aviation (Carley, 2009; EC, 2010). The overwhelming majority of these texts are basically declarations of intent, with little binding value, though three agreements have been implemented by means of directives: seafarers' working time (1999), working time of mobile staff in civil aviation (2000) and the conditions of railway mobile workers (2005). The remainder cover areas like equal opportunities, the use of new technologies, training, work organisation and so on.

In 2004, a new SSDC was launched to cover local and regional government, with representatives from the Employers' Platform of the Council of European Municipalities and Regions (CEMR-EP) and the European Federation of Public Service Unions (EPSU). The themes it prioritised were a statement on telework and the diffusion of good practice across the sector, with respect to good HRM and work practices (EIRO, 2004). This was followed in 2010 by the launch of a further SSDC, covering central government administration, with representatives of the European Public Administration Network (EUPAN) and the Trade Unions' National and European Administration Network (TUNED), which is affiliated to EPSU. During an earlier trial phase of informal social dialogue in the sector (2008–9), outputs had included a joint position on work-related stress, a framework agreement on harassment and violence at work and a conference on improving trust in central government (EIRO, 2010).

These developments tend to demonstrate that the SSDCs focus principally on the 'soft' end of HR issues with a mainly advisory or educative role in promoting good practice. Their influence on the growth and practice of NPM at EU level can, therefore, be described as severely limited.

Conclusions

The introduction of NPM, privatisation and the marketisation of public services have led to profound changes in the status of employees, their employment conditions and, generally, employment relations across the public sector in Europe. Employment rights and job security, which have traditionally applied across the European public sector and have moulded employment relations specific to this sector, are under pressure. A certain degree of convergence between the public and private sectors may be observed, though there has been considerable variation in the way in which NPM has been implemented and its impact on employment conditions and relations mediated. While some countries have experienced structural change, with for example the decentralisation of collective bargaining and an increase in flexibility, other countries – such as France and Germany – have adopted a more moderate approach in 'maintaining' the major features of their public sectors. However, with due regard for these variations, there will continue to be, certainly in the long term, considerable repercussions for employees and their conditions. Generally, NPM and the privatisation and marketisation of the public sector will continue to alter work practices and lead to a gradual disappearance of privileges and, hence, the type of loyalty that has been most common for the many (white-collar) workers affected. The sector will come increasingly to resemble the private sector and more adversarial employment relations are likely to appear.

Consultation within the public sector at domestic levels remains a major element of policymaking, reflecting certain objectives with respect to economic development and the protection of employee rights. To that extent, it might be seen as a major influence on the pace and nature of reform. The way in which, for example, the Netherlands has aimed to modernise the public sector is based on this principle of social dialogue and social partnership, with an underlying aim of increasing efficiency and transparency. The challenge for social partners, at various levels, when compared with the private sector, is therefore to accommodate the needs of a modern public sector with the principles of social partnership. Social dialogue, as a major element of European policymaking, therefore seems an ideal vehicle for developing a different approach towards NPM from the one adopted specifically in the UK, where the public function of, for example, the railways has retrenched to such an extent that the sector can barely compete with the use of private cars. Indeed, these challenges should be reflected too at the level of European social dialogue, where the network of SSDCs – if enhanced – could also assist in influencing the nature of public sector reform. The conclusion is therefore that the notion of public sector, and how it best serves various functions in society, needs profound rethinking. Social dialogue could be a major vehicle to stimulate this rethinking.

References

Allen, K. (2004) *Max Weber: A Critical Introduction* (London: Pluto Press).

Bach, S. and Della Rocca, G. (2000) 'The management strategies of public service employers in Europe', *Industrial Relations Journal*, 31:2, 82–96.

Blum, J. and Manning, N. (2009) 'Public management reforms across OECD countries', in T. Bovaird and E. Löffler (eds) *Public Management and Governance* (London: Routledge).

Bordogna, L. (2003) 'The reform of public sector employment relations in industrialized democracies', in J. Brock and D. Lipsky (eds) *Going Public: The Role of Labor-Management Relations in Delivering Quality Government Services* (Urbana-Champaign (US): Industrial Relations Research Association).

Bouckaert, G. and Van Dooren, W. (2009) 'Performance measurement and management in public sector organizations', in T. Bovaird and E. Löffler (eds) *Public Management and Governance* (London: Routledge).

Bourgon, J. (2008) *The Public Sector of 2025 – Themes, Challenges and Trends: Human Resource Management Trends in OECD Countries* (Quebec City: United Nations Public Administration Network) online at http://unpan1.un.org/intradoc/groups/public/documents/un/unpan034107.pdf [accessed 11 January 2011].

Bovaird, T. and Löffler, E. (2009) 'Understanding public management and governance', in T. Bovaird and E. Löffler (eds) *Public Management and Governance* (London: Routledge).

Carley, M. (2009) 'Social Dialogue', in M. Gold (ed.) *Employment Policy in the European Union: Origins, Themes and Prospects* (Basingstoke: Palgrave Macmillan).

Casey, B. (2009) 'Employment Promotion', in M. Gold (ed.) *Employment Policy in the European Union: Origins, Themes and Prospects* (Basingstoke: Palgrave Macmillan).

Dribbusch, H. and Schulten, T. (2007) 'The end of an era: structural changes in German public sector collective bargaining', in P. Leisink, B. Steijn and U. Veersma (eds) *Industrial Relations in the New Europe: Enlargement, Integration and Reform* (Cheltenham: Edward Elgar).

EIRO (2004) 'New Social Dialogue Committee in Local and Regional Government', online at http://www.eurofound.europa.eu/eiro/2004/03/feature/eu0403203f.htm [accessed 28 December 2010].

EIRO (2005) 'Industrial relations in the public utilities', online at http://www.eurofound.europa.eu/eiro/2005/02/study/tn0502101s.htm [accessed 28 December 2010].

EIRO (2008a) 'Industrial Relations in the Public Sector: Role of Trade Unions', http://www.eurofound.europa.eu/eiro/studies/tn0611028s/tn0611028s_4.htm. Accessed 20 November 2010.

EIRO (2008b) 'Industrial Relations in the Public Sector: Commentary', http://www.eurofound.europa.eu/eiro/studies/tn0611028s/tn0611028s_8.htm. Accessed 20 November 2010.

EIRO (2010) 'Central government administrations to get Sectoral Social Dialogue Committee', online at http://www.eurofound.europa.eu/eiro/2010/01/articles/eu1001039i.htm [accessed 28 December 2010].

Elias, N. (1939) *Der Prozess der Zivilisation* (Berlin: Suhrkamp)

European Commission (2010) 'Sectoral Social Dialogue', online at http://ec.europa.eu/social/main.jsp?catId=480&langId=en [accessed 28 December 2010].

Farnham, D. and Horton, S. (1996) *Managing People in the Public Services* (Basingstoke: Palgrave Macmillan).

Gold, M. (2009) 'Overview of EU employment policy', in M. Gold (ed.) *Employment Policy in the European Union. Origins, Themes and Prospects* (Basingstoke: Palgrave Macmillan).

Hall, P. and Soskice, D. (eds) (2001) *Varieties of Capitalism: The Institutional Foundations of Comparative Advantage* (Oxford: Oxford University Press).

Harrop, K. (1999) 'The political context of public services management', in A. Rose and A. Lawton (eds) *Public Services Management* (London: Financial Times/Prentice Hall).

Hemerijck, A. and Huiskamp, R. (2002) *Public Sector Reform under EMU: A Literature Review* (Dublin: European Foundation for the Improvement of Living and Working Conditions).

Horton, S. (2009) 'Human resource management in the public sector', in T. Bovaird and E. Löffler (eds) *Public Management and Governance* (London: Routledge).

James, P. (2004) 'Industrial relations in the public sector: collective bargaining reform and the issue of convergence', in P. Dibben, G. Wood and I. Roper (eds) *Contesting Public Sector Reforms: Critical Perspectives, International Debates* (Basingstoke: Palgrave Macmillan).

Keller, B., Due, J. and Andersen, S. (2001) 'Employer associations and the public sector', in C. Dell' Aringa, G. Della Rocca and B. Keller (eds) *Strategic Choices in Reforming Public Service Employment: An International Handbook* (New York: Palgrave Macmillan).

Knill, C. and Lehmkuhl, D. (2002) 'The national impact of European Union regulatory policy: three Europeanization mechanisms', *European Journal of Political Research*, 41, 255–280.

Lane, J.-E. (2009) *State Management. An Enquiry into Models of Public Administration and Management* (Abingdon: Routledge).

Martínez Lucio, M. (2007) 'Trade unions and employment relations in the context of public sector change: the public sector, "old welfare states" and the politics of managerialism', *International Journal of Public Sector Management*, 20:1, 5–15.

Mériaux, O. (2007) 'Reforming employment relations in the French Administration Services: is the status of civil servants an obstacle to efficient HRM?' in P. Leisink, B. Steijn and U. Veersma (eds) *Industrial Relations in the New Europe: Enlargement, Integration and Reform* (Cheltenham: Edward Elgar).

Minford, P. (1991) *The Supply Side Revolution in Britain* (Aldershot: Edward Elgar/ London: Institute of Economic Affairs).

Mossé, P. and Tchobanian, R. (1999) 'France: the restructuring of employment relations in the public services', in S. Bach, L. Bordogna, G. Della Rocca and D. Winchester (eds) *Public Service Employment Relations in Europe: Transformation, Modernization or Inertia?* (London: Routledge).

OECD (2010) 'Better regulation in Europe: Netherlands', online at http://www. oecd.org/document/21/0,3343,en_2649_34141_44912917_1_1_1_1,00.html [accessed 20 November 2010].

Pollert, A. (2007) *The Unorganised Vulnerable Worker and Problems at Work: The Weakness of Individual External Remedy and the Case for Union Organising* (Liverpool: Institute of Employment Rights).

Pollitt, C. and Bouckaert, G. (2004) *Public Management Reform: A Comparative Analysis* (Oxford: Oxford University Press).

Proeller, I. and Schedler, K. (2005) 'Change and continuity in the Continental tradition of public management', in E. Ferlie, L.E. Lynn and C. Pollitt (eds) *The Oxford Handbook of Public Management* (Oxford: Oxford University Press).

Rainey, H.E. and Chun, Y.H. (2005) 'Public and private management compared', in E. Ferlie, L.E. Lynn and C. Pollitt (eds) *The Oxford Handbook of Public Management* (Oxford: Oxford University Press).

Stuart, M. and Martínez Lucio, M. (2007) 'Testing times: remaking employment relations through "new" partnership in the UK', in P. Leisink, B. Steijn and U. Veersma (eds) *Industrial Relations in the New Europe. Enlargement, Integration and Reform* (Cheltenham: Edward Elgar).

Traxler, F. (1995) 'Farewell to labor market associations? Organized versus disorganized decentralization as a map for industrial relations', in C. Crouch and F. Traxler (eds) *Organized Industrial Relations in Europe: What Future?* (Avebury: Aldershot).

3
The Economic and Financial Context: Paying for the Banks

Jean Shaoul

> Over the last decade, the UK's economy became unbalanced, and relied upon unsustainable public spending and rising levels of public debt. For economic growth to be sustainable in the medium term, it must be based on a broad-based economy supporting private sector jobs, exports, investment and enterprise.
>
> Treasury, 2010a: 6

British public sector workers, like their counterparts in many other countries, face a future of cuts in public service funding, jobs, pay and working conditions as a result of austerity measures imposed in the wake of the global financial and economic crisis. The corollary is that millions of people, who have paid for public services and social insurance via taxes throughout their working lives, face a cut in their 'social wage'.

The Spending Review (Treasury, 2010a), announced by the Conservative–Liberal Democrat coalition in October 2010 and coming on top of budget cuts announced by the previous Labour government and the Coalition Government earlier in the year, is the most savage package of spending cuts seen in the UK since the 1930s. Departments will see their budgets cut each year after 2010–11, by £60bn, £67bn, £72bn, £80bn a year, as the government seeks to cut the budget deficit to 2.1 per cent of GDP by 2014–15, down from £155bn or 11 per cent of GDP in 2010–11. This equates to a cut of about 20 per cent by 2014–15. Pay for public sector workers earning more than £21,000 a year is to be frozen for two years. Half a million jobs in the public sector and a similar number in the private and so-called third sectors that depend on public contracts will go (Hawksworth and Jones, 2010).

Welfare is to be 'reformed' (Department for Work and Pensions, 2010), 'saving' £0.7bn, £3.8bn, £8.8bn and £10.6bn for the years 2011–12 to 2014–15 respectively, or £18bn a year by 2015 (Treasury, 2010a). A number of benefits will be abolished and/or consolidated into one 'universal credit'. Stringent new conditions will be applied to those who remain unemployed, with some losing their benefit entitlements if they do not accept work.

Millions of families will face destitution as the recession takes its toll, while those in work will be forced to accept lower wages and conditions to avoid a similar fate as Britain takes protectionist measures to compete with its low-wage rivals. Further measures can be anticipated as the recession impacts on the broader economy and the full extent of the financial sector's past and continuing speculation becomes apparent. More fundamentally, these cuts, large though they are, do not address the problem of Britain's mounting public debt, which is expected to rise from 36 per cent of GDP in 2008 to 68 per cent in 2015. This assumes that no further bailouts are required and/or the Treasury's forecast for GDP is not blown off course.

As the opening quote shows, the argument is that public expenditure has become unaffordable and a drain on the economy. The underlying assumptions are that the public sector is profligate and inefficient and must be curtailed in the interests of all. While neither the argument nor the assumptions are new, indeed they have been the leitmotif for public policy for the last 35 years, the clear implication is that public services are responsible for the UK's indebtedness and should therefore be reined in. It is crucial therefore to understand the validity or otherwise of these claims since they provide the context for understanding employment relations in the public sector. This chapter therefore examines post-war expenditure on the public sector, the policies carried out by successive governments, particularly those of the 1997–2010 Labour governments, and the factors that have led to the most drastic spending cuts in the post-war period. While the evidence and analysis relate to the UK, similar pressures prevail elsewhere.

The chapter is structured in several sections. The first section examines public expenditure in the immediate post-war period until 1997, including the measures taken to 'roll back the state' between 1976 and 1997. The second outlines public expenditure and policy under the first 10 years of New Labour, while the third describes the measures taken to deal with the financial and economic crises after the subprime mortgage industry collapsed in August 2007 by first the Labour government and then the incoming Coalition Government in 2010. The final section draws out the implications.

Public expenditure trends until 1997

State expenditure encompasses revenue expenditure by central government, local authorities and public corporations (state enterprises, the NHS, BBC, universities and other bodies) on goods and services; transfer payments such as pensions, unemployment and housing benefits, sick and disability allowances, and subsidies; capital investment; and debt interest and net lending. General Government Expenditure (GGE) is the usual measure of total public expenditure. GGE (at today's prices) has nearly tripled since 1986 (Table 3.1). While this appears relatively straightforward to specify, interpretation of the relevant data is difficult due to conceptual, definitional and measurement problems, not least because the data series have changed over time and it is difficult to get consistent data (as subsequent charts will show).

The usual starting point is to examine the way GGE has varied over time using the ratio of total public expenditure to GDP, which corrects, to some extent at least, for inflation. At the beginning of the twentieth century, total GGE/GDP was about 10 per cent, increasing hugely during World War I (WWI) to 45 per cent, falling to about 27 per cent in the interwar period, and rising again to 61 per cent during World War II (WWII). After falling sharply in the immediate aftermath of the war,

Table 3.1   Public expenditure and GDP

	Public expenditure nominal (£bn)	Public expenditure real (£bn)	Public expenditure as % of GDP
1967–68	18.30	245.80	45
1970–71	22.70	254.90	43
1975–76	55.70	329.50	50
1980–81	112.40	335.50	47
1985–86	166.50	364.10	45
1990–91	227.50	369.30	39
1995–96	311.40	431.30	42
2000–01	364.00	449.10	37
2005–06	524.00	569.00	41
2009–10	671.00	671.00	45
Average			42*

Note: *Public expenditure as % GDP averaged 42% over the period 1967–2010.
Source: *Public Expenditure Statistical Analyses 2010 at 2008–09 Prices,* Office for National Statistics.

it fell fairly continuously to about 33 per cent until the early 1960s. Thereafter, it grew throughout the 1960s and early 1970s, peaking at nearly 50 per cent in the mid-1970s as expenditure rose faster than GDP (Table 3.1).

When the UK faced bankruptcy in 1976, the IMF demanded a halt to the rising GGE/GDP as the price for a bailout and the Labour government cut public expenditure. While the Thatcher governments in the early 1980s are widely believed to have cut public expenditure savagely, Labour's cuts were much greater. Furthermore, and perhaps surprisingly, despite the privatisation of most of the state enterprises during the 1980s and early 1990s, and determined efforts to restrain public expenditure, particularly after 1987, GGE/GDP was still about 43 per cent in the 1990s. It fell to just below 40 per cent at the end of the twentieth century, before reaching 40 per cent again in 2005. Over the last 50 years, it has averaged 42 per cent (Table 3.1).

Several points should be noted. In general, expenditure varied inversely with the state of the economy, rising in recession and declining in the economic upswings, as the tax yield increased and welfare payments declined relative to GDP. Over the whole post-war period, public expenditure grew at the same rate as GDP. This is because the overall increase in public expenditure disguised significant changes in the composition of expenditure.

The largest single component was expenditure on goods and services, accounting for approximately half of all expenditure by the state, although varying over the post-war period. It was a function of previous legislation that placed obligations upon the state to carry out certain activities, such as educating school children. Because it was difficult to reduce it by more than one or two percentage points while maintaining the same volume and quality of services, there had been an emphasis on greater managerial control, performance measurement, audits and inspections to secure increased 'efficiency' and 'value for money'.

The second most important item of expenditure was the transfer or welfare payments, which grew from 21 per cent in 1946 to 37 per cent of GGE in 1996, with most of the increase occurring after 1976 as the UK's economic decline led to increasing poverty. While some of these payments, pensions and child benefits depended on demographic factors, others such as benefits to those without work were highly dependent upon the level of economic activity and the business cycle. Reducing these payments, which were based on strict rules of entitlement, therefore entailed changing eligibility and the types and size of payments.

The 'other; expenditure, including debt servicing and public corpora-tions, was largely dependent upon wider government policy and was therefore less amenable to direct control.

The smallest item of government expenditure was capital expenditure on infrastructure, including road, school, hospital and house building, and so on. Capital investment is traditionally the easiest to reduce since the impact is not felt in the short-term at least. This has fallen over the years, with the end of the public house building programme in the early 1970s, the decision to halt the already inadequate building pro-gramme of schools, hospitals and other public works in 1976 to meet the demands of the IMF, and the privatisation of the big investors, the capital-intensive infrastructure industries, in the 1980s and early 1990s. However, terminating the building and public works programme led to a serious backlog of maintenance and investment in every public service by 1997.

Public expenditure grew broadly in line with the national economy, growing in real terms and with relatively little variation, despite the change in governments, until the end of the long boom in the 1970s. This growth reflected the rise of the welfare state in the 1940s and the nationalisation of the capital-intensive industries, and was the prod-uct of the radicalisation of the working class not just in the UK but in Europe as a whole. As the historian Judt points out in his history of Europe (2005), European leaders established minimum conditions for the welfare of the broad mass of the people and the nationalisations of key industries in order to create favourable conditions for busi-ness to secure markets. They sought to ensure against a return to the revolutionary upheavals that followed WWI and the type of destructive nationalism that had plunged Europe into war.

Although public expenditure was not significantly different from that of the other large European countries for much of the post-war period, it was by the 1990s considerably lower than in its European counterparts, although higher than in the United States of America (USA) and Japan. In part, this was because many of those countries that had in an earlier period spent a smaller proportion of GDP on public goods and services increased their expenditure.

The 1974–76 economic crisis – and the resultant intervention by the IMF – was a turning point in public policy. It marked the end of the post-war system of Keynesian demand management to regulate the economy and the start of attempts to rein in welfare expenditure, as the Labour government responded by instituting a series of cuts and intro-duced a system of annual cash limits for departmental expenditure.

After 1979, the Thatcher government took this further, launching an ideological offensive against 'big government', and making an explicit attempt to 'roll back the state' and curtail public expenditure. This offensive is associated with the ascendance of the New Right agenda and neoliberalism: business friendly policies, the deindustrialisation of the old smokestack industries and the promotion of financial services (Shaoul, 2010).

Firstly, successive governments between 1976 and 2001 introduced institutional measures aimed at curbing public expenditure. In the 1980s, the wage bill, the chief cost, was strictly capped in cash terms in a period of inflation, and wage rises were largely dependent upon productivity bargaining. This meant wage increases at the expense of jobs and intensified work effort for those who remained. In the 1990s, the government set an annual ceiling on public expenditure based on the assumption that real growth in central government expenditure would not exceed 2 per cent a year (Treasury, 1992) and introduced a unified budget to ensure that spending proposals would be considered alongside taxation (Treasury, 1993a).

Secondly, the scope of public sector activities was curtailed by various forms of privatisation. Justified in terms of the assumed greater efficiency of the private sector that would bring benefits to all, its real import was to provide new sources of profits for the corporations and financial institutions (Shaoul, 2000). The government sold off its commercial enterprises cheaply, retaining the debt and liabilities such as clean-up, decommissioning and some pension liabilities and so on, thereby depriving the state of a revenue stream to cover their debts and liabilities and contributing to the subsequent fiscal crisis of the state. It deregulated and liberalised markets, allowing new entrants into services previously provided by the state, such as local transport and care homes for the sick and elderly, before they too were privatised. From the 1980s, many low-paid manual services, such as cleaning, catering and refuse collection, within the local authorities and hospitals, were subject to competitive tender by outside contractors, although an in-house team could also bid (Cutler and Waine, 1994; Walsh, 1995). The range of activities was subsequently extended to the higher paid professional services such as legal and information technology functions. New investment of hospitals and schools would be financed by the private sector that would build and lease back the facilities to the public sector via the Private Finance Initiative (PFI) (Treasury, 1993b).

Thirdly, these institutional changes were accompanied by a series of measures to reduce costs and increase outputs, and a culture that became known as the New Managerialism or the New Public Sector Management (Pollitt, 1990). The New Managerialism took a variety of forms, but broadly speaking involved running public services as though they were businesses by breaking up the public sector into smaller units responsible for their own budgets and, in some sectors, such as schools and hospitals, in competition with each other. It also emphasised the three Es: economy, efficiency and effectiveness, and performance measures which attempted to capture and compare the performance of public sector providers and thereby ratchet up output or throughput with a system of penalties and rewards. This was accomplished by the establishment of extensive inspection and external audit regimes. The effect was to ratchet up the exploitation of the workforce and in some sectors such as schools, to make the workload and stress intolerable.

The driving force behind all these developments was the requirement for new sources of profit and a reduction in restrictions imposed upon the corporations' activities by national governments as they undertook the production of and investment in goods and services on an international scale. The 40 per cent or so of GDP that did not directly yield a profit had to be opened up via privatisation, 'partnerships' and outsourcing to private profit.

While in an earlier period, the corporations had been prepared to tolerate taxation to finance social welfare in the interest of their own long-term survival and when the rate of profit was rising, they were no longer prepared to do so as the rate of profit declined (Armstrong et al., 1984). They sought to claw back a portion of profit previously appropriated by the state in the form of social welfare provision to the working class, since any reduction in tax payable – or more importantly, tax actually paid – represents an attempt to increase their profit or the rate of return on capital employed. The corporations and mega-rich insisted upon, and obtained, a reduction in business taxes and their own personal tax via cuts in Corporation Tax and the top rate of income tax at the expense of ordinary people, contributing to the fiscal crisis of the state. They legally or otherwise minimised their tax payments by relocating their activities to offshore tax havens and other tax dodges. Unpaid tax by the rich and major corporations costs every British worker at least £1000 a year (NAO, 2007). They also obtained income tax reductions for their workers as a low wage subvention. The billions lost in such tax cuts were clawed back via regressive taxes on the consumption of basic goods and services that have hit the poorest families the hardest.

The impact of this sea-change in public policy on public sector staff can be seen by examining the cost of public sector employment. By far the

Table 3.2   Changes in the cost structure of public and social services

	1977		1986		1996	
	Purchases of external goods and services	Labour costs	Purchases of external goods and services	Labour costs	Purchases of external goods and services	Labour costs
General Government Expenditure (GGE) (£m)	5,571	14,209	17,488	34,680	49,360	67,411
GGE as % of operating costs	28	72	34	66	42	58

Note: A high estimate of £22.4bn for health wage costs has been used.
Source: *UK National Income Blue Book* (various years).

largest operating cost, that is the actual cost of running all public services after excluding transfers, capital expenditure and debt servicing, was labour, which includes National Insurance contributions and pension costs as well as wages. Labour costs fell as a proportion of operating costs for two reasons. First, the number of workers employed fell. The number employed had risen from 5.8m in 1961 to about 7.3m in the late 1970s when some 29 per cent of the workforce was employed in the public sector. It declined slightly during the 1980s and then quite substantially in the 1990s until by 1997, there were 5.2m government employees, 12 per cent fewer than in 1961 and 29 per cent fewer than in 1977.

Second, the government moved to external procurement via market testing, compulsory competitive tendering (CCT), and the PFI, and so on. Procurement rose from £10.2bn in 1976 to £70bn in 1996, while labour costs rose from £18bn to £82bn. If we consider only the public and social services, excluding defence, economic and other functions, then the change in cost composition is even starker. As Table 3.2 shows, labour costs fell from 72 per cent in 1977 to 58 per cent in 1996, and procurement rose from 28 per cent to 42 per cent. This growth in procurement reflected the fact that government paid for, but no longer delivered, many services.

Public finance and policy under Labour 1997 to the onset of the banking crisis

For the first few years, the incoming Labour government's strict adherence to its predecessor's spending plans meant a decline in public expenditure relative to GDP to its lowest point for nearly 50 years. The Chancellor of the Exchequer introduced new rules to limit public sector borrowing: keeping the budget deficit to 3 per cent of GDP and public sector net debt to 40 per cent of GDP, even stricter than those of the European Union. He only allowed expenditure to rise in absolute terms after 1999 (Table 3.3) and to surpass GGE/GDP under the last years of the Conservative government in 2005 (Table 3.4). GGE/GDP did not exceed that of the early 1990s until the bank bailouts and the onset of the recession in 2008–9. This increase, however, was quite different from the rest of the post-war period because Labour increased real expenditure quite sharply in a period of prosperity, from £333bn in 1998–99 to £582bn in 2007–8 (Table 3.3), an increase of 75 per cent. The largest increases were in health and education, which accounted for about 61 per cent of the total increase. But significantly, GGE/GDP, which by 2008 had reached 40 per cent, was still below the average 42 per cent of the previous 50 years (Table 3.4). Even more importantly, while public indebtedness did rise, this too, at 36 per cent of GDP in 2008, was no greater than normal (Table 3.4). It was however different in that it rose during a period of economic growth.

While spending on pensions and welfare rose during Labour's 13 years, they fell as a proportion of public expenditure from 36 to 33 per cent in 2008 (*see* Table 3.5), due largely to the growing economy. It rose thereafter to 35 percent with the onset of the recession. At the same time, the Labour government took a number of measures aimed at reducing welfare and increasing the number in work. In 2009, this resulted in nearly 378,000 coming off benefits (Toynbee, 2010).

Public sector employment broadly followed Labour's spending. As Table 3.5 shows, employment continued falling until 1998 and then began to grow, reaching the level prevailing in the last years of the Conservative government by 2001 and surpassing the 1991 level in 2005. In all, the headcount grew from 5.1m in 1997 to 5.8m in 2008, an increase of 11 per cent (or adjusted for full-time equivalent (FTEs) workers, 3.8m to 4.3m), at a time when public expenditure grew by 42 per cent. Despite the increase, public sector employment at 20 per cent of the total workforce in 2008 was still less than in the early 1990s. (The reasons for this will be discussed later.) The biggest increases in employment between 1997 and 2008 were in health (27 per cent), police (24%) and education (24%), accounting for around three quarters of the increase in public sector employment.

According to the Annual Survey of Hours and Earnings (ASHE), the average gross annual wage in the public sector rose from £16,322 in

Table 3.3 Public expenditure by sector, 1995–2010

Real prices (£bn)	1995	1996	1997	1998	1999	2000	2001	2002	2003
Pensions	43	45	49	52	62	66	68	73	80
Health-care	38	39	41	43	47	50	54	60	66
Education	37	37	37	38	40	42	45	50	53
Defence	26	25	25	25	27	28	29	29	30
Welfare	61	63	64	63	55	59	62	65	66
Protection	15	15	15	16	18	18	19	21	24
Transport	12	12	10	9	9	9	9	11	15
Central government	6	7	7	6	9	10	10	11	15
Other spending	35	35	38	38	36	35	40	44	53
Interest	24	27	28	30	29	25	26	22	21
Balance	5	5	4	5	2	3	4	3	–3
Total spending	299	309	318	325	333	344	367	390	421
Public net debt (PND)	290	322	348	353	352	345	312	316	347
GDP	733	782	830	879	929	977	1,022	1,076	1,140

Source: Public Expenditure Statistical Analyses 2010, Office for National Statistics.

Table 3.4 Key public expenditure ratios, 1995–2015

	1995	1996	1997	1998	1999	2000	2001	2002	2003
Total spending (£bn)	299	309	318	325	333	344	367	390	421
Public net debt (PND) (£bn)	290	322	348	353	352	345	312	316	347
GDP (£bn)	733	782	830	879	929	977	1,022	1,076	1,140
Interest (£bn)	24	27	28	30	29	25	26	22	21
Total spending/ GDP (%)	41	40	38	37	36	35	36	36	37
PND/GDP (%)	40	41	42	40	38	35	31	29	30
Interest/total spending (%)	8	9	9	9	9	7	7	6	5
Welfare + pensions/total spending (%)	35	35	36	36	35	36	35	36	35

Source: Calculated from Table 3, *Public Expenditure Statistical Analyses 2010*, Office for National Statistics.

2004	2005	2006	2007	2008	2009	2010	Increase 1999–2008 (%)	Increase 1999–2010 (%)
82	86	90	93	99	110	117	60	89
75	83	90	95	102	110	120	117	155
59	67	72	75	76	80	86	90	115
32	33	35	37	38	42	44	41	63
74	78	83	86	90	98	109	64	98
26	28	29	30	32	34	35	78	94
16	16	17	20	21	21	22	133	144
6	19	22	22	22	25	25	144	178
5	63	68	73	76	88	84	111	133
23	24	26	28	31	31	31	7	7
–3	–7	–8	–10	–5	–8	–3	–350	–250
455	492	524	549	582	629	669	75	101
383	424	463	500	525	617	772	49	119
1,203	1,254	1,326	1,399	1,448	1,396	1,474	56	59

2004	2005	2006	2007	2008	2009	2010	2011	2012	2013	2014	2015
455	492	524	549	582	629	669	690	702	713	724	740
383	424	463	500	525	617	772	932	1,059	1,162	1,235	1,284
1,203	1,254	1,326	1,399	1,448	1,396	1,474	1,539	1,620	1,710	1,803	1,902
23	24	26	28	31	31	31	43	47	52	58	63
38	39	39	39	40	45	45	45	43	42	40	39
32	34	35	36	36	44	52	61	65	68	68	68
5	5	5	5	5	5	5	6	7	7	8	8
34	33	33	33	33	33	34	34	35	34	33	33

Table 3.5 Public sector employment trends

('000s)	Construction	Armed forces	Police	Public admin	Education	NHS	Other health and social	Other	Total public sector
1991	189	311	224	1,271	1,310	1,220	458	999	5,982
1992	172	304	226	1,279	1,225	1,225	454	960	5,845
1993	160	285	228	1,242	1,125	1,204	439	914	5,597
1994	153	262	228	1,209	1,100	1,189	449	844	5,434
1995	146	241	227	1,177	1,122	1,193	451	814	5,371
1996	135	230	230	1,166	1,122	1,197	447	745	5,272
1997	128	220	230	1,142	1,127	1,190	447	694	5,178
1998	122	219	229	1,127	1,137	1,202	435	696	5,167
1999	119	218	227	1,140	1,158	1,212	431	703	5,208
2000	116	217	225	1,146	1,214	1,239	428	706	5,291
2001	105	214	229	1,153	1,241	1,285	414	741	5,382
2002	90	214	238	1,181	1,250	1,348	406	761	5,488
2003	83	223	248	1,223	1,306	1,416	387	751	5,637

2004	83	218	262	1,238	1,342	1,476	401	730	5,750
2005	77	210	274	1,255	1,361	1,531	406	733	5,847
2006		204	274	1,280	1,370	1,522	383	746	5,779
2007		197	283	1,267	1,384	1,490	382	731	5,734
2008		193	285	1,224	1,393	1,510	380	738	5,723
2009*		197	294	1,209	1,411	1,578	374	952	6,015
2010*		197	294	1,201	1,431	1,599	376	899	5,997
Increase		-114	70	-70	121	379	-82	-100	15
1991-2010 (%)		(-37)	(31)	(-6)	(9)	(31)	(-18)	(-10)	(0)
Increase		-23	64	59	304	409	-71	205	819
1997-2010 (%)		(-10)	(28)	(5)	(27)	(34)	(-16)	(30)	(16)
Increase		-27	55	82	266	320	-67	44	545
1997-2008 (%)		(-12)	(24)	(7)	(24)	(27)	(-15)	(6)	(11)

Sources: Labour Force Survey; Returns from public sector organisations, ONS.

Notes:
* includes nationalised banks
* headcount, not seasonally adjusted

Table 3.6 Average annual wage in the public sector

	Number of male public sector workers ('000s)	Number of female public sector workers ('000s)	Total public sector workers ('000s)	Female workers as a % of total (%)	Mean gross annual wage in public sector (£)	Mean gross annual wage in private sector (£)
1999	1,893	3,306	5,199	64	16,322	18,475
2000	1,923	3,289	5,212	63	17,061	19,844
2001	1,815	3,267	5,082	64	17,519	21,075
2002	1,780	3,279	5,059	65	18,216	21,923
2003	1,914	3,345	5,259	64	19,142	22,563
2004	1,900	3,438	5,338	64	20,236	23,536
2005	1,921	3,575	5,496	65	21,771	24,485
2006	1,938	3,703	5,641	66	22,525	25,482
2007	2,014	3,814	5,828	65	23,073	26,251
2008	1,972	3,750	5,722	66	23,925	27,596
2009	2,004	3,721	5,725	65	25,232	27,414
2010*	2,241	4,222	6,463	65	25,892	27,195
Increase since 1999 (%)	18	28	24		59	47

Source: Annual Survey of Hourly Earnings, Public Sector, Table 13.7a (various years).
Note: *Includes workers in nationalised banks and numbers employed are indicative only.

1999 (the earliest year that this data series is available) to £23,925 in 2008 (*see* Table 3.6 and Chapter 5, in this volume). This compares with the average gross annual wage in the private sector of £18,475 in 1999 and £27,956 in 2008. In other words, the pay gap widened from about £2000 in 1999 to £3600 in 2008. In part at least, this gap reflects the fact that women constitute 65 per cent of the public sector workforce and many work part-time. Since public spending rose, the total labour costs rose from just 24 to 27 per cent of government expenditure, despite both the larger number employed and the higher wages. In other words, the increase in public expenditure was not eaten up by the workforce.

The Labour government continued and extended many of the Conservatives' policies. It sought to enable the private sector to deliver public services, such as health and education. Firstly, it expanded the system of performance targets, reporting and inspections for public services. Failure on the part of schools, local authorities and hospitals to deliver on their targets led to turn round teams and/or contracts for the private sector to take over their management. For example, by 2003, there were at least 44 'interventions' by the Department for Education and Skills (DfES), involving outsourcing to private firms and some not for profit organisations (Ball, 2007).

Secondly, although Labour revised the system of CCT for local authorities and the NHS, it retained and encouraged outsourcing on the basis of best overall value. In 2002, it brought in new arrangements to allow Local Education Authorities to contract out all the functions other than the strategic ones of planning and budget approval. The process was also driven by the government's system of sticks and carrots under various policy initiatives such as Best Value Reviews, and the DfES 'New Models' pilot. Some local authorities bundled together a range of services including, for example, housing benefit, IT, human resources, financial services as well as education, and/or joined with other neighbouring authorities to form a 'strategic partnership' and outsourced the package as one contract (Ball, 2007). According to a survey commissioned by the Department for Business Enterprise and Regulatory Reform (Oxford Economics, 2008), by 2007–08, of the £300bn spent on services (excluding, welfare and transfer payments, interest and capital expenditure), £159bn was spent on pay and £141bn on procurement. That is, just 53 per cent was spent in house. Of the £141bn spent on procurement, the report estimated that £79bn went to the 'public services industry'.

Thirdly, as New Labour famously boasted, it got the PFI up and running, rebranding it as Public Private Partnerships (PPP). Under PFI/PPP, the private sector builds, finances and operates the infrastructure underpinning public services such as roads, prisons, hospitals, schools and its administrative services. That is, it not only finances and builds the infrastructure but also runs all the non-core or non-professional services, thereby extending the role of the private sector in public service delivery. For example, it introduced legislation to enable hospital trusts to enter into PFI contracts with the private sector. PFI became 'the only show in town' for public services in desperate need of new infrastructure after 20 years of little capital investment. The government expanded the policy to include joint ventures with the private sector, for example the Local Investment Finance Trust (LIFT) for primary care facilities, and Building Schools for the Future (BSF) in education. Such partnerships go far beyond the initial investment programme. To take but one example, the private partner managing a BSF contract may also control schools that are not part of the original BSF investment, manage revenue streams from multiple public agencies over and beyond schools and children's services, and initiate proposals for public funding for these services for up to 15 years. In effect, BSF provides the mechanism to privatise in all but name many of the functions of local government. This in turn would mean that local government would become a super commissioner of services paid for by public monies, operating as a special purpose vehicle subcontracting its work to private companies: a case of 'hollowed out government' (Rhodes, 1994).

As of February 2010, there were 667 signed PFI/PPP deals with a capital value of £56bn (Treasury, 2010b), although the government routinely cites much larger figures. The largest spending departments were Transport (capital value of £11.8bn signed deals) and Health (£11.3bn), Defence (£8.8bn), and Children Schools and Families (£6bn). Total commitments for all PFI projects between 1995 and 2048, including both the cost of repaying the capital investment and the cost of the associated services, were estimated at £267bn. However, both the list and the costs are incomplete. Based on estimates at financial close, they are subject to upward revision in the light of inflation and contractual changes that have already led to major increases within a few years. For example, hospitals' annual payments rose by an average of 20 per cent, with some rising as much as 50 per cent and 70 per cent (Shaoul et al., 2008a).

These annual payments are significant for several reasons. As essentially fixed costs that must be paid, they commit public authorities to substantial long-term outgoings, while locking in governments to particular forms of service delivery under conditions where needs and technologies may change (Lonsdale, 2005). But should their revenue decline, then the axe must fall on the core professional services and budget, reducing access.

Furthermore, PFI is very expensive. Firstly, a conservative estimate (Shaoul et al., 2008b) shows that 20 per cent of the hospital trusts' annual payments and between 20 and 40 per cent of the various transport authorities' annual payments are attributable to the additional annual cost of private over public finance because of the higher cost of private over public debt and the profit margins. This serves to destabilise the public authorities whose financial position is at best precarious. Secondly, there is no evidence that the service element is any cheaper than public sector provision (Shaoul, forthcoming). Indeed, quite remarkably, the Treasury's own review retreated from government's previous insistence on including soft services in PFI contracts, saying, 'PFI has not led to a step change in soft service delivery', and acknowledged that VFM [value for money] was reduced in PFI contracts with a large service element (Treasury, 2006: 8–9). Lastly, more than half of all PFI projects by capital value have now failed and have had to be bailed out, renegotiated or taken back into the public sector at enormous cost (*see* Shaoul, forthcoming, for an analysis of the PFI/PPP outcomes).

In other words, the increasing payments to the financial institutions and corporate sector entails a reduction in the 'social wage', or public goods and services that are largely the product of direct and indirect taxes and social insurance paid by working people. But in addition to their financial rewards, the private consortia running these projects are acquiring ever greater control over both taxpayers' monies and public policy (Shaoul et al., 2007). This is because these policy initiatives and programmes were designed by, awarded to and evaluated by financial advisors such as the financial and business services consultancies and the global accountancy firms. They were not the result of popular demands. To cite but one example, PwC produced a report (2007) advising the government on how to develop a 'Market for Disabled Children's Services'.

The government's use of consultants has gone up markedly in recent years and the National Audit Office (NAO), the parliamentary spending watchdog, reported (2006) that spending on consultants across the public sector had reached £2.8bn in 2005–6, up from £2.1bn in 2003–4, an increase of one-third in two years. It said many consultants' services did not represent value for money, and recommended that public bodies should start with the presumption that their own staff are best suited to do the work, saying, 'Public bodies must be smarter when it comes to understanding how consulting firms operate and in sharing information about their performance.' Although another report (NAO, 2010a) said that total spending on consultants had fallen in recent years, central government alone had spent £789m on consultants and £215m on interim managers, that is, managers on short term appointment, in 2009–10. This growth in the use of consultants reflects the sidelining of the civil service and the creeping privatisation of public services and more importantly of public policy control and implementation, particularly in relation to the PFI (Shaoul et al., 2007) *see* Chapter11, in this volume.

These various measures, together with the expansion in public spending after 2000, generated a vast increase in disguised subventions to the corporate sector and created a parastatal workforce, employed by private companies that have become de facto public authorities. But the parastatal sector is not very visible in official statistics, which do not record the extent of outsourcing or the number of people employed by such firms providing public services on government contracts.

According to the *Financial Times* (Timmins, 2010), the private provision of public services, as reflected in the UK public services industry, rose from about £42bn in 1995–96 to £80bn in 2007–08 in current prices. Only in Sweden and Australia was this a higher proportion of GDP. A recent report (Froud et al., 2009), reworked the data provided in the *Annual Business Inquiry* published annually since 1998, and estimated that the number of people employed by both the state and the parastatal sector grew from 6.2m in 1998 to 7.5m in 2007. Of this, the parastatal sector employed 1.7m people in 2007, particularly in health, education and social services. Many of these are employed on low wages and conditions lower than the previous rate for the job when carried out in the public sector. The report notes that such jobs are typically carried out by women and are often part-time. In other words, there was little genuine private sector job creation. Most of what was created was dependent upon increased public expenditure channelled in the direction of business, masking the emasculation of the UK economy, despite decades of successive governments' business friendly policies (Froud et al., 2009) *see also* Chapter 8, in this volume.

Taken together, this means that much of the increase in public expenditure between 2001 and 2008 has been eaten up, not by public service workers, but by the additional costs of outsourcing, administering internal and quasi-markets, the PFI/PPP, rail subsidies to the private railways that would not otherwise be able to pay dividends to their shareholders (Shaoul, 2006), and all the rest of the 'new public management'.

Financial and economic crisis 2007 to 2010

Expenditure relative to GDP really began to take off after 2007–8 (*see* Table 3.5), as the credit crunch following the collapse of the subprime mortgage industry in the US in August 2007, and the collapse and sub-sequent nationalisation of Britain's mortgage lenders, Northern Rock and Bradford & Bingley, a few weeks later, took its toll. The government bailout of Northern Rock added at least £127bn to the public sector's liabilities, a sum equal to 8.6 per cent of GDP in 2007–8, increasing total public sector net debt to GDP to about 48 per cent (NAO, 2009). These two bailouts alone were worth more than the £110bn spend on health-care, by far the largest spending area, for 2008–9. It was double the £60bn worth of capital investment in hospitals, schools, transport, and so on, by the private sector via PFI since 1997. Yet the turn to private finance for public infrastructure was in part at least justified in terms of accessing the finance that the government could not provide.

In September 2008, the collapse of Lehman Brothers in the USA precip-itated an international banking crisis that included some of Britain's best known high street banks and mortgage lenders. The government stepped in to guarantee all deposits up to £50,000 in order to prevent a flight of capital from Britain's lenders. Over the subsequent months, the govern-ment introduced a rolling package of measures including the takeover of some of the banks, secret loans, rescue packages to recapitalise the banks and building societies, including the UK subsidiaries of international banks, and to ensure that the banking system remained liquid. It also provided them with guarantees for up to three years in order for them to refinance their loans, equivalent to an open-ended commitment to use the earnings of working people to support the banks far into the future. The Bank of England, backed by the Treasury, provided at least £500m of liquidity to the markets, swapping three-month Treasury bonds in return for the banks' worthless assets for 'as long as necessary', and later cut interest rates to almost zero. These measures were discussed and agreed behind closed doors, without any discussion in parliament – much less with the public – on the conditions or on accountability.

Table 3.3 shows the impact of these subventions on public debt, which rose rapidly after 2008, from £525bn to £772bn in 2010. It is set to rise to £1.2tn by 2012, a sum equal to 68 per cent of GDP (Table 3.4), and to keep rising, as is the cost of debt servicing. Figure 3.1 shows very graphi-cally that this rising debt/GDP ratio is the product of the bank bailouts, as it rises steeply after the financial crisis of 2007–8. But there is a further point: these ratios assume economic growth. But it is far from clear that the private sector will be able to pick up the slack created by the public sector squeeze in the light of the cuts, the impact of the recession includ-ing the multiplier effect on suppliers, and 'the weaker state of our key exports markets in the US and Europe' (Hawksworth and Jones, 2010).

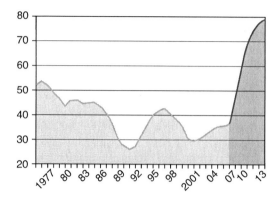

Figure 3.1   Public sector net debt as percentage of GDP
Source: Public Expenditure Statistical Analyses 2010, Office for National Statistics.

According to the NAO (2009), by the end of 2009, the cost of the bailout had reached £850bn, more than any undertaking by a British government except the two world wars. The IMF (Horton et al., 2009) calculated that the 'direct up front financing' cost to the UK taxpayer as at April 2009 was £289bn, including the cost of the Bank Recapitalisation Fund, the Special Liquidity Scheme and the cost of nationalising the mortgage lenders and banks. Moreover, the IMF calculated the potential cost, including the Bank of England/Treasury loans and guarantees, at about £1.2tn or about 82 per cent of GDP.

This was not so much the nationalisation of the banks, however partial, as financial commentators claimed, but the nationalisation or public ownership of the banks' liabilities, or, to put it another way, the privatisation of the UK Treasury. The banks would continue to be run in the interest of the financial elite and subject to no direct control by government. To give some indication of the scale of what is involved, the assets – their now worthless loans – of just the four high streets banks were more than four times the value of Britain's GDP (NAO, 2009). This means that the government's real liabilities may be nearer to £5tn, which could bankrupt the British government in the same way as Ireland, Greece and Iceland.

Conclusion

While since 1979, successive governments have had a common policy of privatisation, after 2000 New Labour increased public spending and with that public service jobs. While the workforce and the public did benefit, the corporate and financial sectors were the indirect and less visible beneficiaries. However, this changed with the onset of the financial crisis in the autumn of 2007, as the government bailed out the banks rather than allowing them to fail. In other words, public spending continued to increase, but the banks were the main and explicit beneficiaries. But since the banks are by no means out of the woods, further support measures, and thus cuts, can be expected. Indeed, as the NAO (2010b) notes, the government's Asset Protection Scheme is set to last to 2099, not just for a few years as in similar schemes elsewhere.

Both the former New Labour government was, and the Conservative–Liberal Democrat coalition is, determined that the massive subvention to the banks should be paid for by a deliberate policy of mass job losses in the public sector while further opening up essential services to private profit, aimed at driving down wages and conditions. The government's claims that public expenditure – meaning public services – had become unaffordable and a drain on the economy, and that austerity is the price to be paid for returning Britain to 'prosperity' are, as this analysis has shown, incorrect. The cuts are not the result of profligate public services but are the direct result of the £1.2tn bailout of the UK banks carried out in the aftermath of the 2008 global financial crash. In other words, it is the banks that are unaffordable, not public services. They should be taken over and run as public utilities that provide cheap credit for productive and socially useful purposes.

The austerity measures are a deliberate attempt to roll back the welfare state and re-order social relations on the basis of 'not letting a good crisis go to waste'. While the Coalition Government insists 'there is no money' for hospitals, education, pensions and welfare benefits, the bankers continue to receive massive rewards, including those in banks dependent on the state. Indeed, the only section of society that is 'ring-fenced' from this assault are those responsible for the financial and economic crisis in the first place. At the same time, however, the Labour government could find billions for the criminal and unpopular occupations of Iraq and Afghanistan. The Conservative–Liberal Democrat coalition for its part has not only continued to support these military campaigns but has also played a leading – and very expensive – role in the NATO assault on Libya. The cost will come at the expense of public services.

In short, the Coalition Government is set to reduce public service workers' jobs and their terms and conditions to compensate for the bailout, which it fully supported. This will play a major role in transforming public sector labour relations in the coming period. It begs the question: in whose interests is the economy to be run, the bankers' or the public's?

References

Armstrong, P., Glyn A., Harrison, J. (1984) *Capitalism since World War II: The Making and Breakup of the Great Boom* (London: Fontana Paperbacks).

Ball, S. J. (2007) *Education PLC: Understanding Private Sector Participation in Public Sector Education* (Abingdon: Routledge).

Froud, J., Leaver, A., Williams, K., Johal, S., and Buchanan, J. (2009) 'Undisclosed and unsustainable: problems of the UK national business model', *CRESC Working Paper* series, working paper no 75, online at http://www.cresc.ac.uk/publications/undisclosed-and-unsustainable-problems-of-the-uk-national-business-model (accessed 21/06/11).

Cutler, T. and Waine, B. (1994) *Managing the Welfare State: The Politics of Public Sector Management* (Berg: Oxford).

Department for Work and Pensions (2010) *Universal Credit: Welfare that Works,* White Paper, CM 7957 (London: The Stationery Office).

Hawksworth, J., and Jones, N.C. (2010) *The Spending Review: Sectoral and Regional Impact of the Fiscal Squeeze* (London: PwC).

Horton, M., Kumar, M. and Mauro, P. (2009) *The State of Public Finances: A Cross-Country Fiscal Monitor,* International Monitory Fund Staff Position Note (Washington: IMF).

Judt, T. (2005) *Post War: a History of Europe since 1945* (London: Heinemann).

Lonsdale, C. (2005) 'Post–contractual lock in and the UK Private Finance Initiative: The cases of National Savings and Investments and the Lord Chancellor's Department', *Public Administration,* 83:1, 67–88.

NAO (2006) *Central Government's Use of Consultants: Report by Comptroller and Auditor General,* HC 128, Session 2006–7 (London: The Stationery Office).

NAO (2007) *Management of Large Business Corporation Tax: Report by Comptroller and Auditor General,* HC 614, Session 2006–7 (London: The Stationery Office).

NAO (2009) *Maintaining Financial Stability across the United Kingdom's Banking System: Report by Comptroller and Auditor General,* HC 91, Session 2009–10 (London: The Stationery Office).

NAO (2010a) *Central Government's use of Consultants and Interims: Report by Comptroller and Auditor General,* HC 488, Session 2010–11 (London: The Stationery Office).

NAO (2010b) *The Asset Protection Scheme: Report by Comptroller and Auditor General,* HC 567, Session 2010–11 (London: The Stationery Office)

Oxford Economics (2008) *The Public Services Industry in the UK, Report Commissioned for the Department of Business Enterprise and Regulatory Reform* (London: BERR)

Pollitt, C. (1990) *Managerialism and the Public Services: The Anglo-American Experience* (Oxford: Basil Blackwell).

PwC (PricewaterhouseCoopers) (2007) *Market for Disabled Children's Services: Report for the Department of Children, Schools and Families* (London: DCSF).

Rhodes, R. A. W. (1994) 'The hollowing out of the state: the changing nature of public services in Britain', *The Political Quarterly,* 65:2, 138–151.

Shaoul, J. (2000) 'Privatisation: Claims, Outcomes and Explanations' in G. Philo and D. Miller (eds) *Cultural Compliance* (London: Longman).

Shaoul, J. (2006) 'The cost of operating Britain's privatised railways', *Public Money and Management*, 26:3, 151–158.

Shaoul, J. (2010) 'Defeating neo-liberalism: a Marxist perspective and programme', in K. Birch and V. Mykhnenko (eds) *The Rise and Fall of Neoliberalism: The Collapse of an Economic Order?* (London: Zed Books).

Shaoul, J. (forthcoming) 'The inefficiency, cost and risks of Public Private Partnership', in P. de Vries and E. B. Yehoue (eds) *The Routledge Companion to Public Private Partnerships* (London: Routledge).

Shaoul, J., Stafford, A. and Stapleton, P. (2007) 'Private control over public policy: financial advisors and the private finance initiative', *Policy and Politics*, 35:3, 479–96.

Shaoul, J., Stafford, A. and Stapleton, P. (2008a) 'The cost of using private finance to build, finance and operate the first 12 NHS hospitals in England', *Public Money and Management*, 28:2, 101–8.

Shaoul, J., Stafford, A., Stapleton, P. and MacDonald, P. (2008b) *Financial Black Holes: Accounting for Privately Financed Roads in the UK* (Edinburgh: Institute of Chartered Accountants of Scotland).

Timmins, N. (2010) 'Private Sector "not yet better or cheaper"', *Financial Times*, 19 October.

Toynbee, P. (2010) 'No losers – really? Soon they will emerge by the million', *The Guardian*, 13 November.

Treasury (1992) *Autumn Statement*, Cm 2096 (London: HMSO).

Treasury (1993a) *Financial Statement and Budget Report 1994–95*, HC31 (London: HMSO).

Treasury (1993b) *Breaking New Ground* (London: HMSO).

Treasury (2006) *PFI: Strengthening Long-term Partnerships* (London: The Stationery Office).

Treasury (2010a) *Spending Review*, Cm 7942 (London: The Stationery Office).

Treasury (2010b) *PFI Signed Projects* (London: The Stationery Office).

Walsh, K. (1995) *Public Services and Market Mechanisms: Competition, Contracting and the New Public Management* (Basingstoke: Palgrave Macmillan).

4
Public Sector 'Ethos'

Jane Lethbridge

Introduction

The term public sector 'ethos' encapsulates the defining characteristics of what working in the public sector actually involves and why it is different from working in the private sector. However, it is also a subjective term that can be interpreted in both positive and negative ways. For many public sector workers, it is what makes their work special and different from working in the private sector. For others, it is what makes the public sector appear bureaucratic, out of touch and unresponsive to service users. This chapter uses the word 'ethos' in inverted commas, because it is a contested and nebulous term.

Commentators have remarked that the public sector 'ethos' is in danger of being lost in current public sector reforms, especially in the area of human resource management (Matheson, 2002). The focus of these reforms has been predominantly on improving the effectiveness and efficiency of the public sector. This has been done through the introduction of private sector business systems. That focus has often ignored workers within the public sector, who, if mentioned, are seen as part of the 'problem'. Steijn (2002b) has argued that human resource management has been a neglected subject in the debates about public sector reforms.

This chapter will start by considering various definitions of public sector 'ethos' that characterise the way things are done within the public sector and highlighting the contribution of public sector workers to the 'ethos'. This is approached by examining what motivates public sector workers in several different countries. A wider discussion of the impact of public sector reforms, particularly the increased involvement of the private sector in the delivery of public services and how it has affected the public sector 'ethos' will follow. Public sector motivation has recently been challenged by the move towards looking at public service users as customers, a process aided by the reconceptualisation of public sector 'ethos' by the New Labour administration. The last part of the chapter will discuss the implications of the United Kingdom (UK) Coalition Government's proposals in the *Comprehensive Spending Review*, published on 20 October 2010, for the future of the public sector 'ethos' in the UK. This will discuss the proposals in respect of four initiatives: shrinking the size of the state, payment by results, Total Place and reforms to education services, before concluding that these new developments will make it much more difficult for public servants to pursue the values that make up the public sector 'ethos'.

Public sector 'ethos'

A dictionary definition of the word 'ethos' is: 'the distinctive character, spirit, and attitudes of a people, culture, era, etc' (*Collins English Dictionary*, 2009). 'Ethos' is sometimes framed in relation to how decisions are taken and the nature of the role of the individual, as a player, within the public sector. In this sense, 'ethos' should be considered as having two essential components: the way in which decisions are taken and the role of people working within this setting.

The public sector 'ethos' in the UK can be traced to the creation of a neutral civil service in the mid-nineteenth century. This was informed by the belief in government as public service in pursuit of the public interest. In 1854, the Northcote–Trevelyan Report, commissioned as a response to the expansion of government business, set out the case for a politically neutral civil service. Although not implemented immediately, by the end of the nineteenth century, the Report had informed the establishment of a civil service, where civil servants were appointed on merit through open competition, not on patronage. This recognised that politicians were subject to short-term pressures and that public administration needed officials who could ensure the public interest. In order to do this successfully, officials had to be politically neutral, show financial and moral integrity and be uninterested in making money (Civil Service, 2010).

Civil servants are expected to adhere to four core values: integrity, honesty, objectivity and impartiality, which includes political impartiality. 'Integrity' is putting the obligations of public service above personal interests; 'honesty' is being truthful and open; 'objectivity' is basing advice and decisions on rigorous analysis of the evidence; and 'impartiality' is acting solely according to the merits of the case and serving equally well governments of different political persuasions. This is part of a code of employment for civil servants. These can be seen as a set of public sector values, which can be defined as 'inner impulses not only to do what is right but to do it well' (Barberis, 2001). Plant (1993) set out the case for a public service ethic consisting of motivation, trust, impartiality and judgement. The element of trust has many different dimensions, covering trust between citizens, between government and citizens, between government and the public sector, between people who work in the public sector and between the public sector and future partners. Written at a time when the contracting out of public services was just beginning, Plant's attempt to define a public sector ethic is a significant milestone in the debate about public sector 'ethos'. His first characteristic is motivation and this is a subject of much human resource literature, which will be considered in the next section.

Public sector workers' motivation across Europe

Public sector workers' motivation has been subject to research in North America and Europe. Some of the results help to inform a wider appreciation of the concept of public sector 'ethos'. Perry and Wise (1990) define public service motivation as 'an individual's predisposition to respond to motives grounded primarily or uniquely in public institutions or organisations' (Perry and Wise 1990: 368). Through extensive research, Perry developed a multi-dimension public sector motivation scale that has been used to explore the different dimensions of public sector motivation. Three transcendental values have been found to contribute to the development of public service motivation: spirituality, doing good for others, and life changing events (Perry et al., 2008).

Although there is an extensive body of research into public service workers' motivation in the United States, further research has been done in Europe, to explore the extent to which public sector workers' motivation has common characteristics across countries, even when political systems are significantly different. Steijn (2002a) found that the motivation of Dutch civil servants was closely linked to their sense of job satisfaction, although he reported that the level of job satisfaction was in decline in the public sector. In a later study, Steijn (2008) continued with a study of public sector workers' motivation but he drew on the concept of 'person-environment fit', which refers to a 'fit between a person and the environment (organisation, group, job) in which they work' (Steijn, 2008: 14). He used this as a way of exploring what influences workers in their working environment and how this can be linked to motivation. Steijn found that Dutch civil servants had a greater degree of 'person-environment fit' than private sector workers. He also found that private sector workers with a high degree of 'person-environment fit' tended to search for jobs in the public sector.

Cerase and Farinella (2009) in a study of the Italian revenue service examined whether public sector motivation evolved over time in response to a person's working environment or whether it was a predetermined factor. They found that public sector workers' motivation was one of several factors that informed a positive perception of change but the relationship was strongest where the worker related to public service as a duty (Cerase and Farinella, 2009). They suggested that further research, a longitudinal study, was needed.

A comparison of UK and Germany found that the focus on public interest varied. In the UK, the prime focus was on government but in Germany the focus was on provincial and local levels. Vandenabeele et al. (2006) argue that institutions and their administrative systems have a significant impact on public sector workers' motivation, which they describe as 'the belief, values and attitudes that go beyond self-interest and organisational interest, that concern the interest of a larger political entity and which induce through public interaction motivation for targeted action' (Vandenabeele et al. (2006). This more recent European research can contribute to a wider understanding of public sector motivation.

The redefinition of public sector workers' motivation can be linked to another research theme of organisational theory. Lundquist (1996) distinguished values of democracy and rationality within the public sector 'ethos' and this perspective complements attempts to locate the public sector 'ethos' in wider debates about the development of reflexivity, whether in the individual or as part of a collective endeavour (Cunliffe and Jun, 2005). Another approach takes the development of critical thinking in public administration and argues that the basis for a public sector 'ethos' is the translation of critical thinking into action (Martin, 2002). This can link to the promotion of public services and their associated values. Quill (2009) explores some of the contemporary ethical issues and argues for a 'reflective' form of loyalty to the public sector, which enables the practitioner to remain a 'critical and reflective' individual as well as a public administrator.

From public sector motivation to customers

The concept of public sector 'ethos' has not been without its critics, with criticism centred on 'self-interest', articulated through public choice theory. Le Grand (2006) has been one of the most vocal commentators who perceives public sector providers of public services to be motivated by bureaucratic procedures and rules and regulation rather than the interests of service users. Public choice theory provides a theoretical framework for a direct attack on the concept of public sector 'ethos'. Its exponents argue that public sector workers do not work for the public interest; rather self-interest is the driving force of politics and bureaucracies. Political parties make promises to obtain votes; politicians make deals to secure support; and bureaucrats want to maximise their own interests in terms of jobs and budgets. Public choice theory, originally propounded by Tullock (1965), has had a powerful influence on public sector reform. It informed the introduction of market forces to government, including contracting out of public services, the creation of internal markets and full privatisation of public services.

Public choice theory has led to the redefinition of public service users as customers. This apparent change of language has had a profound influence on the public sector 'ethos'. Considering public service users as customers changes the relationship between providers of public services and service users.

The New Labour administration from 1997 wanted to modernise the concept of public sector 'ethos' (Koumenta, 2009). It did this with a subtle change in language that served to provide some apparent support for the concept of 'ethos'. New Labour started to talk about public service 'ethos', rather than public sector 'ethos'. This was part of a strategy to widen the range of public service providers, with services still being free at the point of access, although not necessarily provided directly by the public sector. Customer service was added to the list of component parts of 'ethos'. Clarke et al. (2007) explored how public sector workers and service users identified themselves as producers and consumers, which highlighted the relationship between language and power.

The (2002) Public Accounts Committee reported on the differences and similarities between public and private sector workers providing services and in so doing produced a new vision of public service 'ethos'. In 2002, Prime Minister Blair said that 'in public services, customer satisfaction has to become a culture, a way of life, not an added extra' (Blair, 2002). The implication for public sector 'ethos' was that the customer should define the type of demand for services and the outcomes rather than the public sector worker or provider. The limitation of this more private sector approach is that the options for the customer are limited if they decide that the quality and standards of public services are not acceptable. It is also questionable whether government can continue to respond to constantly expanding demands (Needham, 2006).

The growth of a consumerist perspective in public services also needs to be seen in the context of the growth of advocacy of consumer and non-governmental sector groups, which articulate the needs of different interest groups, whose needs have not always been met by public services. The development of these groups has not been a recent phenomenon, but the involvement of what is known as the voluntary and community sector with government has been formalised over the last decade. A series of local and national compacts have established agreements between the government at national and local level with the voluntary and community sectors. Perhaps the most important critique of the introduction of consumers to public services is that it refocuses on an individualistic approach and moves away from a collective sense of responsibility, which informed the creation of the welfare state (Needham, 2006).

Public sector reforms and public sector 'ethos'

In a prescient article, Plant (1993) argued: 'Because it is a contested and nebulous term, relations of trust (in the private sector) are more circumscribed than in the context of large scale delivery in the public sector' (Plant, 1993: 566). The public sector also delivers more complex services. Many of the dimensions of public sector reform, which include managerialism, the introduction of a corporate culture into public sector organisations, performance-related pay and the questioning of professionalism and self regulation are seen to have contributed to the decline in public sector 'ethos' (Barberis, 2001).

A study of how public–private partnership arrangements have influenced the public sector 'ethos' looked at the changes that have taken place in the different dimensions of public sector 'ethos' in the health and housing sectors. The four dimensions considered were accountability, bureaucratic behaviour, public interest, motivation and loyalty. Hebson et al. (2003) found that the contract system of decision making was replacing a more transparent arrangement of accountability and bureaucratic behaviour. Public and private managers were found to have different priorities and the process of monitoring a contract did not lead to high-trust relationships. The greater scope for managerial discretion led to a breakdown of trust and public sector managers became more manipulative to secure value for money.

For non-managerial workers, terms and conditions have often worsened. Although the Transfer of Undertakings (Protection of

Employment) (TUPE) Regulations provides some protection for workers who are transferred to a private sector company, that company may introduce a reorganisation for technical, business or organisational reasons or workers may be transferred to another company taking on a public sector contract (Page, 2004). The case of care services, which have been privatised over the past decade, shows how the terms and conditions of workers have deteriorated (TUC Commission on Vulnerable Employment, 2008). Although working for performance-related targets has replaced working for the public interest, there was evidence that principles of working for the public interest and public accountability have not been completely eroded (Hebson et al., 2003: 498). To what extent this will continue, when the overall motivation is presented as meeting performance targets is unclear.

Pratchett and Wingfield (1996) see a change in public sector 'ethos' as moving from a process-focus towards a more output-focus and present this as a challenge to public service values. Brereton and Temple (1999) are critical of the use of codes to instil a shared set of values, which could inform an 'ethos' because they fail to highlight how different groups now define the public interest. Their research into the alliances between workers in the public and private sectors points towards the creation of public service values, which both public and private sector workers can subscribe to and are more likely to emerge from a multi-sectoral consensus about the public interest in particular sectors and neighbourhoods (Brereton and Temple, 1999).

Barberis (2001) provides an alternative view and sees the definition of a civil service code as trying to inform and nurture citizenship that will inform a public sector 'ethos' (Barberis, 2001: 124). He argues the need to place more emphasis on citizenship, which would contribute to defining the public interest and so inform 'what is right'. The processes that could facilitate this interaction are not set out, although Jorgensen and Bozeman (2007) attempt to show how public sector values evolve. They conclude that government has a special role in guaranteeing public sector values, through political authority, but they are not the exclusive preserve of government. They are also based in society and culture.

The concept of public sector 'ethos' has undergone extensive questioning over the last twenty years, during the period of public sector reform. As a concept, it has underpinned the civil service but the New Labour government contributed to its reconceptualisation, moving from public sector 'ethos' to public service 'ethos', as noted above. Research has found that there have been changes to the manifestation of the public service 'ethos' as the role of the private sector in delivering public services has increased. However, the head of the UK Civil Service in 2009, Sir Gus O'Donnell, said:

> In the 21st Century we are witnessing a return of public sector ethos. The Civil Service – an organisation that makes a difference to society and people's lives – is more important than ever.
>
> (O'Donnell, 2009)

This view was strengthened by the Constitutional Reform and Governance Act 2010, which put the Civil Service and its core values of integrity, honesty, objectivity and impartiality on a statutory basis. No changes can be made to core Civil Service values and principles without Parliamentary scrutiny and approval (Civil Service, 2010).

Although public services have been the subject of extensive research from think-tanks across the political spectrum in the United Kingdom, there are three agencies that have made significant contributions to re-conceptualising public services and the public service 'ethos'. The Institute of Government is an independent charity with cross-party and Whitehall governance support. Headed by a former Permanent Secretary, Sir Michael Bichard, the aim is to increase government effectiveness. It is funded by the Gatsby Charitable Foundation, one of the Sainsbury Family Charitable Trusts, a large charitable donor. Its chief executive has headed several public sector agencies and has a strong reputation as an innovator within the public sector.

Another initiative that is contributing to re-thinking public services is the 2020 Public Services Trust based at the Royal Society of the Arts (RSA). Like the Institute of Government, it also has cross party support and is looking at the future of public services. It aims to 'understand the challenges of public services in medium term'. In 2008, it set up the Commission 2020 Public Services, chaired by Sir Andrew Foster, a former Chair of the Audit Commission. Its aim was 'to recommend the characteristics of a new public services settlement appropriate to the future needs and aspirations, and the best practical arrangements for its implementation'(2020 Public Services Commission, 2010).

A third player is the Serco Institute, part of the company, Serco plc, which is described as an 'international service company that combines commercial know-how with a deep public service ethos' (Bichard, 2010). Serco plc was created to take advantage of the contracting out process. Its aim is to create and support the development of 'sustainable public sector markets'. As part of a company, Serco Institute highlights the contribution of the private sector to public services. Together, these three organisations have contributed to the debate about the future of public services, underpinned by a broad based range of providers. They have also attempted to redefine the concept of public service 'ethos'.

2010 Coalition Government and the future

After the May 2010 election in the UK, a coalition of the Conservative and Liberal Democrat parties formed a government. Known as the 'Coalition', this government started to introduce a series of new policies that will have a fundamental impact on the public sector and on the provision of public services. In an announcement in June 2010, which set out a pre-budget forecast, the rationale for the new policies was given as the need to 'balance the budget' and reduce the size of the public sector deficit (HM Treasury, 2010a). As part of this strategy, the size of the public sector will be dramatically reduced. For more on the economic and financial situation, *see* Shaoul (this volume).

The reasons presented for the reduction in the public sector are articulated as 'underpinned by a radical programme of public service reform, changing the way services are delivered by redistributing power away from central government and enabling sustainable, long-term improvements in services' (HM Treasury, 2010b: 8). It will be informed by a greater diversity of public service provision through payment by results, encouraging independent provision and through helping 'communities, citizens and volunteers to play a bigger role in shaping and providing services'. The implications of these proposals will now be explored in relation to the following tendencies:

- shrinking the size of the state
- payment by results
- Total Place
- the creation of 'free' schools.

Shrinking the size of the state

It is important to recognise that the Coalition did not just start from a blank slate. The New Labour government of 1997–2010, pursued a comprehensive set of policies that initially were designed to 'modernise' the public sector and gradually led to an expansion of private sector involvement in the provision of public services. Part of this process, was a growing involvement of the private sector in the process of government. Private sector advisers have actively worked with civil servants in government departments. There are numerous examples of both politicians and civil servants moving to the private sector after they left office or retired from the civil service (Player and Leys, 2008). This movement from the public to the private sector has implications for the continued impartiality of the civil service and the public sector in the context of an environment where the private sector is securing a significant influence in government.

In October 2010, when the Coalition Government set out its comprehensive spending review, several government departments were required to reduce their budgets by up to 25 per cent over the following four years (HM Treasury, 2010b: 45). Only the budgets of two government departments, health and international development, were apparently ring-fenced. The reality of this ring-fencing will only become clear after the extensive health service reforms have been implemented and similarly when the international development department's relationship with the Foreign Office and its policies have been redefined to support national business interests.

In a speech made in 2006, David Cameron, then Conservative leader of the opposition, specifically presented his views on the importance of the public service 'ethos'. He said:

> Public service – the concept of working for the good of the community – is a high ideal. We see it in our doctors and nurses, our police officers and our soldiers. But we also see it in many, many areas of our civil service and local government. Yet this is rarely, if ever, acknowledged. ... And when I hear Ministers bashing bureaucrats – or declaring that their departments are 'not fit for purpose' – I wish they'd have the decency to admit that very often it's their policies that are at fault, not the people who work for them. Instead of using public servants as scapegoats we should acknowledge their successes. The truth is that public servants are privately dedicated to what they do. To them, it's not just work – it's their vocation. Often it's not just their job – it's their life. ... We believe we can improve public services by trusting public servants more.
>
> (Cameron, 2006)

This speech is revealing in that it shows an attempt by Cameron, four years ago, to soften the image of the Conservative party by acknowledging the value of public sector workers. It is difficult to reconcile this with the position taken by the Conservative party in 2010 when it became the major party in the Coalition Government and specifically the Chancellor of the Exchequer's announcement that 500,000 public sector workers would lose their jobs over the next four years.

As well as the potential loss of jobs, which will leave almost all government departments operating with reduced staff, the responsibility for implementing many of these cuts was given to local government. This was presented as a new 'settlement for local government that radically increases local authorities' freedom to manage their budgets, but will require tough choices on how services are delivered within reduced allocations' (HM Treasury, 2010a: 8).

What was missing in these radical proposals was any sense of democratic accountability. Voters did not vote for these proposals, because they were not presented as part of any election manifesto. Local government was given a task of implementing cuts to front-line services as a result of central government requirements, not as a result of a mandate from local voters.

In the light of earlier discussions about how to involve citizens in the definition of public sector 'ethos', the demands for people to play an active role in the planning and delivery of services raises questions about whether the involvement of citizens in public services will contribute to the quality of these services. It appeared that it was more likely to be a way of reducing public sector expenditure and making people take on the responsibility of planning and providing services themselves.

The implications for the public sector 'ethos' are profound. There will be a reduction in the number of public sector workers, including civil servants, with some functions being outsourced to private sector companies, such as Serco. This will extend the influence of the private sector into the administration of government. Depending on the sequencing of the budget reductions, it is still unclear whether there will be a direct transfer of workers from the public to the private sector or whether public sector workers will be made redundant and then new services contracted out to the private or not for profit sectors, so employing new workers on reduced terms and conditions (*see* Chapter 8, in this volume).

The planned decentralisation of the funding and delivery of public services has particular implication for the public sector 'ethos'. Although the involvement of local people in the planning of services has been acknowledged as important for achieving services that meet local needs, extensive decentralisation can lead to a fragmentation of service provision across a country. There is some evidence drawn from developing countries, which have implemented decentralisation policies over the past two decades, that there is a still an important role for central government to play, even when many services are decentralised. Their experience also shows that local government often lacks the human and financial resources to take over the provision of all public services (Rivera, 2003; Hampwaye, 2008).

The reduced role of government in service provision may well lead to a lack of accountability and transparency in the funding of public services. If local groups, civil society organisations and businesses are all involved in service provision, how will decisions about funding and resource allocation be made available to local citizens? Further evidence from many developing countries shows that a few local sectoral interests can become more dominant in local resource allocation processes than disadvantaged groups (Klugman, 1994; Lakshminarayanan, 2003; Mukhopadhyay, 2005). Ultimately, the public sector has been the arbiter of social justice. If the public sector is no longer involved in this process, who will be responsible for ensuring social justice at local level and between regions?

Payment by results

The terms 'payment by results' or 'outcome-based commissioning' describe an approach to assessing ways of paying for contracted services by focusing on the outcomes achieved rather than process or output measurements. Although the origins of this approach can be found in development aid and funding, promoted by the World Bank, it was discussed by the New Labour administration as well as by the Coalition Government. A report published by the Serco Institute suggested services such as primary care, waste and recycling contracts, managing the asylum system and campaigns against drug misuse and reoffending-could adopt a 'payment by results' approach (Cumming et al., 2009).

Payment by results means that a government will commission and pay for results, but will not dictate how the results are achieved. Successful application of this approach depends on how outcomes are defined and how tightly contracts are drawn up and managed, moving the risk from state to provider (Barker, 2010). In dealing with aspects of social policy, it is often difficult to define outcomes without some acknowledgement of the context within which individuals are operating. Experience from public–private partnerships have shown that although there may be a rhetoric of moving risk away from the state to the private sector, in reality it is the state that has to be ultimately responsible. If a provider fails in contractual or financial terms, the state has to take over the risk.

Payment by results could lead to further undermining of public sector 'ethos'. Public sector 'ethos' is effectively a process and a 'way of doing' things. Payment by results will focus on the results and will not consider how the results are achieved. Furthermore, the delivery infrastructure might be reduced as the delivery of public services will be left to the discretion of providers. Public sector commissioners of services will have little influence over the process of delivery. This has implications for disadvantaged groups' access to services. Unless such access is written into the outcome specification, there will not be a requirement to see that access to services by diverse groups in the community is ensured. A contractual system will also be cost based and many providers will be aiming to deliver a contract with reduced costs. This will determine the quality of the service, *see* Chapter 8 in this volume for a fuller discussion.

The issue of the 'unintended consequences' of a set of actions is not considered in 'payment by results'. Public services cover social and economic policies that are not independent and separate, but are affected by a range of factors. Any social intervention will be influenced by a set of factors, as well as having the potential to impact on these factors. For example, criminal justice interventions are affected by social and economic factors within and outside a local neighbourhood.

Total Place

Total Place was an initiative that was promoted by the Institute of Government from 2009. Introduced as a series of 13 pilot schemes in England, the aim was to map total public spending and devolve control to public service providers (Grint, 2009). Adopting a spatial approach to planning and spending, the Total Place approach aimed to unify government spending across neighbourhoods. It was sponsored by the Department of Communities and Local Government and backed by the Cabinet Office and the Treasury. The underlying rationale was that future cuts in public spending would be necessary and that more effective ways of managing and delivering public services had to be found (Bichard, 2010). Although introduced under the New Labour government, the approach is one that addresses the Coalition agenda of reducing public sector expenditure. At the time of writing, there has been no formal announcement that the Total Place scheme will continue, but the learning from these existing pilot sites remains relevant.

The implications for public sector 'ethos' were that there would be an opportunity to re-shape services in a way that broke down the barriers between different budgets and government departments. It would also offer new ways of involving different providers and service users with a focus on local delivery. The negative effects would be a reduction in jobs and a further reduction in the services provided by the public sector. There was uncertainty about the extent to which front-line staff would retain a sense of ownership of services that they were responsible for delivering. The introduction of outcome based commissioning could contribute to an undermining of front-line staff. Staff motivation could become an important issue that would need to be addressed in the future.

An evaluation of Total Place by the Office of Public Management (OPM) found that the most successful pilot projects were those that had taken the longest time to establish relationships between local stakeholders, including local people. These sites also had clear focus and outcomes. In the OPM's view, an additional agenda of 'efficiency gains' might make it more difficult to engage local communities (OPM, 2009).

Free schools

One of the most high-profile policies announced in 2010 by the new Secretary of State for Education, Michael Gove, was the creation of 'free schools' that parents and other interested groups could set up. They would be government-funded, non-fee paying, but independent from local education authority control (Kershaw, 2010). The concept of 'free schools' was based on the experience in Sweden and the 'charter schools' initiative in the United States. Evaluations of both these initiatives indicate mixed results that show some of the limitations, as well as possible benefits. One of the problems with drawing from initiatives in different countries is the context within which they have been established.

Allen (2010) writing about the Swedish 'free school' system points out that in 1992, Sweden introduced a voucher system so that privately run schools could receive public funding for each student. At the same time, there were some significant changes in the supply side of schools. Teachers' pay and conditions were deregulated. School financing was decentralised and there was increased school discretion over the curriculum, testing and overall goals. These changes provided local schools with more control over setting their own goals and determining their own curricula. The results of the Swedish 'free schools' show a moderate positive impact on municipal educational performance at the age of 15–16. The main beneficiaries have been students from highly educated families, but students from less educated families or immigrant families have not clearly benefitted. Moreover, the advantages have not translated into any greater educational success at 18 or beyond for any group of students (Allen, 2010).

'Free schools' have to be approved by the Secretary of State for Education. They do not have any connection with local education authorities, which are linked to local democratic systems of account-ability and, which over the past 60 years have provided a structure for allocating education funding at local level, according to need. Accordingly free schools, as stand-alone bodies, will serve to undermine the comprehensive nature of the public sector and, indirectly, public sector 'ethos'.

Conclusion

In the UK, the term public sector 'ethos' was fundamental to the concept of a neutral civil service responsible for serving the public interest within government. More recently there has been a change in vocabulary from public sector 'ethos' to public service 'ethos'. This has been accompanied by the change from services users to consumers and signifies a changed relationship between users of public services and providers. Public sector 'ethos' has been the subject of research, in many countries. It has often been addressed in relation to public sector work-ers' motivation and this provides a useful starting point to examine changes emanating from public sector reform.

The proposed changes to the public sector in the United Kingdom include a reduction in the size of the public sector, merging state agen-cies, blurring public–private boundaries, and commissioning through payments by results. The public sector 'ethos' will be affected through a reduction in accountability of public service arrangements, more lim-ited control over the form of public service delivery, and the uneven distribution of public services that will result from a reduced role of government. To what extent public service workers will be motivated to deliver public services when their focus is likely to be on meeting performance targets is unclear at this point. Research into public sec-tor workers' motivation shows that such motivation contributes to the intrinsic values that shape public sector 'ethos'. A recent code of conduct for UK civil servants identified four Ps as important: pride, pas-sion, pace and professionalism. It is strongly arguable that the reforms proposed by the Coalition Government will make it more difficult for public servants to pursue these values.

References

2020 Public Services Commission (2010) 2020 Vision: A far sighted approach to improving public services London: 2020 Public Services Trust.
Allen, R. (2010) 'Replicating Swedish "free schools" reforms in England', *Research in Public Policy*, 10, 4–7.

Barberis, P. (2001) 'Civil society, virtue, trust: implications for the public service ethos in the age of modernity', *Public Policy and Administration*, 16:3, 111–126.

Barker, A. (2010) 'Payment by results: hitting targets', *Ethos Journal*, Spring, 16–17.

Bichard, M. (2010) 'Shaping the future', *Ethos Journal*, Spring, 1–2.

Blair, T. (2002) *The Courage of our Convictions: Why Reform of the Public Services is the Route to Social Justice* (London: Fabian Society).

Brereton, M. and Temple, M. (1999) 'The new public service 'ethos': an ethical environment for governance', *Public Administration*, 77:3, 445–474.

Cerase, F. and Farinella, D. (2009) 'Public service motivation: how does it relate to management reforms and changes in the working situation of public organizations? A case study of the Italian Revenue Agency', *Public Policy and Administration*, 24:2, 281–308.

Civil Service (2010) The Civil Services: A Partial History, www.civilservice.gov.uk.

Clarke J., Newman, J. and Westmarland, L. (2007) 'Creating citizen-consumers? Public service reform and (un)willing selves', in S. Maasen and B. Sutter (eds) *On Willing Selves: Neoliberal Politics and the Challenge of Neuroscience* (Basingstoke: Palgrave Macmillan).

Collins English Dictionary (2009) 'ethos', in *Collins English Dictionary: Complete and Unabridged*, 10th edn (London: HarperCollins).

Cumming, L., Dick, A., Filkin G. and Sturgess, G. (2009) *Better Outcomes* (London: 2020 Public Services Trust at the RSA).

Cunliffe, A. and Jun, J. (2005) 'The need for reflexivity in public administration', *Administration and Society*, 37:2, 225–242.

Grint, K. (2009) *Total Place: Interim Research Report*, online at www.localleadership.gov.uk/totalplace/.../Total-Place-interim-review-report-Prof-Keith-Grint-Warwick-Business-School.pdf [accessed 13 January 2011].

Hampwaye, G. (2008) 'The limits of decentralisation in urban Zambia', *Urban Forum*, 19:4, 347–361.

Hebson, G., Grimshaw, D. and Marchington, M. (2003) 'Public Private Partnerships and the changing public sector ethos: case study evidence form the health and local authority sectors', *Work, Employment and Society*, 17:3, 481–501.

HM Treasury (2010a) *Budget 2010: HC 61 22 June 2010 Copy of an Economic and Fiscal Strategy Report and Financial Statement and Budget Report, June 2010 as Laid Before the House of Commons by the Chancellor of the Exchequer When Opening the Budget* (London: HM Treasury).

HM Treasury *Spending Review 2010 CM 7942 Presented to Parliament by the Chancellor of the Exchequer* (London: HM Treasury).

Jorgensen, T. and Bozeman, B. (2007) 'Public values: an inventory', *Administration and Society*, 39:3, 354–381.

Kershaw, A. (2010) 'Sweden's free schools model has "limited impact"', *Press Association*, 23 June.

Klugman, J. (1994) 'Decentralisation: a survey of literature from a human development perspective', Occasional Paper 13 (United National Development Programme (UNDP)) Online at http://hdrnet.org/497/1/oc13.htm [accessed 13 January 2011].

Koumenta, M. (2009) 'Modernisation, Privatisation and the Public Service Ethos in the UK', paper presented at *Labour Market Policy for the 21st Century:*

A Conference in Honour David Metcalf, 14 December (London School of Economics: London).

Lakshminarayanan, R. (2003) 'Decentralisation and its implications for reproductive health: the Philippines experience', *Reproductive Health Matters*, 11:21, 96–107.

Le Grand, J. (2006) *Motivation, Agency and Public Policy: Of Knights and Knaves, Pawns and Queens* (Oxford: Oxford University Press).

Lundquist, L. (1996) cited in S. Montin 'Teaching public administration in Sweden', *Public Administration*, 77:2, 421–429.

Martin, E. (2002) 'The role of critical social analysis in public policy and administration: a service learning course application in race, inequality and public policy', *Contemporary Justice Review*, 5:4, 351–369.

Matheson, A. (2002) 'Public sector modernisation: a new agenda', paper prepared for the *26th Session of the Public Management Committee of the OECD* (Paris: 30–31 October).

Mukhopadhyay, M. (2005) 'Decentralisation and gender equity in South Asia: an issues paper', online at http://extranet.kit.nl/net/KIT_Publicaties_output/ShowFile2.aspx?e=824 [accessed 27 June 2011].

Needham, C. (2006) 'Customer care and the public sector ethos', *Public Administration*, 84:4, 845–860.

O'Donnell, G. (2009) *Sir Gus O'Donnell Roland Smith Lecture*, 18 February, Lancaster University.

Office for Public Management (OPM) (2009) *Total Place: Lessons Learnt* (London: Office for Public Management).

Page, J. (2004) 'Business takeovers: your employment rights (TUPE)', online at http://www.hackneytuc.org.uk/node/59 (Hackney TUC, London) [accessed 13 January 2011].

Perry, J., Coursey, D., Brudney, J. and Littelpage, L. (2008) 'What drives morally committed citizens? A study of the antecedents of public service motivation, moral commitment and trust in public service', *Public Administration Review*, May/June, 445–458.

Perry, J. and Wise, L. (1990) 'The motivational basis of public services', *Public Administration Review*, 50:3, 367–373.

Plant, R. (1993) 'A public service ethic and political accountability', *Parliamentary Affairs*, 56, 560–579.

Player, S. and Leys, C. (2008) *Confuse and Conceal: the NHS and Independent Sector Treatment Centres* (London: Merlin Press).

Pratchett, L. and Wingfield, M. (1996) 'Petty bureaucracy and woolly minded liberalism? The changing ethos of local government', *Public Administration*, 74:4, 639–656.

Public Accounts Committee (2002) *The Public Service Ethos*, 7th Report, Session 2001–2 (London: Stationery Office).

Quill, L. (2009) 'Ethical conduct and public services: loyalty intelligently bestowed', *The American Review of Public Administration*, 39:3, 215–224.

Rivera, W. (2003) 'The invisible frontier: the current limits of decentralisation and privatisation in developing countries', in A. Cristovao and L. Zorini (eds) *Proceedings of the 4th European IFSA Symposium* (Florence: Agenzia Regionale per lo Sviluppo e L'innovazione nel Settor Agricole e Forestale).

Steijn, B. (2002a) 'HRM and job satisfaction in the Dutch public sector', abstract for the *EGPA-Conference in Potsdam, study group on Public Personnel Policies*, 4–7 September.

Steijn, B. (2002b) 'HRM in the public sector: a neglected subject. Modernisation review – the HRM perspective', paper prepared for the *Human Resource Management Working Party Meeting* (OECD headquarters, Paris 7–8 October).

Steijn, B. (2008) 'Person-environment fit and public services motivation', *International Public Management Journal*, 11:1, 13–27.

TUC Commission on Vulnerable Employment (2008) *Hard Work, Hidden Lives: The Full Report of the Commission on Vulnerable Employment* (London: TUC).

Tullock, G. (1965) *The Politics of Bureaucracy* (Washington: Public Affairs Press).

Vandenabeele, W., Scheepers, S. and Hondeghem, A. (2006) 'Public service motivation in an international comparative perspective: the UK and Germany', *Public Policy and Administration*, 21:1, 16–31.

Part III
Issues

5
Rewarding Public Servants: Continuity and Change

Geoff White

This chapter considers the changing nature of the reward relationship between employers and their employees in the UK public sector focusing primarily on central and local government and the NHS. The 'effort bargain' (Behrend, 1957) in the public sector has traditionally been different to that in the private sector. Given that public sector employment has always been associated with bureaucratic institutions with a strong emphasis upon the so-called public sector 'ethos', as opposed to the overriding profit motive and income maximisation of private sector employment, this difference is not surprising (*see* Chapter 4 in this volume for a fuller discussion). In accordance with public sector values, personnel policies have prioritised careers, equity of treatment and recognition of service, rather than strong financial incentives and competition between staff. Similarly, reward policies in the public sector have tended to incorporate clear grading and promotion structures, collective determination of pay and conditions, service-related pay progression and relatively generous benefits compared to those in the private sector. The recruitment and retention of staff have been paramount considerations and have often taken precedence over issues of motivation.

Over the past two decades the differences between private sector and public sector reward systems have become more exaggerated, even though governments of all political persuasions have made repeated attempts at reform of public sector reward systems to make them more like those in the private sector, often as part of much wider organisational reforms. Yet despite these attempts significant differences in practice remain.

This chapter begins by looking at the key factors that shape reward in the public sector. Then it traces the development of public sector reward starting with the position in the 1970s, followed by the reforms first of the Conservative governments 1979–1997 and then of the Labour governments 1997–2010. It next focuses on differences in public/private sector reward: pay determination, pay comparability, pay practices and non-financial rewards. Finally the chapter examines current issues, pensions and executive rewards, and some concluding observations are made.

Factors shaping public sector rewards

Chapter 1 in this volume traces the historical development of the public sector. Here we focus on the key factors that shape public sector reward. First, there is a strong accent on public accountability compared to private sector organisations, because they are under the direct political control of government, because they are paid for by tax payers and because they exist primarily for the benefit of citizens. While their individual objectives are complex and sometimes in conflict, they are all essentially managed through a political process (Pollitt, 1993). In this respect, all public sector organisations operate within very different constraints to private sector ones and this becomes clear when we look at their reward systems.

Second, public sector organisations are often large scale in the scope of their delivery of services, (even if some of this delivery is through decentralised structures), and hence often administratively complex, with particular issues concerning the role of leadership and management. They are also labour intensive, so that when we speak of investment in public services we are primarily speaking about the cost of the staff who deliver those services.

Third, the public sector is a virtually monopolistic employer of many occupations – there is limited demand for teachers, doctors, nurses and social workers outside the public sector – which has important ramifications when we seek to make pay comparisons. The final and possibly most important characteristic concerning public service employees for reward issues is the public service 'ethos' governing their behaviour as employees (*see* Chapter 4 in this volume).

Traditional features of public sector reward

By the end of the 1970s the traditional structures and components were in place in all parts of the public sector. In terms of pay determination this meant virtually all components of the reward package were determined through collective negotiations at national level with the resulting agreements being implemented by all employers covered by the sector. While there might be several bargaining groups within each sub-sector – for example there were eight civil service bargaining groups – all of these bargained at the national level and often shared some components such as pension arrangements. Each bargaining group would have its own grading structure with separate wage rates or salary scales. In some cases job evaluation was used to grade staff, but in many cases it was not.

For non-manual workers pay progression arrangements were strongly linked to the concept of seniority with service-related incremental progression through long grades. Such systems were generally designed to reward loyalty and the gaining of experience in the job although in certain cases they related also to the concept of 'wage for age' pay, with separate pay rates for younger workers. In earlier days there were also separate pay rates for males and females but these ceased essentially in the 1960s in respect of equality for like work, but not work of equal value (*see* Chapter 6 in this volume). There was very little use of payment by results or incentive pay for non-manual workers although there were some 'proficiency allowances' for typists in the civil service, for example.

For manual workers, wage structures tended to reflect those of private sector manual workers with simple single wage rates based on skill level and, in the more industrial situations such as armouries and dockyards, possibly forms of payment by results or bonus schemes. Indeed the introduction of bonus schemes in the 1960s in local government was often more to do with raising very low basic earnings than to do with raising productivity (NBPI Report 1966 cited in Clegg 1976: 393). For these workers there was no concept of pay progression, other than the negotiated increase to basic rates or promotion to a higher grade. In the case of maintenance craftsmen, pay rates were often linked to those of the industry-wide agreements covering their private sector counterparts.

In terms of conditions of service, benefits were generally as good, if not better, than the private sector and there was a clear view that lower pay for public servants than their private sector equivalents could be compensated for by other factors, such as good leave and sick pay provision as well as relative job security, career development and job satisfaction, at least for the professional workforce. Certainly for manual workers there were also some distinct advantages to working in the public sector where working conditions were likely to be better.

A key attraction of public sector work has traditionally been the provision of defined benefit 'final salary' pension schemes. Separate pension schemes are available for civil servants, school teachers, NHS staff, local government, police and fire services and for the armed forces. These schemes provide a guaranteed pension in retirement based on length of service and salary at retirement. In total there are today 12m active, deferred or pensioner members and dependants of public service pension schemes. Around one in five people in the UK has some entitlement to a public sector pension and in 2008–09 payments were £32bn, around a third of the basic state pension cost (Hutton 2010a: 7). The average size of the pension in payment was £7800 in 2010.

Most importantly, non-financial reward, recognition and the intrinsic rewards of public service were seen as key aspects of the public sector 'effort bargain'. From the 1980s onwards there was also possibly more engagement with the principles of equal pay and equal opportunities among public sector employers than among their private sector counterparts, an integral part of the 'model employer' approach to human resource issues (Corby, 1999).

A final key element of public sector pay determination prior to 1979 was the concept of pay comparability, whereby government would attempt to ensure that public sector pay levels continued to have some fixed relationship with private sector levels. For instance until 1981 the civil service had an elaborate system of comparisons through the standing Pay Research Unit (PRU), which collected relevant pay and conditions data to inform negotiations in the Whitley Council. Elsewhere the principle of pay comparability was less well established; although it was relatively common for boards of inquiry to be established to deal with particularly difficult industrial disputes over pay – for example, for teachers and nurses (White, 2003). The Pay Comparability Commission, established in the dying days of the Labour government in 1979 to deal with the 'winter of discontent' and under the chairmanship of Professor Hugh Clegg, was perhaps the summit of pay comparability, producing many well-researched reports for various groups. Pay Review Bodies (PRBs) were established for three particular groups (armed forces; senior salaried staff – including in the civil service, military and judiciary; and doctors and dentists) (White, 2003). PRBs make independent recommendations on pay after consulting the relevant parties, typically government, employers and unions, which the government then decides whether to accept.

There has also been a distinct pattern to the relationship between public sector and private sector pay. While in general public sector pay movements have followed those of the wider economy, the patterns in the public sector have been more complex. Compared to private sector pay movements, which have generally closely mirrored economic cycles, public sector pay has been more subject to political decision making. In general, in the public sector 'one observes a pattern of pro-longed falls in relative pay, and sometimes absolute pay too, followed by large, expensive, "catching up" awards' (Trinder, 1991: 43). Trinder identified the cycles as ranging in length between three to five years with periods of decay in pay relativities to the private sector, usually the result of government pay restraint policies, being followed by expensive 'catching up' awards (Brown and Rowthorn, 1990). The Confederation of British Industry (CBI) (1994) pointed to the problems that arose as a result of this counter-cyclical pattern. Large public sector 'catching up' awards often came at embarrassingly inconvenient times for both the private sector (where pay increases were already falling) and the Government. The CBI commented that 'catch up occurred when the private sector had already entered downturn and when settlements were falling' (CBI, 1994: 5).

Government attempts at reform 1979–1997

In the period 1979–1997 there were significant changes to the size, structure and organisation of the public sector (*see* Chapter 1 in this volume). This chapter focuses on the initiatives in reward policy and practice. Three main episodes of public sector pay policy have been identified during this period of Conservative administrations (Bach and Winchester, 1994; White, 1996). First, in the early 1980s, following the Conservative victory in 1979, the government imposed strict controls on public expenditure through a system of cash-limited 'pay provision' figures, which were gradually reduced in size. These cash limits were abandoned as the economy recovered from the recession of the early 1980s and skill shortages in the public sector began to appear. Second, from 1986 there was a policy of trying to make the national agree-ments more flexible and responsive to local circumstances through the adoption of pay policies based on 'merit, skill and geography'. Under this policy attempts were made to link pay increases more closely to individual performance, to the market rate for the job and to the local labour market.

The government had some success in meeting its first objective – link-ing pay more closely to merit. The first groups to have individual per-formance-related pay (IPRP) were in the civil service where government had the power to dictate policy. The existing system of Pay Research was unilaterally ended and, following industrial action, new pay arrangements were put in place for all civil service groups that included elements of IPRP. Elsewhere forms of IPRP were introduced for NHS senior managers and in local government some Conservative-controlled authorities introduced such schemes for some staff. The government also had some success in meeting its second objective – linking pay to skill. Skill shortages, which emerged in the tight labour markets of south-east England, were addressed through targeted pay supplements and new types of employee benefit, such as cars and private medical insurance.

In the case of its third objective, however, the government made little headway. The decentralisation of pay bargaining to regional or local level was strongly resisted by unions and by some employers who feared the potentially inflationary effect of decentralisation. Indeed the Government itself did not follow its own rhetoric in deciding to establish two new national PRBs – one for nurses and paramedicals in 1983, the other for school teachers in England and Wales in 1991.

The third period of Conservative pay policy started in 1993 and ended in 1997 when Labour won the general election. This period followed a severe economic depression in the early 1990s that led to a major U-turn on public sector pay policy. Retreating from its avowed policy of decentralised pay, the government re-introduced a central pay policy with a limit of 1.5 per cent on all public sector pay increases in 1993. This was followed by a freeze on departmental budgets for three years but with the flexibility for pay awards to be funded out of efficiency savings (i.e. self-financing). This 'pay freeze' was continued from 1996.

At the same time the government introduced further reorganisational restructuring of the public sector with the abolition of national pay negotiations for the civil service and the delegation of pay bargaining to over 150 individual departments and agencies, except for the most senior staff who were covered by the Senior Salaries Review Body (Kessler et al., 2006). In the NHS it introduced autonomous NHS Trusts and made some attempt to introduce a system of two-tier bargaining whereby a national pay award would be topped up at individual Trust level (Corby et al., 2003). This system was attempted in 1994 with enabling agreements to allow Trusts to make pay additions. In 1995 the PRB for nurses, midwives, health visitors and professions allied to medicine awarded a national pay increase to be uprated by a local increase of between 0.5 and 2 per cent locally. Following industrial action, a complex agreement was reached under which the national rates would be uprated each year to reflect the outcome of the previous year's local agreements, although these complicated arrangements only lasted until 1996. Few NHS trusts took advantage of these freedoms.

While local government had been the most resistant part of the public sector to changes in reward systems, a small minority of around 30 councils had exited from the national pay bargaining arrangements (Bryson et al., 1993). These councils, which were overwhelming Conservative-controlled and largely concentrated in London and southeast England, had sought to develop their own arrangements to cope with the tight labour market in which they found themselves. Some took the opportunity to develop new grading structures while others introduced forms of pay progression related more to merit than to service. In the remaining councils covered by national bargaining there was increasing concern, shared by the unions, that the existing pay determination arrangements left them open to challenges under equal pay for work of equal value legislation. As a result a new national 'Single Status' agreement was reached with the unions in 1997 that merged the manual and non-manual salary scales on to a single pay spine and provided more flexibility for councils to develop their own job-evaluated and 'equal pay proofed' grading structures and progression systems (Perkins and White, 2010).

Change of climate in 1997

The election of a Labour government in May 1997 heralded a change in the fortunes of the public sector with manifesto commitments to reverse Conservative policy, especially in education and the NHS, with new investments in public services (*see* Chapter 3 in this volume). In terms of public sector pay policy there was also a change in rhetoric, although the previous Conservative public sector expenditure controls remained in place for Labour's first two years in office. In many ways the new rhetoric echoed many of the objectives of the previous government but with an emphasis upon 'pay modernisation'. The difference was that agreement to these reforms with the unions was to be sought through negotiation and 'partnership working', rather than through central diktat and imposition.

In its white paper (Cabinet Office, 1999: 2), the Labour Government stated that: 'Public servants must be rewarded fairly for the contribution they make. We must make sure that our approach to pay encourages more of the best people to join and stay'. To that end it proposed reform of 'outdated' pay systems that gave uniform increases to all, irrespective of contribution; revising pay and grading systems to deal with recruitment and retention problems for key groups of staff; making better use of non-pay incentives; and more linkage of pay to performance.

In 1999 the standing terms of reference of four of the then five independent PRBS – which set the pay for particular groups of public servants – were changed to reflect these new government priorities (White and Palmer, 2009). The new criteria for pay increases were to be recruitment, retention and motivation; departmental output targets; expenditure limits; and inflation targets. They were further amended in 2003 (except for the armed forces) to have regard to labour markets and discriminatory and other legal obligations on employers. A new review body was also created for prison officers in 2001.

While government rhetoric continued to stress affordability and curbing inflation, in reality between 1999 to 2001 there was some relaxation of government pay policy and PRB awards were implemented in full from due settlement dates. Public sector pay awards averaged 3 to 4 per cent in line with the private sector (White and Palmer, 2009). As inflation fell dramatically (the average Retail Prices Index (RPI) figure was 1.6% in 1999), public sector workers began to see real improvement in base pay levels. In 2002, however, the government evidence to the PRBs exerted a new downward pressure on public sector pay. From 2003 there was a continuing policy of restraint, although the impact of this varied across different public sector groups. One significant feature of the period since 1997 was the continued strong economic performance of the UK, with historically low inflation, which only came to an end in 2008. This led to a remarkable degree of continuity in overall pay settlement levels, with awards clustering around 3 to 3.5 per cent in most years, despite inflation averaging 4.3 per cent in 2007.

A major development under Labour was the return to an acceptance of joint regulation of pay and conditions, albeit to a limited extent. The 1997 Single Status Agreement in local government became the model for future 'pay modernisation' projects in both the NHS and the higher education sector (although strictly speaking higher education establishments are considered in the national statistics to be 'not-for-profit private corporations' rather than public sector). The key aspects of the three agreements in local government, the NHS and higher education were the creation of a single pay spine for all non-clinical staff; the merger of separate bargaining groups into 'single table' arrangements; the use of job evaluation to create new local grading structures that were 'equal pay proofed'; more flexibility in pay progression arrangements (with the use of more 'contribution-based pay' or competency-related systems); harmonisation of working hours for staff on the same levels; and an acceptance of the need for some degree of market-based pay to deal with specific labour shortages (Perkins and White, 2010).

The NHS Agenda for Change agreement was described as 'one of the most complex and lengthy pay negotiations in the world (Bevan et al., 2004: 8). The agreement involved negotiations with 17 separate trade unions covering all non-clinical staff (doctors and dentists have separate pay arrangements) and a final deal was not reached until late 2004. The rationale 'was not just to pay staff more, but to secure changes in working patterns and productivity that would translate into benefits for patients' (King's Fund, 2007: vi).

In local government progress in implementing the 1997 'Single Status' agreement was problematic. Following industrial action in 2002 and a settlement finally brokered by ACAS, an independent Local Government Pay Commission was established to consider pay relativities and to identify barriers to implementation (Kessler and Dickens, 2008). The commission identified the key issue in local government as being one of equal pay, rather than relative low pay. It therefore recommended that the parties to the agreement set a deadline for implementation of the 1997 agreement at local level, the result of which was a 2004 agreement to complete implementation by April 2006.

Public/private sector differences

In this section we focus on the differences in public/private sector reward: pay determination, pay comparability, pay practices and non-financial rewards. Equal pay initiatives are considered in Chapter 6 in this volume.

Chapter 10 in this volume, 'Organised Labour', looks at both trends in union density in the public and private sectors and at the coverage of collective bargaining. Here the reader is briefly reminded that, according to Kersley et al. (2006), the percentage of workplaces where the pay of any of the workers was determined by collective bargaining was 77 per cent in 2004 for the public sector, compared to 11 per cent for the private sector, a decline of six percentage points in the private sector since 1998 and two percentage points in the public sector. According to the Labour Force Survey 68.1 per cent of public sector employees had their pay affected by a collective agreement in 2009 against 17.8 per cent of employees in the private sector. The equivalent figures for 1996 were 74.4 per cent of public and 23.2 per cent of private sector employees (Achur, 2010).

The locus of collective pay determination has also changed in the private sector. Public sector workers are much more likely to be covered by multi-employer, industry-wide pay determination than by the single

Table 5.1 Locus of decision making within main types of pay determination in the public sector, 1984–2004

	1984	1990	1998	2004
Collective bargaining	94	71	64	71
Most distant level of negotiations				
Multi-employer bargaining	82	58	40	50
Multi-site, single employer bargaining	11	12	18	15
Workplace bargaining	*	*	1	1
Don't know	1	1	5	4
Not collective bargaining	6	29	36	29
Most distant level of decision-making				
External to organisation	3	16	29	23
Management at a higher level in organisation	1	6	5	6
Management at workplace level	*	*	2	*
Don't know	*	6	0	0
Weighted base	717	587	508	446
Unweighted base	812	617	579	452

*Less than 0.5 per cent but not zero.
Note: Staff covered by Pay Review Bodies are considered to be 'not collective bargaining' in WERS.
Source: WIRS/WERS *Data: Workplaces with 25 or More Employees*. Cited by Bach, S. Kolins Givan, R. and Forth, J. in Brown et al. (2009).

employer or workplace level pay decision-making. Multi-employer pay setting has almost disappeared from the private sector but remains the norm for most public servants. Indeed the 2004 WERS found that that there had been a slight increase in the proportion of staff covered by public sector multi-employer agreements from 1998 to 2004 (although this was largely due to the re-classification of groups covered by PRBs). Only in the civil service had sector-wide arrangements been replaced by pay delegation to departments and agencies with the Treasury retaining a strong grip over these individual negotiations through setting the parameters and vetting agreements. Even so, during this period there was an increase in the proportion of public sector pay set unilaterally by employers (Kersley et al., 2006).

Two outcomes of decentralising pay determination have been identified: first, increased variations in the size of pay settlements and, second, increased pay dispersion (OECD, 1997). A study of civil service pay decentralisation in three countries by Bender and Elliott (2003) found that pay dispersion had increased as a result, both within and between departments, especially in the UK. They noted, however, that IPRP may

have played a greater role in this widening of within-grade pay dispersion. The gender pay gap also increased in the UK civil service.

Pay comparability

While devices to secure some form of comparability between public
and private sector pay have either been abolished, as in the case of the
civil service, or amended as in the case of the PRBs, comparisons of pay
in the two sectors continue to be an important part of the public and
political debate. Much of that debate has revolved around levels of earnings in the two sectors, rather than the rate of increase. The raw data
indicate that median pay levels tend to be ahead in the public sector but
this observation, while accurate, disguises some important differences
in the two sectors. Since the privatisation of the public sector corporations in the 1980s and 1990s, the public sector consists overwhelmingly
of non-manual staff and a higher proportion of professionals compared
to the private sector. The figures also show that women are better paid
in the public sector, while men are better paid in the private sector,
largely because of the prevalence of female professionals in the public
sector, but also because of stronger action in the public sector to combat
pay discrimination on gender grounds.

In general, the lowest paid public sector workers are better paid than
their private sector counterparts while the highest-paid are lower paid
than their private sector comparators, although there has been a widening dispersion between the top and bottom of the earnings distribution over the last ten years (Hutton 2010b), with larger pay growth at
the top. The data on public and private sector pay comparisons has
recently become more complicated with the inclusion of finance sector
staff transferred to public ownership through the banking bail-out. The
Office for National Statistics (ONS) now publishes two monthly sets of
average weekly earnings data, one including these staff and one excluding them.

As mentioned above, the traditional pattern of the relationship of
public service pay to the economic cycle has been counter-cyclical
(Trinder, 1991). In other words, while public sector pay has generally
followed the fortunes of the wider economy, it has been subject to
political intervention to such an extent that periods of falling behind
the private sector have been followed by expensive 'catching up' awards
to bring public sector pay back into competition with the private sector. The inefficiency of these cycles has been commented upon by various government inquiries on public sector pay (e.g. Megaw, 1982 and

Edmund-Davies, 1978). The CBI (1994) also pointed to the problems that arise as a result of this counter-cyclical pattern.

This counter-cyclical pattern was common in the 1980s and 1990s but in the 2000s there appeared to be a shift to a more stable relationship to private sector pay (White and Palmer, 2009). Using three measures of public and private sector pay growth over the period 1997 to 2008, White and Palmer (2009) looked at the rate of increase (rather than the level of earnings). The ONS Average Earnings Index data indicates that increases in public sector earnings (on an annualised basis) lagged in the early years of New Labour but then remained ahead of the private sector from 2003. In contrast, the more detailed ONS Annual Survey of Hours and Earnings data shows a continuing public sector lag with annual increases only coming close in 2005. In terms of pay awards, the IDS databank also indicated a public sector 'catch-up' between 1999 and 2003, but the private sector caught up from 2004 and in 2007 overtook the public sector.

Since 2008, the counter-cyclical pattern has emerged again. The effect of the global economic recession has ended the generally stable pay pattern of the last ten years and private sector pay awards have fallen significantly, with a third of employers freezing pay levels (IDS, 2009). The public sector has continued to exhibit larger awards but this is primarily because of the lag from continuing multi-year agreements for some large groups of public servants such as teachers and NHS staff. Following the election of a Conservative–Liberal democrat Coalition Government in

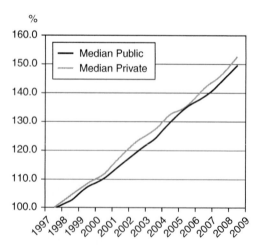

Figure 5.1   ASHE Data, 1997–2009, Median increases
Source: ONS (data adjusted to take account of discontinuities).

May 2010, a two-year pay freeze for public servants was announced but with the proviso that staff earning below £21,000 per annum can be paid a lump sum of £250 (IDS, 2010a). As mentioned before, a major reason for the pattern of continuity between public and private sector pay movements between 2003 and 2008 was the historically low level of inflation prevailing over this period. Pay 'modernisation' in the public sector also contributed to keeping public sector pay levels competitive with the private sector but the costs of these exercises for employers was significant and progress was not uniform across the sector.

Pay practices

There have also been limited changes to the composition of the total pay package in the public sector. Analysis of pay agreements indicates that many public sector workers continue to be paid on pay spines comprising a scale of service-related increments that can be applied to each grade. Therefore, in addition to the annual basic pay award, a proportion of staff (i.e. those not yet at the ceiling of their pay grade) receive guaranteed, service-related increments. In contrast, pay in the private sector (and at more senior levels in the public sector) is increasingly individualised, even under collective bargaining, with individual workers receiving a pay increase based on an assessment of their individual value (either in terms of their 'contribution' or their market position).

Both individual and collective annual bonuses are much more common in the private sector than the public and in some sub-sectors (e.g. financial services) these can add substantially to annual earnings (although in general the size of any median growth in earnings through merit pay is roughly equivalent to incremental pay drift). According to WERS 2004 (Marsden, 2007), 10 per cent of public sector workplaces were using merit pay compared to 16 per cent of private sector workplaces (in employment terms 21% compared to 26%), not a very large difference. A survey of pay progression arrangements by IDS (2010b) found that 67 per cent of public sector employers used incremental progression compared to just 13 per cent in the private sector and the majority were still using service. Similarly the 2010 Annual Reward Survey by the Chartered Institute of Personnel and Development (CIPD) indicates that 66 per cent of public sector respondents used pay spines or increments (CIPD, 2010a), although the same survey also indicated that 50 per cent used performance as the main criteria for pay progression. The CIPD survey states that 'public service employers are more likely to take into account length of service than private sector services firms' (CIPD 2010a: 9).

The CBI argues that 'an inappropriate gap has opened up between reward practices in the public and private sectors' (CBI, 2006: 6). It also states that 'job grading structures in the public sector put too much emphasis on control and predictability while those in the private sector tend to emphasise flexibility' (CBI, 2006: 14). Only in the civil service and in some local authorities has there been a move towards more individual and flexible pay progression and grading systems, although teachers in England and Wales also have a form of 'pay for contribution' under which a performance threshold must be passed for entry on to an upper scale. In the NHS there has been a move towards a form of competency-based career framework with progression linked to knowledge and skills.

The use of job evaluation (JE) to design grading structures is also much more common in the public sector than the private, again reflecting the more transparent reward systems found in the public sector. Not only is JE more common in the public sector than the private sector, but its use has grown dramatically. Between 1984 and 2004, the proportion of public sector workplaces using JE grew from 18 to 44 per cent (Bach et al., 2009: 323). This was largely the result of the pay modernisation agreements in local government and the NHS, where the requirement for equal pay proofing led to the design of sector-specific JE schemes (Hastings, 2009).

Turning to other aspects of the reward package, the traditional benefits of public sector employment such as job security, flexible working, interesting work, and good conditions of service, including a generous final salary occupational pension scheme have continued. On the other hand, public sector workers have not generally received typical private sector benefits such as medical insurance, company cars, profit sharing and stock options. Efforts have occasionally been made to 'price' individual aspects of these packages – for example the Megaw enquiry concluded that the civil service pension was 'worth' eight per cent of salary and took that into account in recommending pay levels (Megaw, 1982). Armed Forces pay is similarly abated to take account of the value of the pension scheme. There has, however, been little effort to compare benefits because while it might be simple to compare single items within a package it is less easy to assess value between different items, or to put a value on intangible benefits like interesting and challenging work. As White and Palmer (2009: 6) argue, there is also the issue that 'the employers' cost of provision is not necessarily a proxy for employee value'.

Econometric analysis using data from the UK Labour Force Survey has shown that on average the annual pay of NHS nurses and midwives consistently lies around £2000 per annum lower than that of employees with the same characteristics employed in the private sector. This led the NHS Pay Review Body to the conclusion that 'to some extent at least, the relative value of the rest of the nursing employment package is already factored into their pay rates' (NHS Pay Review Body, 2008: 86). In other words, nurses place a value of at least £2000 per annum on the rest of their employment package, including the intangible elements.

Work by the Institute of Fiscal Studies (IFS) shows that public sector pension arrangements are particularly valuable to employees when compared to similar defined benefit schemes in the private sector (Disney et al., 2007). However, further research by IFS, which looked specifically at the scheme for school teachers, found that changing the pension scheme is not a 'no-cost' option and that teachers' career earnings line would need to be brought closer to that of private sector equivalents in order to maximise earnings earlier in their working life, thus enabling them to make adequate pension provision. Otherwise, teaching would be disadvantaged as a potential career option for graduates (Disney et al., 2009).

An attempt to compare total reward packages by the ONS (Levy et al., 2010), using the ASHE, found that total reward for full-time employees was higher in the public sector than the private sector, largely because of the large proportion of public sector employees who belong to employer pension schemes. Almost three-fifths of full-time private sector employees do not belong to a pension scheme, compared to just one in ten in the public sector. A comparison on a 'like-for-like' basis, comparing full-time employees with pensions in both sectors, however, showed the reverse with a private sector lead. Distributional analysis shows that the gap between the private and public sectors is particularly noticeable at the upper end of the distribution.

Non-financial reward

While there remains a general continuity with the past in terms of public sector reward practices, other non-financial aspects of the 'effort bargain' may have changed. Work–life balance practices appear to have improved. For example, flexitime increased from 38 per cent of workplaces in 1998 to 44 per cent in 2004, while over the same period job sharing increased from 29 to 30 per cent; home working increased from 10 to 14 per cent; and financial assistance with childcare or provision of a workplace nursery increased from seven to 10 per cent of workplaces. In all of these practices except home working, the public sector leads the private sector (Bach et al., 2009: 328). Similarly extra-statutory sick pay is generally more generous than in the private sector.

In terms of the more intangible rewards of public service, arguably the situation has worsened for public servants. In 2004 public sector workers were generally more trusting of management and more satisfied and committed than those in the private and were eight per cent more motivated than their private sector counterparts sector (Guest and Conway, 2004). The exception was central government where employees were less likely than those in the NHS or local government to report that they worked in a high quality workplace, although motivation levels were still higher than in the private sector. But contrary evidence emerged during the latter half of the 2000s. As Bach (2010: 159) states: 'Critics of the modernisation agenda have suggested that the use of targets in conjunction with more flexible and Taylorist forms of work organisation have eroded professional influence and been used to intensify work'. In particular, professional staff have complained about loss of autonomy and increased surveillance by management. Staff surveys have indicated workforce worries about work pressures and difficulties in reconciling work and home responsibilities and, despite the increase in flexible working, staff are still not satisfied with their work–life balance (Bach et al., 2009).

There have also been concerns about the target- and league table-driven agenda followed by government (Givan, 2005). The Audit Commission identified the paperwork necessary for the target-driven agenda as the most important factor in public sector staff turnover (Audit Commission 2002 cited in Bach, 2010). The most recent CIPD survey of employee attitudes (CIPD, 2010b), however, continues to indicate that public sector workers are more satisfied with their job than those in the private sector. However, perceptions of leadership are much worse than in the private sector with negative scores on every item, especially consultation, confidence and trust. Public sector workers are also least likely to feel informed and most likely to report that their workload is too much, (*see* Chapter 9 in this volume on Leaders).

Current issues

The economic recession that began in 2008 heralded major changes for the public sector. The public expenditure reductions announced by the incoming Coalition Government on top of those already announced by the outgoing government imply major job losses across the public sector workforce and a decline in workforce numbers has already begun. In addition the pay freeze announced by the government to take effect from 2011 for two years will reduce the rate of pay growth considerably – although, as mentioned earlier, those staff earning below £21,000 per annum will see a small lump sum of £250 and those in receipt of service-related increments will probably continue to see some pay growth. The main issue for unions and employees is now job security rather than reward issues. In the latest CIPD Employee Outlook Survey in Autumn 2010 (CIPD, 2010b), half of public sector staff say that their organisation is planning redundancies, up from 40 per cent three months earlier. Nevertheless, reward issues are not being totally ignored with the Coalition identifying pensions and executive reward as priorities.

In the case of public sector pensions, a review by Lord Hutton (the former Labour Work and Pensions Secretary) for the Independent Public Service Pensions Commissions established by the Coalition Government, has argued that the calculation basis for public sector pensions should be changed from final salary, possibly to career-average (Hutton, 2010a). He also recommended that the age at which the pension becomes payable should be increased. The key issue identified by Hutton was that the increasing longevity of pensioners was placing increasing strain upon the financing of the schemes. Contrary to previous evidence (see above), Hutton also maintained that there was no proof that pay was lower for public servants to reflect higher levels of pension provision. He also, however, pointed out that the cost of these schemes was already reducing and that the past reforms, the current pay freeze and the planned reductions would reduce the future cost of pensions. Of course, it is worth noting that in the private sector there has been a major decline in defined benefit, 'final salary' schemes as companies have sought to dispense with the burgeoning costs of such schemes. This withering away of private sector pension schemes has left the public sector schemes exposed and seemingly now too generous.

The other area of current interest is the remuneration levels of public sector chief executives. Fuelled by campaigns by both the Tax Payers Alliance on the right and the trade unions on the left, the reward packages of these senior staff have become a political issue. Reviews of their pay packages have been undertaken by the House of Commons Public Administration Committee (PAC, 2009 and 2010) and, at the invitation of the previous Prime Minister, the Review Body on Senior Salaries (RBSS, 2010). Furthermore, the Coalition commissioned the journalist Will Hutton to investigate the possibility of some form of imposed ceiling based on some pay multiple, for example a 20:1 ratio to the lowest-paid person in the organisation. His interim report (Hutton, 2010b) found that earnings dispersion in the overall public sector had widened from 1997 and that pay ratios between the lowest and highest paid employee had also increased in all sectors apart from the civil service. But Hutton also points out that it is the private sector where the problem begins and that the share of top percentile wages (i.e. those earning above £117,523 per annum) earned by public sector workers has been declining and now accounts for less than one per cent of those above this figure.

Conclusions

This chapter has sought to investigate the differences and trends between reward systems in the public and private sectors. The pattern of public sector remuneration was established at the end of WWII and continued under the post-war consensus until 1979. The election of a radical Conservative administration in that year heralded much wider changes to the public sector than simply pay systems and by the election of the next Labour administration in 1997, several aspects of reward had begun to change. Nonetheless, for those public employees still employed in the public sector, there was a remarkable degree of continuity with the past. While in 1979 the reward systems of the public sector were not that different from the private sector, especially for non-manual workers, by 1997 significant changes had occurred in the private sector – in pay determination systems, in grading, in pay progression systems and in benefits provision.

The divide in reward practices has become much more exaggerated since the 1990s. While policy under Labour signalled some respite for public servants from Conservative public sector pay policy, in reality this was more rhetoric than reality and New Labour continued to espouse many of the same ambitions for public sector reward as the Conservatives – more decentralisation of reward decisions, greater linkage to local labour market conditions and more pay based upon contribution than service. Again, however, the reforms had limited impact on the traditional reward package for the public servant, which remained essentially determined through national negotiations with trade unions, where grading systems are narrow (a feature increased as a result of pay modernisation) and pay progression still largely linked to service. Conditions of service also remain generous in comparison to those in the private sector, especially in the provision of family-friendly benefits, sick pay and of course in pension provision. Only in the civil service did the reforms to reward systems make much progress, largely because here the government could enforce its will through direct control. In the NHS and local government, the major concern was with the risk of equal pay challenges and this led to rather timid attempts by management to seek wider reforms of the reward system.

The fact that the public sector remains a bastion of trade union organisation may explain this lack of management progress, but some commentators have also pointed to the overwhelming lack of enthusiasm for reform among public service managers as a key barrier to change. Whether the period 2010–15 will bring radical reform of public sector reward remains to be seen. but there can be no doubt that the public sector spending reductions announced in November 2010 will have a major effect on employment, pay levels relative to the private sector and work intensification.

References

Achur, J. (2010) *Trade Union Membership 2009* (London: Department for Business Innovation and Skills/National Statistics Office).

Audit Commission (2002) *Recruitment and Retention: A Public Service Workforce for the Twenty-first Century* (London: Audit Commission).

Bach, S., Bryson, A., and Forth, J. (2009) 'The Public Sector in Transition', in W. Brown, A. Bryson, J. Forth and K. Whitfield (eds) *The Evolution of the Modern Workplace* (Cambridge: CUP).

Bach, S. (2010) 'Public sector industrial relations: the challenge of modernisation', in T. Colling and M. Terry (eds) *Industrial Relations: Theory and Practice*, 3rd edn (Chichester: Wiley).

Bach, S. and Winchester, D. (1994) 'Opting out of pay devolution? The prospects for local pay bargaining in UK public services', *British Journal of Industrial Relations*, 32:2, 263–282.

Behrend, H. (1957) 'The effort bargain', *Industrial and Labour Relations Review*, 10:4, 503–515.

Bender, K.A. and Elliott, R.F. (2003) *Decentralised Pay Setting: A Study of the Outcomes of Collective Bargaining Reform in the Civil Service in Australia, Sweden and the UK* (Aldershot: Ashgate Publishing).

Bevan, S., Horman, L. and Turner, N. (2004) *Case Study Report Prepared for the Public Services Forum* (London: The Work Foundation).

Brown, W. and Rowthorn, B. (1990) 'A Public Service Pay Policy', *Fabian Society Pamphlet 542* (London: Fabian Society).

Bryson, C., Gallagher, J., Jackson, M., Leopold, J. and Tuck, K. (1993) 'Decentralisation of collective bargaining: local authority opt outs', *Local Government Studies*, 19:4, 558–583.

Cabinet Office (1999) *Modernising Government*, Cm 4310 (London: The Stationery Office).

CBI (1994) *People, Paybill and the Public Sector: Improving Performance and Service* (London: CBI/Hay Management Consultants).

CBI (2006) *For What It's Worth: Managing Public Sector Reward 2008–11* (London: CBI).

CIPD (2010a) *Annual Reward Management Survey* (Wimbledon: CIPD).

CIPD (2010b) *Employee Outlook: Autumn 2010* (Wimbledon: CIPD).

Clegg, H. A. (1976) *The System of Industrial Relations in Great Britain*, 3rd edn (Oxford: Blackwell).

Corby, S. (1999) 'Equal opportunities: fair shares for all?' in S. Corby and G. White (eds) *Employee Relations in the Public Services* (London: Routledge).

Corby, S., Druker, J., Meerabeau, E., Millward, L., and White, G. (2003) 'Finding a cure? Pay in England's National Health Service', *Employee Relation*, 25:5, 502–516.

Disney, R., Emmerson, C. and Tetlow, G. (2007) *What is a Public Sector Pension Worth?* (London: Institute for Fiscal Studies).

Disney, R. Emmerson, C. and Tetlow, G. (2009) *The Value of Teachers' Pensions* (London: Institute of Fiscal Studies).

Edmund-Davies (1978) *Committee of Inquiry on the Police: Reports on Negotiating Machinery and Pay*, Chair: Lord Edmund-Davies. Cmnd 7293 (London: HMSO).

Givan, R. (2005) 'Seeing stars: human resources indicators in the National Health Service', *Personnel Review*, 34:6, 634–647.

Guest, D. and Conway, N. (2004) *Employee Well-being and the Psychological Contract 2004* (London: CIPD).

Hastings, S. (2009) 'Grading systems, estimating value and equality', in G. White and J. Druker (eds) *Reward Management: A Critical Text*, 2nd edn (Abingdon: Routledge).

Hutton, J. (2010a) *Independent Public Service Pensions Commission: Interim Report* (London: HM Treasury).

Hutton, W. (2010b) *Hutton Review of Fair Pay in the Public Sector. Interim Report* (London: HM Treasury) online at http://www.hm-treasury.gov.uk/d/hutton_interim_report.pdf [accessed 20/12/10].

IDS (2009) 'Pay prospects 2010: planning for recovery', *IDS Pay Report 1034*, October.

IDS (2010a) 'Pay freeze takes hold across the public sector', *IDS Pay Report 1053*, July.

IDS (2010b) 'Pay Progression', *IDS HR Study 929* (London: IDS).

Kersley, B., Alpin, C., Forth, J., Bryson, A., Bewley, H., Dix, G. and Oxenbridge, S. (2006) *Inside the Workplace: Findings from the 2004 Workplace Employment Relations Survey*, (London: Routledge).

Kessler, I., Heron, P. and Gagnon, S. (2006) 'The fragmentation of pay determination in the British civil service: a union member perspective', *Personnel Review*, 35:1, 6–28.

Kessler, I. and Dickens, L. (2008) 'Dispute resolution and the modernisation of the public services in Britain: the case of the Local Government Pay Commission', *Journal of Industrial Relations*, 50:4, 612–629.

King's Fund (2007) *Realising the Benefits? Assessing the Implementation of Agenda for Change*, Report authored by J. Buchan and D. Evans (London: King's Fund).

Levy, S., Mitchell, H., Guled, G., and Coleman, J. (2010) 'Total reward: pay and pension contributions in the private and public sectors', *Economic & Labour Market Review*, 4:9, September.

Marsden, D. (2007) 'Pay and rewards in public services: fairness and equity', in P. Dibben, P. James, I. Roper, and G. Wood (eds) *Modernising Work in Public Services: Redefining Roles and Relationships in Britain's Changing Workplace* (Basingstoke: Palgrave Macmillan).

Megaw, J. (1982) *Inquiry into Civil Service Pay* (London: HMSO).

NBPI (1966) *Pay and Conditions of Manual Workers in Local Authorities, the National Health Service, Gas and Water Supply* (London: National Board for Prices and Incomes).

NHS Pay Review Body (2008) *NHS Pay Review Body Report 2008* (London: OME).

OECD (1997) *Employment Outlook, 1997* (Paris: OECD).

PAC (2009) *Public Administration Committee, Sixth Report: Top Pay in the Public Sector*, 21 September (London: House of Commons).

PAC (2010) *Public Administration Committee, Eleventh Report: Top Pay in the Public Sector*, 24 March (London: House of Commons).

Perkins, S. and White, G. (2010) 'Modernising pay in UK public services: trends and implications', *Human Resource Management Journal*, 20:3, 244–257.

Pollitt, C. (1993) *Managerialism in the Public Services*, 2nd edn (Oxford: Blackwell).

RBSS (2010) *Initial Report on Public Sector Senior Remuneration 2010* (by the Review Body on Senior Salaries), Cm 7848, (London: OME).

Trinder, C. (1991) 'Policies to reduce "cycles"', in J. Hawkins (ed.) *International Pay Policies* (London: Public Finance Foundation).

White, G. (1996) 'Public sector pay bargaining: comparability, decentralisation and control', *Public Administration*, 74:1, 89–111.

White, G. (2003) 'The Pay Review Body System: its development and impact', *Historical Studies in Industrial Relations*, 9, 71–100.

White, G. and Palmer, S. (2009) 'Public sector pay in the UK: patterns and trends since 1997', paper presented at the *EIASM 2nd European Reward Conference* (Brussels, December).

6

Equality in the Public Sector: The Sky Darkens

Susan Corby

Introduction

According to the *Oxford Thesaurus*, synonyms for equality are parity or sameness, but the question is parity or sameness with whom. Equality has many dimensions, but parity/differentials in respect of pay are dealt with in Chapter 5, in this volume. This chapter focuses on the six legally protected grounds: gender, race/ethnicity, disability, sexual orientation, religion or belief and age. Inevitably, however, the main focus is on gender and race/ethnicity as these two grounds have been legally protected for over 30 years, whereas the four other grounds are relative newcomers.

Equality takes several guises. At its narrowest, equality can be conceived as treating like as like: equality as consistency and the focus is on process and the removal of unfair barriers and irrelevant group characteristics. It stems from a liberal ideology that asserts the individual's right to universally applicable standards of justice and provides, for example, for a man and a woman to be assessed on the same criteria in a recruitment exercise. A broader conception is equality of opportunity or starting gate equality (McCrudden et al., 1991), whereby special measures are taken to bring the under-represented group up to a position where they can compete for jobs with the over-represented group, for instance women-only assertiveness training or work placements for ethnic minorities, but selection is on merit. Equality of opportunity can also include family-friendly measures, such as maternity leave and flexible working, so that working women are not hampered by their domestic responsibilities. Importantly also equality of opportunity includes the positive legal duties laid on public bodies to promote equality.

Merit, however, is socially constructed and the broadest conception of equality entails a focus on outcomes and equality of results: discrimination persists until, for instance, the presence of women, ethnic minorities and disabled people in the various parts of the labour force reflects their presence in society as a whole. Yet such outcomes can only be achieved quickly by quotas, which are currently both controversial and unlawful (Fredman, 2002; Jewson and Mason, 1986).

The argument of this chapter is that from 1997–2010 New Labour advanced equality for public sector workers both rhetorically and in practice, but its approach was confused: it adopted measures to advance equality of opportunity, but largely adopted criteria of success based on equality of results, which it failed to achieve. The Conservative–Liberal Democrat Coalition Government seems to be adopting a more cautious approach, focusing on equality of opportunity but not seeking to achieve equal outcomes (May, 2010). Moreover, while the Coalition has said that it will 'promote equal pay and take a range of measures to end discrimination in the workplace' (Cabinet Office, 2010: 18), it has also said that its 'most urgent task ... is to tackle our record debts' (ibid.: p. 7), thus subordinating equality initiatives to economic imperatives. Additionally, its promotion of 'radical devolution of power and greater financial autonomy to local government and community groups' could undermine equality policies driven from the centre.

The plan of this chapter is as follows. Initially the post-war developments on public sector equality are traced in broad terms, with advances from 1945 and a retreat from the mid-1980s to 1997. Then the approach of the New Labour administration from 1997 is examined: its legislative measures, including the creation of public sector duties, and its voluntary measures. Next, New Labour's limited progress towards equality of results is considered. Subsequently, we look at the Coalition Government's approach to equality, discussing the threats to progress stemming from the Coalition's economic policies and its plans to devolve power. Finally, some concluding observations are made.

Historical background: the rise and fall of equality initiatives

Post WWII: the rise of equality initiatives

In the three decades following the end of the WWII, the public sector expanded primarily because of the establishment of the National Health Service (NHS), the nationalisation of a number of basic industries including coal, steel and railways, and the extension of education through the growth of universities, the formation of polytechnics and the raising of the school leaving age. By 1977 over 7m people worked in the public sector (Shaoul, 1999). This expansion coincided with a period when the government sought to be a model employer (Hepple, 1982), giving a lead to private sector employers. Accordingly, the government introduced equal pay between men and women in the civil service in 1955 and, shortly afterwards, in other areas of public sector employment, including education and local government well before the Equal Pay Act of 1970 (Deakin and Morris, 2005). Furthermore, five years before the Sex Discrimination Act of 1975, a civil service committee proposed virtually unprecedented measures to enable women to combine a civil service career with domestic responsibilities (Civil Service Department, 1971).

As to local government, from the late 1970s some local authorities adopted innovative equal opportunity strategies, such as Manchester's opening up of certain posts only to disabled people (Leach, 1989) and the Inner London Education Authority's contract compliance. In a nutshell, contract compliance entailed making compliance with equality procedures and practices a condition of securing a contract to provide goods and services to the Authority. Contract compliance was then copied by 19 other local authorities and resulted in significant numbers of private sector companies changing their employment practices (Institute of Personnel Management, 1987).

Mid-1980 to 1997: equality in retreat

The equality initiatives outlined above were concentrated in central and local government, rather than elsewhere in the public sector, and were curtailed by the Conservative government led by Mrs Thatcher. Thus the Local Government Act 1988 outlawed contract compliance with regard to sex and disability and circumscribed it in respect of race (Godwin, 2004) and required local authorities to put certain services out to tender with negative effects on equality. Women, especially part-time women, suffered a decline in net pay or were more likely to lose their jobs, compared to their male colleagues and there was a decrease in the number of disabled workers (Escott and Whitfield, 1995). Similarly ministerial pressure to contract out ancillary services in the NHS impacted adversely on women (Kelliher, 1996). Furthermore, rate-capping in 1987 resulted in equality initiatives being reduced because of budgetary constraints (Corby, 1994; Leach, 1989).

Nevertheless, there were some public sector equality initiatives under the Conservative Government although such initiatives were purely voluntary. For instance in 1987 an agreement for local authority manual grades, designed on equal value principles was concluded and in 1991 the then Health Secretary imposed yardsticks to encourage the advancement of women in the NHS by the year 2000 as a contribution to a general programme on gender equality covering all public and private sector organisations (Corby, 1995). Similarly from the 1990s, targets and programmes were drawn up to aid the advancement of women, ethnic minorities and disabled people in the civil service. Such actions, however, resulted in only limited progress by the time that the Conservatives were replaced by New Labour in 1997 (Cabinet Office, 1998).

New Labour 1997–2010

When New Labour came to power in 1997, it sought to make equality an integral part of its strategy to reform the public services under its so-called modernising agenda, thus giving equality a higher priority than hitherto, but it elided equality of opportunity with equality of outcome. Thus in its seminal document, *Modernising Government,* it said:

[The public service] is committed to achieving equality of opportunity ... It should reflect the full diversity of society. At present it does not. Women, people from ethnic minority groups and people with disabilities are seriously under-represented in the more senior parts of the public service. Addressing this is a top priority.

(Cabinet Office, 1999: 59)

Legislative measures

In fulfilment of its commitment, New Labour legislated to foster equality and diversity. Partly this was a response to European Union directives, for instance protection against discrimination on grounds of sexual orientation, religion or belief and age, but partly legislation has been purely government generated. Such legislation included so-called family-friendly measures: increases in the maternity provisions and the right to request flexible work on return to work after childbirth. The most innovative, however, was the imposition of equality duties on public sector bodies.

New Labour began to legislate to impose positive equality duties on public bodies first in respect of racial equality in 2002, then in respect of disability equality in 2006 and gender equality in 2007. The Equality Act, passed by New Labour in 2010, took this further by creating a single equality duty, comprising the previous three duties and adding duties in respect of age, sexual orientation, religion or belief, pregnancy, maternity, gender reassignment and harassment on a protected ground (IDS, 2010). Labour lost office, however, before it could implement the Act.

Looking at the three duties under New Labour, what did they entail? In short, they required public bodies to carry out an equality impact assessment and publish an equality scheme, renewable every three years, both in respect of the provision of public services, whether directly or through a contracted-out service, and in respect of employment. Thus, on race, the public body was required to collect ethnic monitoring data on such matters as staff in post, applications and selection for employment, training and promotion and those taking grievances or being disciplined. Then it had to analyse the collected data and carry out an impact assessment of its policies, procedures and practices and finally it had to propose measures to remove any barriers and advance equality by proactive and anticipatory action. In the event of non-compliance, the Equality and Human Rights Commission (EHRC) could issue a non-compliance order and follow this up with a court order.

These positive duties provided a basis for the public sector to move away from the fault-based model of discrimination law, with its reliance on individuals making complaints in an adversarial legal system and with remedies designed to compensate the individual after the event. Under the public sector duties, the duty bearer, whether or not responsible for creating discrimination, became responsible for eliminating structures, policies and practices that were found to have had an adverse impact on the protected group.

These duties have the potential to be a powerful tool and to make equality a key goal in the public sector because as noted above, they covered employees, service users and procurement/contractors. Some notes of caution, however, should be sounded. First, they only imposed an obligation on public bodies to give 'due regard' to equality, that is, to balance the importance of equality against other considerations, 'thus incorporating the requirements of relevance and proportionality' (O'Cinneide, 2005: 229).

Second, on gender, a public body was required 'to consider the need to include objectives that address the causes of any differences between the pay of men and women that are related to sex' (Equal Opportunities Commission, 2007: para 3.40). The duty did not require public authorities to carry out an equal pay review, even though such a review (which entails comparing the pay of men and women doing work of equal value, identifying and analysing any pay gaps and eliminating gaps that cannot be satisfactorily explained on grounds other than sex) had been recommended in a statutory Code of Practice (Equal Opportunities Commission, 2003). In a survey undertaken in 2008 it was found that less than half the public sector bodies surveyed had either completed an equal pay review, had one in progress or were planning to conduct one (Adams et al., 2008).

Third, some public bodies focussed mainly on process compliance. Fourth, heavy workloads rather than lack of commitment, was the reason for a lack of meaningful action in respect of the gender equality duty in local government according to research by Conley and Page (2010).

In 2008–09 several pieces of research were conducted jointly by the EHRC, the Improvement and Development Agency (IDeA) for local government, the Local Government Association and the Society of Procurement Officers in respect of equality in local authority procurement. The researchers found that the extent to which equality considerations were integrated into the various stages of the procurement process varied, as did the extent of corporate commitment and leadership, which were important in establishing positive attitudes to equalities among officers. Also, there was variation in the frequency and scope of equality impact assessments and only 37 per cent said that they monitored the equalities aspects of contracts once they were let. In short a mixed picture (Local Government Association, 2008).

Finally, while the duties have proved a powerful lever for change in Northern Ireland, the Greater London Authority, the Scottish Parliament and the Welsh Assembly, there has been considerable political support there. For instance Chaney (2002: 30) found that the Welsh Assembly had given unprecedented priority to equality with 'a series of wide-ranging institutional reforms'.

As O'Cinneide (2003) points out, however, the duties may be less effective in a less favourable political context and research by Hussain and Ishaq (2008) in respect of the race equality duty in Scottish local authorities supports that view. They concluded that while 10 (one-third) of the local authorities could be classed as proactive, the remainder were 'doing no more than making sure they comply with the law' (Hussain and Ishaq, 2008).

Voluntary measures in the sub-sectors

Against a background of New Labour's focus on legislating for equality in the public sector, with new public duties and the embedding of equality into the procurement process, there were various national level voluntary initiatives in sub-sectors and these are traced. Of course, however impressive the initiative is at national level, the extent to which there is commitment and action down the line varies, but space precludes a full discussion of local variations. Accordingly, first, the chapter traces equality initiatives in central and local government and the NHS, where there was a track record of action to further equality objectives before New Labour came to power. This chapter then considers the uniformed services where there are embedded attitudes that have been unhelpful to progress on equality.

The civil service, as noted above, has a long pedigree on women's equality and it introduced ethnic monitoring in the 1980s. In 2005, the Cabinet Office launched 'Delivering a Diverse Civil Service: A 10-Point Plan'. The plan resulted in diversity targets being set by departments and agencies in support of service-wide targets, with progress towards these targets being monitored by the Cabinet Office, a board level diversity champion in each department and a new development scheme (Leaders Unlimited). In 2008, the civil service adopted a new strategy to build on the 10-point plan, 'Promoting Equality, Valuing Diversity'. Measures included ensuring that diversity was integral to permanent secretaries' performance appraisal and to departmental capability reviews, talent management for instance, through mentoring schemes and new, more stretching targets. Progress was measured quantitatively, for instance, by staff survey results, take-up of flexible working and diversity training, as well as qualitatively through feedback from unions and focus groups (Cabinet Office, 2008).

Some local authorities also have a long pedigree on equality, but recently there has been more widespread action, partly in response to the positive legal duties outlined above and partly because local government centrally introduced an Equality Standard, initially in 2001 but revised in 2007, to include both employment and service delivery. The Standard has five levels. First, a commitment to a comprehensive equality policy; second, assessment and community engagement; third, setting equality objectives and targets; fourth, information systems and monitoring against targets; and fifth, achieving and reviewing outcomes. Claims that levels three and five have been achieved have to be validated by external assessment (IDeA, 2007).

Turning specifically to gender pay equality, in 1997 local government employers and unions agreed a new job-evaluated pay structure, the Single Status Agreement, based on a single spine to replace different pay scales for different job families and to put into effect equal pay for work of equal value principles. After a fitful start, there was agreement that all local authorities would introduce the new pay structure by July 2007, but some did not meet that deadline (*Labour Union Digest*, 2010), *see* Chapter 5 in this volume.

One of the main obstacles to gender pay equality in local government has been money. A job evaluation exercise is not cost-free, but the main costs relate to pay protection for men and to back pay for women which, in law, can be for up to six years from the date of the equal pay claim (five years in Scotland) and local authorities have been deluged with such claims by no win/no fee solicitors. Unlike trade unions, no win/no fee solicitors do not have an on-going relationship with the employer, but are only concerned with back pay. Moreover, whereas unions have a responsibility to take account of the interests of all their members, no win/no fee solicitors are only responsible for their claimants' interests. In *GMB* v *Allen*[1] the Court of Appeal found that the union had discriminated against its female members by not pressing for the full amount of back pay to which they were entitled in return for the employer offering pay protection to others (mostly men). As a result, the only safe approach now for unions, if they are to avoid legal liability for discrimination, is to bring proceedings on behalf of every member who might have an equal pay claim and eschew negotiations (Cavanagh, 2008).

It would, however, be erroneous to demonise no win/no fee solicitors. They stepped into an arena where women's work had not been valued equally with men, where employers, often with union collusion, had tailored productivity and bonus systems to the work done by manual men (Hastings, 2000) and where the law is problematic, with the result that cases can take over a decade to resolve (Corby, 2009). They also stepped into an arena where local authorities have been slow to act, essentially because they have had to fund their equal pay liabilities by using their capital receipts, as central government has refused to provide funding (*Labour Union Digest*, 2010).

No win/no fee lawyers have been active not only in local authorities, but also in the NHS as well, pursuant to the NHS adopting a new job-evaluated pay structure, known as Agenda for Change. Introduced in 2004 and covering all staff except doctors, dentists, very senior managers and general practitioner staff, it aimed to replace a job families' structure and put staff on a single pay spine, incorporating equal pay for work of equal value (*see* Chapter 5 in this volume). As in local government, however, the new NHS pay structure made clear a history of gender bias and many equal pay claims have been lodged to recover back pay.

On equality more generally, the NHS has sought to be an exemplar employer. As a result 'there is no shortage of advice and guidance on equality and diversity in the NHS workforce' (NHS Employers, 2008: 3). Such advice includes: *The Vital Connection* (Department of Health, 2000), *Equalities and Diversity in the NHS: Progress and Priorities* (Department of Health, 2003), *Sharing the Challenge, Sharing the Benefits in the Medical Workforce* (Department of Health, 2004), *Positively Diverse: Quick Guide* (NHS Employers, 2005), *Tackling the Challenge: Promoting Race Equality in the NHS in England* (Healthcare Commission, 2009) and *Sexual Orientation: A Practical Guide for the NHS* (Department of Health, 2009).

While there have been many initiatives to foster equality in the civil service, local government and the NHS, the uniformed services have been much slower to act. There is danger in those uniformed occupations, where the assistance of a colleague may literally be a matter of life and death, and personnel often live closely together in police or prison housing, in fire stations and barracks. There is an assumption that homogeneity is a necessary prerequisite of collegiality and this leads to an occupational norm of a white, heterosexual male. Nevertheless, there are some signs of change.

In the police, following the Stephen Lawrence Inquiry report (Macpherson, 1999) and the BBC television programme, *The Secret Policeman,* in 2003, there was a formal investigation by the Commission for Racial Equality (CRE) (CRE, 2005). In response, a new equality, diversity and human rights strategy was developed, recruitment targets were set and interventions to address barriers to promotion were introduced (Home Office, 2008). In a similar vein the Prison Service, after the CRE issued a highly critical report of race equality, drew up a national race equality plan and established a management board to oversee delivery (Ministry of Justice, 2008).

In the Fire Service, where over 98 per cent of fire-fighters were white and male in 2002 (Independent Review, 2002), an equality and diversity strategy was published in 2007 and a national action plan developed in 2009 with recruitment targets, a monitoring system, a network of equality champions and a scheme for developing those with high potential (Communities and Local Government, 2009).

As to the Armed Forces, again the CRE issued a highly critical report and only lifted its threat of a non-discrimination notice after a five-year voluntary partnership between the CRE and the armed forces was agreed in 1998 in respect of black and ethnic minorities, but it was not until 2000 and following a case to the European Court of Human Rights[2] that the ban on homosexuality was lifted. More recently however, there have been some signs of change. For instance in 2005 a new procedure was published in respect of allegations of harassment, including on the basis of race, gender and sexual orientation and an equality and diversity so-called directive was issued for the army (Dannatt, 2008). Nevertheless, the extent of change should not be exaggerated. For instance at the time of writing, women and transsexuals are still not allowed to serve on submarines or in close-combat units (Henley, 2010).

Not equality of results

The legislation and the stream of voluntary measures described above have not produced equality of results in the public sector. According to the Annual Survey of Hours and Earnings (2010) the gender pay gap for full-time employees in the public sector (based on median hourly earnings excluding overtime) was 10 per cent in 2010. For all public sector employees, regardless of whether they were full-time or part-time, the gender pay gap was 19.2 per cent. Comparing men and women in the same professions in the public sector, the gender pay gap, based on average annual salaries, was over 20 per cent for medical practitioners and over 10 per cent for primary school teachers, secondary school teachers and teachers in further and higher education (Connolly and Holdcroft, 2009). Although the gender pay gap for the public sector was significantly narrower than the private sector gap, the statistics indicate there is still some way to go before equality of results between men's and women's pay is achieved.

The gender pay gap apart, women, ethnic minorities and disabled employees were under-represented at the top of organisational hierarchies. For instance in the civil service in 2009, 53 per cent were women, but only 32.8 per cent were in the senior civil service; 8.9 per cent of civil servants were from ethnic minorities, but only 4.2 per cent were in the senior civil service; and those who had declared themselves disabled were 7.1 per cent of all civil servants, but only 4.3 per cent were in the senior civil service (ONS, 2010). In the NHS 13.7 per cent of the non-medical workforce in England were from ethnic minorities in 2009, but only 8.0 per cent were managers or senior managers and 2.1 per cent were qualified ambulance staff. Women comprised 81.1 per cent of the non-medical workforce in England, while 59.8 per cent were managers and 33.8 per cent were qualified ambulance staff.[3] Moreover, while the prison service achieved the target of employing 6.3 per cent of black and minority ethnic (BME) staff by 2009, 'management positions seem to evade BME males' (NOMS, 2009: 4).

In short, despite legislation and a plethora of voluntary initiatives to provide for equal opportunity, this has not led to equality of results and, on the present statistical trend, equality of results will only be achieved after very many years. This is not surprising. There is an inherent conceptual confusion between those who are concerned to eradicate unfair barriers and those who are concerned with a fair distribution of rewards (Jewson and Mason, 1986). If the aim is equality of results in less than, say, a decade, then there has to be positive discrimination.

The Coalition Government

The Coalition Government's agreement states that the government 'will promote equal pay and take a range of measures to end discrimination in the workplace' (Cabinet Office, 2010: 18). This is rather a bland statement, however.

The Coalition has implemented certain politically uncontroversial parts of the Equality Act 2010, which New Labour passed at the end of its period of government, for instance the harmonisation of the different strands of discrimination law, discrimination because of association with a protected person (e.g. a mother caring for a disabled child) and discrimination because of perception (e.g. perception of homosexuality even if in fact that person is not homosexual). It has also implemented that part of the Act that makes it clear that the protected ground of gender includes pregnancy and gender reassignment and that ethnicity includes caste.

As to the public sector, the Coalition Government is implementing the Act's single equality duty[4] for public sector bodies, incorporating the existing public duties in respect of race, disability and gender, but adding the other protected grounds of age, religion or belief and sexual orientation (but not a socio-economic duty as envisaged by New Labour). Although at the time of writing the government has yet to formulate the regulations fleshing out the Act's general public sector duty with specific duties, it has said it will have 'significantly different' arrangements from the previous government and not 'impose burdensome additional processes on public bodies' (Government Equalities Office, 2010: 19).

Moreover, monitoring under the new single equality duty is to be less extensive than those in Labour's three separate public duties. For instance under the Coalition's proposals public authorities/bodies will not be required to ethnically monitor the number of applicants for training and promotion, nor to publish workforce equality data unless they have 150 or more employees, a significant reduction on New Labour's requirements. Nevertheless, even under the Coalition Government's regulations, public bodies with 150 or more employees will be required to publish data annually on the gender pay gap, the proportion of staff from ethnic minority communities and the distribution of disabled employees through an organisation's structure. To that end, the EHRC is seeking to develop a system of reporting gender pay differentials (Government Equalities Office, 2010).

As to other provisions in the Equality Act, the Coalition Government is banning pay secrecy clauses in contracts, though this is essentially a private sector issue as most pay scales are published in the public sector (IDS, 2010) and extending positive action. Under the pre-existing legislation so-called positive action can be taken to encourage people from a particular group to take advantage of opportunities for work and training where under-representation of that group has been identified. Examples include women-only assertiveness training or recruitment advertisements placed in the ethnic minority press, but selection has to be on merit. S.159 of the Equality Act takes this further. Where there is a tie break, that is, one person is overall as 'qualified' as another, the person with the protected ground can be treated more favourably, for instance in terms of recruitment or promotion. This provision is in line with the decision of the European Court of Justice in Marschal.[5] It does not amount to quotas or positive discrimination, which remain unlawful in Great Britain.[6] Moreover, employers are not obliged to use this power. It is permissive, not obligatory.

So far we have looked at areas where the Coalition Government will implement Labour's provisions, but there are areas where the Coalition Government will go further than Labour and which affect both the public and private sectors. First, it has said it will legislate to extend the right to *request* flexible work to all workers. This fits in with 'the espoused concerns to improve people's general non-material well-being and family life' (Williams and Scott, 2010: 15). Second, it is ending the default retirement age of 65 as from October 2011. Furthermore, it seems likely that the Coalition will introduce measures to allow parents to share their maternity and paternity leave between them (subject to the two weeks compulsory maternity leave for women), but 'it is doubtful whether this will be a legislative priority of the new administration' (Rubenstein, 2010: 2).

These legislative provisions, however, must be set against the neoliberal economic background and the Coalition Government ordering cuts of at least 20 per cent in the budgets of public sector bodies (except health and overseas aid) (*see* Chapter 3, in this volume). First, public sector cuts will have a disparate impact on women, as twice as many women than men work in the public sector (Matthews, 2010). Second, equality is not resource-free. There need to be public servants to draw up action plans, oversee the introduction of equality measures, carry out equality impact assessments, monitor and assess progress, but such posts carry a cost and are likely to be cut in order to save front-line services.

As the IDeA for local government commented, a comprehensive equality duty will include the 'earmarking of specific resources for improving equality practice' (IDeA, 2007: 26). Under New Labour there was money for equality initiatives. For instance in 2009 the Department for Communities and Local Government gave a £2m capital grant to be divided among those Fire and Rescue Authorities who were prepared to commit to certain diversity targets to be achieved by 2013. Other initiatives, such as equality awareness training for managers and mentoring schemes for ethnic minorities, are likely to be jettisoned, as budgetary constraints force departments and other public bodies to focus on their core duties. Also, as noted above, there is some evidence that the public duties are less effective in a less favourable political context (O'Cinneide, 2003) and politicians' priority will be their budgets, given the Coalition's focus on cutting public expenditure.

Furthermore the Coalition looks set to promote localism, which is likely to be detrimental for equality initiatives for two reasons. First, the centre will be disempowered and so no longer be able to drive equality programmes forward. Second, smaller devolved bodies, such as 'free' schools, no longer under the control of local authorities, will not have the economies of scale to provide the resources and expertise to implement equality measures; whereas a local authority, although forced to reduce equality initiatives under a harsh economic climate, will not eliminate them entirely or lose its equality expertise altogether. This applies equally to the NHS, where several hundred general practitioner commissioning consortia are to replace 150 primary care trusts in England (Department of Health, 2010).

Conclusions

This chapter has shown how central and local government action on equality in respect of public sector employees has waxed and waned. For instance, in the 1960s and 1970s, some local authorities adopted innovative equal opportunity strategies and the civil service sought to enable women with domestic responsibilities to continue working. From 1979–1997 however, there was a period of retreat. For instance, the Conservative government enacted legislation to prevent local authorities from taking virtually all equality issues into account when contracting out their services.

In contrast in the period 1997–2010, New Labour moved equality issues up the public sector agenda, both by legislation, particularly introducing the public duties, and by voluntary programmes. In its dying days New Labour enacted the Equality Act 2010, but had no time to bring it into effect. This is largely being done by the Coalition Government that came to power in 2010, but its regulations fleshing out the single equality duty will be less far-reaching than Labour's three separate duties (race, disability, gender).

The Coalition Government has said it will cut so-called red tape and provide 'the competitive environment required for enterprise to thrive' (Cabinet Office, 2010: 10). Like its predecessor, however, the Coalition is requiring the public sector to set an example on equality to the private sector essentially by the imposition of public duties. At the same time, in the interests of economic efficiency the Coalition will allow private sector employers the freedom to decide whether or not they wish to follow the public sector's example. This enables the Government to claim it is helping to build a fairer society and at the same time to ensure that business is not burdened (Government Equalities Office, 2010). Of course, this begs the question of whether equality legislation does impede economic efficiency.

At the start of this chapter, three concepts of equality were set out: equality of consistency, or like versus like; equality of opportunity or starting gate equality; and equality of results. This chapter has shown that New Labour promoted equality of opportunity, but measured outcomes by results and the current government is adopting a similar approach. The governmental assumption is that discrimination prevents the labour market operating efficiently and if unfair barriers are eliminated, there will be equality of opportunity and the best person will win. It ignores the fact that merit is socially constructed and that inequality stems from structural sources (Jewson and Mason, 1986; Young, 1990).

Under the banner of equality of opportunity it is lawful to introduce positive action, but it is not lawful under domestic and EU law to introduce positive discrimination provisions, such as numeric quotas to obtain a distribution within the organisation's workforce reflecting the disadvantaged population. Yet equality of opportunity will not lead to equality of outcome in the foreseeable future without positive discrimination and the use of quotas. Although quotas may be controversial,[7] they have proved to be quick and effective catalysts for change, for instance Labour's experiment in the 1990s with all-women shortlists for parliamentary candidates, Texas's 10 per cent rule for ethnic minorities in university entrance (Vasagar, 2010) and Norway's 2003 law requiring private sector company boards of over 10 members to comprise 40 per cent of women by 2005 (AIPBW, 2010). Moreover, measuring outcomes without the fast action that can be obtained through quotas, can lead to discouragement.

As to localism, whatever the arguments for it, such localism is unlikely to prove conducive to promoting equality. The Government has said that it wants to eschew 'central diktats' on equality, yet small, local bodies are unlikely to have equality knowledge and expertise. Most important of all, however, is the economic context. Against that background there will be less room for equality measures that inevitably cost money. Such costs derive from the people required to plan, implement and monitor measures, as well as from the measures themselves, which are often invisible to the public and do not comprise the front-line services that the Government seeks to protect. Accordingly, the prospect for the furtherance of equality in the public sector is far from rosy.

Notes

1. *Allen and others* v *GMB* [2008] EWCA Civ 810; [2008] WLR (D) 243.
2. *Smith and another* v *United Kingdom* (App. nos. 33985/96 and 33986/96) [2000] ECHR 33985/96.
3. *NHS Hospital and Community Health Services Non Medical Workforce Census* (England: NHS Information Centre, 30 September 2009).
4. S.149 Equality Act 2010.
5. *Marshall* v *Land Nordrhein–Westfalen* [1998] IRLR 39, ECJ.
6. In Northern Ireland, 'affirmative action', that is, quotas, to enable fair participation between Protestants and Catholics, is lawful (McCrudden, 1992).
7. For example, the Supreme Court in the USA ruled quotas unconstitutional in the case *Regents of the University of California* v *Bakke* (1978), which concerned a university admission system that enabled racial minorities to enter medical school with lower scores than white applicants.

References

Adams, L., Hall, P. and Schäfer, S. (2008) *Equal Pay Reviews Survey 2008*, London: Equality and Human Rights Commission.

AIPBW (Association of Professional and Business Women) (2010) 'Women on Boards: the inside story on Norway's 40 % target', online at http://europeanpwn. net/index.php?article_id=150 [accessed 27 July 2010].

ASHE (2010) *Statistical Bulletin* (London: Office for National Statistics).

Cabinet Office (1998) *Equal opportunities in the Civil Service 1995–1999* (London: Stationery Office).

Cabinet Office (1999) *Modernising Government*, Cm 4310 (London: Stationery Office).

Cabinet Office (2008) *Promoting Equality, Valuing Diversity – A Strategy for the Civil Service* (London: Cabinet Office).

Cabinet Office (2010) *The Coalition: Our Programme for Government* (London: Cabinet Office).

Cavanagh, J. (2008) 'Equal pay: why we should feel sorry for public sector employers', *Equal Opportunities Review*, 178, 6–10.

Chaney, P. (2002) 'New and unexplored possibilities – the Welsh legislature's statutory duty to promote equality of opportunity', *Equal Opportunities International*, 21:1, 19–30.

Civil Service Department (1971) *The Employment of Women in the Civil Service* (London: HMSO).

Commission for Racial Equality (2005) *Final Report: Police Formal Investigation* (London: Commission for Racial Equality).

Communities and Local Government (2009) *Fire and Rescue Service: Equality and Diversity Report 2009* (London: Communities and Local Government).

Conley, H. and Page, M. (2010) 'The gender equality duty in local government: the prospects for integration', *Industrial Law Journal*, 39:3, 321–325.

Connolly, S. and Holdcroft, A. (2009) *The Pay Gap for Women in Medicine and Academic Medicine* (London: British Medical Association).

Corby, S. (1994) 'The rise and fall of equal opportunities', *Personnel Management*, December, 34–36.

Corby, S. (1995) 'Opportunity 2000 in the NHS: a missed opportunity for women', *Employee Relations*, 17:2, 23–37.

Corby, S. (2009) 'Pay equity: gender and age' in S. Corby, S. Palmer and E. Lindop (eds) *Rethinking Reward* (London: Palgrave Macmillan).

Dannatt, R. (2008) *The Chief of the General Staff's Equality and Diversity Directive for the Army* (London: Ministry of Defence).

Deakin, S. and Morris, G. (2005) *Labour Law*, 4th edn (Oxford: Hart).

Department of Health (2000) *The Vital Connection* (London: Department of Health).

Department of Health (2003) *Equalities and Diversity in the NHS: Progress and Priorities* (London: Department of Health).

Department of Health (2004) *Sharing the Challenge, Sharing the Benefits in the Medical Workforce* (London: Department of Health).

Department of Health (2009) *Sexual Orientation: A Practical Guide for the NHS* (London: Department of Health).

Department of Health (2010) *Equity and Excellence: Liberating the NHS*, Cm 7881 (London: Stationery Office).

Equal Opportunities Commission (2007) *Gender Equality Duty Code of Practice*, Manchester: Equal Opportunities Commission.

Equal Opportunities Commission (2003) *Code of Practice on Equal Pay* (Manchester: EOC).

Escott, K. and Whitfield, D. (1995) *The Gender Impact of CCT in Local Government* (Manchester: Equal Opportunities Commission).

Fredman, S. (2002) *Discrimination Law* (Oxford: Clarendon Press).

Government Equalities Office (2010) *Equality Act 2010: The Public Sector Equality Duty, A Consultation* (London: Government Equalities Office).

Godwin, K. (2004) 'Contracting for equality', *Equal Opportunities Review*, 130, 8–14.

Hastings, S. (2000) 'Grading systems and estimating value' in G. White and J. Druker (eds) *Reward Management* (London: Routledge).

Healthcare Commission (2009) *Tackling the Challenge: Promoting Race Equality in the NHS in England* (London: Healthcare Commission).

Henley, J. (2010) 'Women on the frontline', *The Guardian*, G2, 23 June, 6–10.

Hepple, B. (1982) 'Labour law and public employees in Britain' in W. Wedderburn and J. Murphy (eds) *Labour: Law and the Community: Perspectives for the 1980s* (London: Institute for Advanced Legal Studies).

Home Office (2008) *Policing Minister's Assessment of Minority Ethnic Recruitment, Retention and Progression in the Police Service* (London: Home Office).

Hussain, A. and Ishaq, M. (2008) 'Managing race equality in the Scottish local councils in the aftermath of the Race Relations (Amendment) Act 2000', *International Journal of Public Sector Management*, 21:6, 586–610.

Improvement and Development Agency (2007) *The Equality Standard for Local Government* (London: IDeA).

Independent Review of the Fire Service (2002) *The Future of the Fire Service: Reducing Risk, Saving Lives* (London: Home Office).

Income Data Services (IDS) (2010) *Equality Act 2010: Employment Law Guide* (London: IDS).

Institute of Personnel Management (IPM) (1987) *Contract Compliance: the UK Experience* (London: IPM).

Jewson, N. and Mason, D. (1986) 'Theory and practice of equal opportunities: liberal and radical approaches', *Sociological Review*, 34:2, 307–334.

Kelliher, C. (1996) 'Competitive tendering in NHS catering: A suitable policy?' *Employee Relations*, 18:3, 62–76.

Labour Union Digest (2010) 'The background to the single status agreement', *Labour Union Digest*, March, online at http://www.labouruniondigest.org.uk/index.php?option=com_content&view=article&id=46&Itemid=53 [accessed 8 July 2010].

Leach, B. (1989) 'Disabled people and the implementation of local authorities' equal opportunities policies', *Public Administration*, 67:1, 65–77.

Local Government Association (2008) *Equalities and Procurement Research: Summary*, online at http://www.lga.gov.uk/lga/aio/1853916 [accessed 9 July 2010].

Macpherson, W. (1999) *The Stephen Lawrence Inquiry*, Cm 4262–1 (London: Stationery Office).

Matthews, D. (2010) 'The changing face of public sector employment 1999–2009', *Economic & Labour Market Review*, 4:7, 28–35.

May, T. (2010) *Equality Strategy Speech*, 17 November, online at http://www.homeoffice.gov.uk/media-centre/speeches/equality-vision [accessed 18 November 2010].

McCrudden, C. (1992) 'Affirmative action and fair participation: interpreting the Fair Employment Act 1989', *Industrial Law Journal*, 21:3, 170–198.

McCrudden, C., Smith, D. and Brown, C. (1991) *Racial Justice at Work* (London: Policy Studies Institute).

Ministry of Justice (2008) *Race Review 2008. Implementing Race Equality in Prisons: Five Years On* (London: National Offender Management Service).

NHS Employers (2005) *Positively Diverse: Quick Guide* (Leeds: NHS Employers).

NHS Employers (2008) *Navigating Equality and Diversity Guidance for the NHS* (London: NHS Employers).

NHS Information Centre (2010) *NHS Hospital and Community Health Services Non-Medical Workforce England 1999–2009* (Leeds: NHS).

National Offender Management Service (NOMS) (2009) *Annual Staff Diversity Review 2008–09* (London: NOMS).

O'Cinneide, C. (2003) 'Extending positive duties across the equality grounds', *Equal Opportunities Review*, 120, August, 12–16.

O'Cinneide, C. (2005) 'Positive duties and disability rights', in A. Lawson and C. Gooding (eds) *Disability Rights in Europe* (Oxford: Hart).

ONS (2010) *Civil Service Statistics* online at http://www.statistics.gov.uk/articles/nojournal/Patterns-of-Pay-1997to2009.pdf [accessed 9 July 2010].

Rubenstein, M. (2010) 'Diary: The Coalition Government and discrimination law', *Equal Opportunities Review*, 201, 2–3.

Shaoul, J. (1999) 'The economic and financial context: the shrinking state', in S. Corby and G. White (eds) *Employee Relations in the Public Services* (London: Routledge).

Vasagar, J. (2010) 'Save top university places for state school pupils, says Cable', *Guardian*, 16 July, 6.

Williams, S. and Scott, P. (2010) 'Shooting the past? The modernisation of Conservative Party employment relations policy under David Cameron', *Industrial Relations Journal*, 41:1, 4–18.

Young, I. (1990) *Justice and the Politics of Difference*, Princeton, NJ: Princeton University Press.

Part IV
The Actors

7
Assistant Roles in a Modernised Public Service: Towards a New Professionalism?

Stephen Bach

Introduction

In the past, when politicians have celebrated the achievements of the public sector workforce they have inevitably pinpointed the contribution of public service professionals such as nurses, teachers and police officers. Recently, however, a striking feature of public service modernisation has been the increased recognition of the contribution of assistant roles, such as teaching and health care assistants that has started to pepper policy documents (Blair, 2002; Cabinet Office, 2008). This higher public profile reflects the extent to which the growth of assistant roles has been integral to work restructuring and public service modernisation. Assistants work alongside public service professionals, often in welfare roles that support vulnerable members of the community. These positions are usually filled by women and traditionally have been low-paid with limited career prospects (Clayton, 1993; Thornley, 1996).

The term 'assistant' is deceptively simple, but disguises considerable variation and uncertainty about the significance of the role. This ambiguity is reflected in a myriad of current and former job titles (e.g. support worker, auxiliary, aide), reflecting their unplanned development over a quarter of a century. In many service areas the role reflects its attachment to a dominant profession; in the United States the title physician assistant reflects its close proximity and support to physicians. In other cases the role is more detached from a specific profession, for example, health care assistants are usually viewed as part of the nursing hierarchy, but unlike the United States they are not titled nursing assistants, opening up the possibility of a role that is not confined to nursing work. These roles frequently have historical antecedents, for example, the teaching assistant role has its origins in the Learning Support

Assistant, which assisted pupils with special needs (Clayton, 1993), but these jobs were largely detached from government policy, reinforcing their role at the margins of the public service workforce.

These occupations are employed across the public services, are integral to workforce modernisation and support high-profile professional staff. This chapter focuses on the most prominent assistant roles that have experienced rapid growth in the last two decades. These include teaching assistants, health care assistants, police community support officers and social work assistants. This chapter considers the public policy context that encouraged the growth of assistant jobs, before examining the evolution of the assistant workforce. It then proceeds to consider the consequences of assistant roles for the assistants themselves, the professionals they work with and service users.

Public policy and the new professionalism

The New Labour government in office between 1997 and 2009 had an ambition to radically transform public services. Its initial White Paper on public service reform stated that: 'Modernising Government means making sure that citizens and businesses come first ... we want public services that respond to users' needs and are not arranged for the provider's convenience' (Cabinet Office, 1999: 23). These sentiments not only signalled a commitment to erode professional job controls but also indicated government distrust of public service professionals (Blair, 2002). The reform of working practices was also prompted by severe shortages of professional staff and government attempts to shed its traditional image as fiscally irresponsible and beholden to the public service unions. Changing labour utilisation, by employing a cheaper and less unionised workforce, furthered the objective of reducing public service reliance on the professions. Finally, the Labour government endorsed the shift towards new public management, which incorporated a higher-profile and more strategic approach towards the management of the workforce, encouraging employers to question existing working arrangements (Bach, 2004; Newman, 2001). This reform agenda started to take shape in the second term of Labour government with school reform in the vanguard of change (Morris, 2001).

A new professionalism?

Promoting the role of assistants and new ways of working has been part of a wider questioning of the role of professionals (Broadbent and Laughlin, 2001). Although differing conclusions are drawn about the resilience of public service professions (Kirkpatrick et al., 2005; Farrell and Morris, 2003) a continuous process of reform, accompanied by periodic scandals weakened claims to professional expertise. The assumption of professional self-regulation was also challenged (Beck, 2008; Gleeson and Knights, 2006). The term 'professionalism' has been colonised by government to signal high standards of customer service and excellent leadership skills, rather than the application of specific forms of professional knowledge as decided by the professions themselves. This 'new professionalism' (Cabinet Office, 2008: 27) implied that a far broader range of staff could be identified as professionals and aspire to professional status (Dent and Whitehead, 2002; Morris, 2001). The Labour government acknowledged that 'a new professionalism capable of driving world-class improvement is likely to represent a challenge to many established working practices' (Cabinet Office, 2008: 28).

The government sought to reassure professionals that their role was not being usurped. The Home Secretary in the foreword to the 2001 White Paper on police reform stated that 'No one need be worried that we are substituting support staff for trained police officers' (Home Office, 2001: foreword). This is precisely the concern of many observers, however, who suggest: 'less qualified staff are used to nibble away at the more routine tasks of professionals' (Law and Mooney, 2007: 237; Worrall et al., 2010). For example, a key element of the 2003 workload agreement in schools was an increased role for support staff, especially teaching assistants, to undertake work usually done by teachers. In contrast to other teaching unions, the National Union of Teachers (NUT) refused to be a signatory to the agreement.

The opposition of the NUT stemmed from a belief that allowing support staff to deliver teaching materials would devalue the status of teachers and the use of cheaper substitutes would threaten the jurisdiction of the teacher in the classroom, opening up the prospects of subordinate occupational groups colonising teaching (Stevenson, 2007; Wilkinson, 2005). Related concerns about substitution are evident amongst nurses. The Royal College of Nursing (2005) has recognised that not all nursing work is undertaken by registered nurses, but they emphasise the difference between the professional judgement and knowledge exercised by registered nurses in comparison to the delegation of specific nursing tasks to health care assistants. Despite these concerns, trade unions and professional associations, with certain exceptions (i.e. NUT, The Police Federation) have recognised the importance of recruiting assistants to safeguard their future and have actively encouraged assistants into membership.

A contrasting interpretation of the consequences for professionals is more sanguine and suggests that professions retain considerable scope to shape the work of support staff, continuing historical precedents in which occupations such as nursing have delegated the more physically demanding 'dirty work' to nursing auxiliaries (Daykin and Clarke, 2000). Attention has been directed at the strategies that professions use to safeguard occupational closure by establishing monopoly of competence over certain areas of advanced knowledge and excluding other occupational groups from their jurisdictions. Professions also create 'subordinate groups', allowing a profession 'to delegate dangerously routine work' (Abbott, 1988: 72).

Assistants: role and profile of the workforce

These differing interpretations of the consequences of assistants signalled a number of different roles for assistants (Kessler et al., 2007). First, assistants have been portrayed as a relief to professionals, relieving them of mundane tasks, enabling professionals to concentrate their expertise on front-line service delivery in schools, hospitals and other public service settings. It was acknowledged that professionals spent too much of their time on administrative tasks and in the case of schools it was argued that the increased use of teaching assistants would 'take burdens away from teachers' (Morris, 2001: 16). This approach was adopted in the 2003 national agreement Remodelling the School Workforce (DfES, 2003). A key element of the agreement was the increased use of teaching assistants to undertake 24 administrative tasks routinely carried out by teachers. A similar logic informed the introduction of Police Community Support Officers (PCSOs) in the 2002 Police Reform Act, in which it was stated that trained support staff would focus on 'reducing the burdens that keep officers off the streets' (Home Office, 2001: foreword).

Second, assistants have been viewed as a substitute, undertaking similar work to professionals, enabling the same work to be undertaken at lower cost. This strategy was not novel, public service employers have frequently sought to reduce expenditure by substituting cheaper assistant type labour for more costly professional labour, for example, using nursing auxiliaries instead of registered nurses (Grimshaw, 1999; Thornley, 1996). Within social services, because of increased workload pressures, social workers have increasingly concentrated on statutory cases, for example, supporting children on the child protection register. This created the need for a role to deal with non-statutory cases and social work assistants have substituted for social workers to fill this void (Kessler et al., 2006).

Third, the Labour Government also cast assistants in the role of apprentices, undertaking some of the routine work of professionals and simultaneously acquiring the skills to progress within their role and ultimately achieve professional status. This was facilitated by the establishment of more transparent career ladders for lower grade staff, illustrated by the NHS 'skills escalator' and in education there has been a similar government commitment to 'clearer career paths and skills escalators for support staff' (DfES, 2005: 98). These career ladders have often involved the establishment of 'bridging' roles that straddle the gap between support roles and professional jobs. This led to the establishment of higher level teaching assistants (HLTAs) and Assistant Practitioners (AP) in the NHS, but to date numbers remain modest. In the case of APs questions arise about how new roles fit into existing workforce structures, their financial affordability, and their professional jurisdiction, especially identifying the boundary with registered nurses (Spilsbury et al., 2009).

Finally, with the emphasis on designing services around the needs of users rather than following established professional practice, assistants have been viewed as co-producers bringing additional skills to bear on service delivery, in partnership with service users. Assistants are often recruited from local labour markets and are more representative of the communities than the professionals they work with, enabling them to provide complementary skills such as knowledge of local dialects (Bach et al., 2006). Similarly, PCSOs break down barriers with community groups 'in a way that police officers have found difficult' (HMIC, 2004: 144). These forms of co-production often arise because assistants have greater opportunity to spend time with their clients than the professionals they work with. This has certainly been the case with health care assistants who have been able to provide emotional support to patients in a way that often eludes overburdened nurses (Bach et al., 2008).

Assistants have therefore been viewed as fulfilling a variety of roles with implications not only for their own role but for the professionals they work with. Irrespective of the role they fulfil, what marked out expansion of the assistant workforce from the 1990s was the active sponsorship by the state. Earmarked resources were made available to facilitate the recruitment of teaching assistants and PCSOs (Home Office, 2004). This type of public commitment signalled a degree of longevity about a role, encouraging employers to incorporate assistants into their workforce plans with encouragement from Skills for Care, The NHS Modernisation Agency and the Training and Development Agency for Schools (TDA).

Evolution of the assistant workforce

Teaching assistants comprise the largest single group of assistants within the public services and their role has evolved to include general support to teachers and pupils that may include specific responsibilities for a child, subject area or age group. The broad category of teaching assistant includes higher level teaching assistants and support staff for special needs and minority ethnic pupils. The vast majority in this category are employed as teaching assistants, predominantly located within primary schools. In 2010, within the local authority-maintained school sector, there were 190,400 full-time equivalent (FTE) teaching assistants in England, comprising a huge increase from the 79,000 employed in 2000 (Department for Education, 2010: Table 1).

In the NHS, the evolution of the health care assistant workforce reflects the longstanding use of nursing auxiliaries. The 1919 Nurses Registration Act gave nurses a protected title, but failed to achieve closure, because registration was not a pre-requisite for employment as a nurse. This enabled the expansion of a non-registered nursing workforce to address nurse shortages arising from poor pay and working conditions. The reforms of nurse education at the end of the 1980s resulted in a change from an apprenticeship-type training towards a university-based model, providing the impetus for the development of a support role to address this labour shortfall. This development was reinforced by the establishment of a specific grade of Health Care Assistant (HCA) and the introduction of vocational qualifications to formalise the HCA role (Thornley, 2003).

The size of the HCA workforce is disputed because of the uncertain boundaries between support worker and HCA roles with different definitions used to distinguish particular roles. Saks and Allsop (2007: 170) estimate that health support workers, defined as those 'who provide face-to-face care or support of a personal or confidential nature to service users', exceeds one million workers, but this figure includes care provided in hospital, community and domiciliary settings. The narrowest definition of support worker, which overlaps most closely with the HCA role, concentrates on staff who provide support 'to doctors and nursing staff'. Using this narrower definition in 2009, there were around

118,000 FTE HCAs in England, compared to around 104,000 a decade earlier (NHS Information Centre, 2010: Table 2b).

The PCSO role is more recent and was introduced in the 2002 Police Reform Act as part of measures to extend the police family and increase the use of civilian staff. PCSOs contribute to neighbourhood policing by providing a visible presence in the community with sufficient powers to deal with relatively minor public order issues (Loveday et al., 2008). In 2010, there were almost 17,000 FTE PCSOs compared to around 150,000 police officers (Home Affairs Committee, 2010), but this represents rapid growth from a zero base line in 2002.

Despite some differences between these occupations, assistants share many similarities in terms of their profile. With the exception of PCSOs, a large majority of assistants are women and a substantial proportion work on a part-time basis (Bach et al., 2007; Kessler et al., 2010). The majority of HCAs, teaching assistants and PCSOs are older than the professionals they work with, although the recent development of career paths has encouraged younger staff to enter these occupations. Assistants are more embedded in their local area and the expansion of PCSO employment has been especially important in this regard, increasing the diversity of the police service workforce and facilitating improvements in community relations (Johnston, 2006). Although some assistants in schools and hospitals enter the workplace with limited formal educational qualifications, they often bring relevant experience, such as caring for elderly relatives or children that provide insights into the role they are to fulfil. This experience often leads them to explore jobs in which they can use their knowledge and skills to assist people in a similar situation. This sense of vocation must not be overstated; in practice these workers have relatively few labour market options and becoming an assistant is rarely a matter of choice alone (Ducey, 2009).

The background of assistants has also been influenced by the degree of regulation. In health and education, the absence of statutory educational requirements has enabled informal recruitment with women who volunteered in schools attended by their children, sometimes invited to transfer into a formal TA role having heard of the opportunity by word of mouth. As these roles have become more central to service provision, they have been developed with formal job descriptions, person specifications and tighter entry requirements. By contrast, in social care, the pace of formalisation has been much quicker with stricter statutory guidance and organisations have trawled more widely for young and well qualified individuals willing and able to progress into professional roles (Kessler et al., 2006).

The crafting of assistant roles

A notable feature of the debate about assistant roles is that advocates and critics share a tendency to portray assistants as 'standard packages' with uniform roles. This excludes the possibility that the same job can vary significantly, influenced by the individual occupying the role, the training opportunities available to them and shaped by broader features of human resources (HR) policy and workplace governance. It is precisely this diversity, however, that detailed studies of assistant roles have highlighted and identifying a uniform trend towards degradation or empowerment does not capture adequately the evolution and variation in assistant roles (Bach et al., 2007).

Amongst TAs, there has been a shift from ancillary activities, such as photocopying and undertaking displays, to a more central involvement in delivering the curriculum. In primary schools TAs often work with particular groups of lower ability pupils or specific individuals in a targeted manner to boost literacy and numeracy and to maintain pupil attention and classroom control (Bach et al., 2006; Blatchford et al., 2009a). HCAs undertake a substantial proportion of direct care work and in addition some HCAs assist with more technical and administrative tasks such as wound care and dressings, venepuncture and undertaking ECGs (Bach et al., 2008; Kessler et al., 2010; Thornley, 2003). The absence of statutory requirements has created few regulatory barriers to limit the role of TAs and HCAs but even when national guidelines have been developed this has not prevented role expansion. The National Policing Improvement Agency (NPIA) identified a number of PCSO roles including Liaison (e.g. domestic violence), Offender Management and Detention Officer that were outside the PCSO core role and recommended that police forces implement and adhere to these standards to curtail 'role drift' (NPIA, 2008).

Regulation and national guidelines have some influence on assistant roles, but it is at the workplace that roles are enacted and the requirements of the job specified. This can be illustrated by the experience of two NHS acute trusts, termed Metro and Tower, and their differing expectations and deployment of HCAs (Bach et al., 2008). Metro had a reputation for nursing workforce innovation and an ethos that resulted in a greater willingness to relax the boundaries between HCAs and registered nurses. By contrast at Tower, nurse leaders emphasised clear demarcations between the work of registered nurses and HCAs and there was a reticence to delegate more technical tasks. These differences were reinforced by differences in the training regime. In particular at

Tower, considerable effort was invested in highlighting and reiterating the differences between HCA and registered nurse responsibilities and competencies. At Metro, a more fluid set of expectations prevailed and this was in part linked to the challenging environment in recruiting and retaining registered nurses. The pragmatic response was to extend the role of HCAs to compensate for nurse staff shortages and to assist in achieving government targets, a labour utilisation strategy that had many historical precedents (Thornley, 1996). Similar aspects of the workplace context influence the overall shape of the TA role. Primary schools that employed more TAs and used them more fully were often characterised by a leadership team ethos in which the head teacher viewed TAs as an integral component of their workforce and adopted an inclusive approach. In cases where the head incorporated TAs into the routines of the school, this led to a greater emphasis being placed on the contribution of TAs, reflected, for example, in the approach towards training and development needs (Bach et al., 2006).

Assistants themselves were not simply passive recipients of work, but actively engaged in job crafting. This involved employees using opportunities to redesign their own jobs, altering the boundaries with other employees' jobs by taking on or removing tasks from their remit, and altering their interactions with other staff (Wrzesniewski and Dutton, 2001). Lower-ranked employees faced distinct challenges in job crafting that relate to convincing other employees to alter their expectations and behaviours to let them job craft (Berg et al., 2010). Line managers and other staff were influenced by the extent to which they trust an individual, based on their knowledge of an individual's competence, experience and attitude; nurses identified 'good' and 'bad' assistants (Bach et al., 2008; for the US: Weinberg, 2003: 67). In hospitals, nurses sometimes reluctantly delegated tasks because they were too busy to undertake the work themselves (Spilsbury and Meyer, 2004). In schools, often individual TAs identified their training requirements informally and lobbied the head to support them, creating opportunities for role development (Bach et al., 2006).

Overall, the increased number and visibility of assistant roles increased scope for development. The extent to which this has occurred has varied between workplaces and has been influenced by the policies and ethos of individual organisations as well as bottom-up job crafting by assistants themselves. It is notable that although trade unions have taken an active interest in the growth of assistant roles, they have had limited engagement and influence in shaping assistant roles at the workplace.

Consequences for assistants

For this expanding workforce important questions arise about the quality of employment and the extent to which these roles comprise low-paid, mundane jobs with few career prospects or if they genuinely represent apprentice roles in which there is scope to develop and progress. In terms of the quality of working life, survey data comparing TAs and social work assistants (SWAs) revealed a generally positive picture. Assistants had not only developed good working relationships with other staff, but they derived particular satisfaction from supporting children and their families either in the classroom or home environment. Even more marked is the fact that in the case of social work assistants their level of job satisfaction exceeded social workers, which arose from the negative attributes of the professional role (i.e. too much paperwork), sentiments that were not confined to social work. Consequently, some of the reservations amongst professional staff about the growth of assistants, stemmed from anxiety that assistants reinforced their own distance from 'the front line' (Bach et al., 2007, 2008).

For assistants, the generally positive view of their working lives was tempered by concerns about inadequate rewards. Assistant roles comprise highly gendered and low wage work, especially in relation to the professionals they support. For example, HCAs are predominantly situated on Band 2 in the NHS pay spine with a range of £13,653–16,753 (as on 1 April 2010) while newly qualified registered nurses are placed on Band 5 (£21,176–27,534). At least HCAs are predominantly employed on a full-time basis. In comparison TAs often work part-time, on a term-time contract basis only. Career development also often fell short of expectations, although concern was not universal and in general a majority of social work assistants viewed the role as a stepping-stone into social work, a realistic aspiration considering their qualifications and significant role overlap with social workers. PCSOs had similar aspirations with survey data from London-based PCSOs indicating that around 60 per cent of recruits viewed the job as a stepping stone to the regular police and an opportunity to 'test the waters' (Johnston, 2006: 393). In education, only around a quarter of teaching assistants aspired to teacher status, but TAs were still keen to develop within their current role. A range of personal factors such as domestic responsibilities and lack of confidence, in conjunction with organisational factors, especially the inability of schools to meet their expectations about pay and development, presented significant barriers to progression (Bach et al., 2006; Hutchings et al., 2009).

It is within the health sector that the most emphasis has been placed on developing job ladders. In the United States, huge sums (in excess of $1bn in New York State alone, by 2005) have been committed to training programmes directed at front-line health workers to facilitate hospital restructuring and to address staff shortages (Ducey, 2009). The health sector has led the way in attempting to improve career trajectories using a variety of technical and soft skills (e.g. communication, customer service) programmes. Fitzgerald (2006) views career ladder strategies as providing opportunities to 'move up' in the US economy and describes many individual initiatives that have enabled entry-level health and education workers to progress to more advanced roles. She also acknowledges difficulties, such as supervisors' reluctance to release their best workers who then moved job, and uncertainties about how far workers are aware of and were suitable for the jobs they were trained to do. Ducey (2009), focusing on healthcare upgrading programmes, argues they miss the point because they rarely resulted in better pay or more respect for caring work. They send out a message that existing nursing aide jobs were not worthwhile, and the metaphor of a ladder disguises the detours and cul-de-sacs faced by health care workers in their attempts to further their careers.

Many HCAs seek to become registered nurses and achieve this goal, but barriers remain in place. Many HCAs do not have a record of academic achievement, and unless encouraged by line managers and colleagues, often lack the self-confidence to continue into nurse training. Moreover, some HCAs view themselves as too old to embark on nurse training or identify other domestic or financial commitments that make it difficult to pursue their ambition. Although the revamped NHS pay system (Agenda for Change) created increased scope for career progression, at trust level managers often do not increase pay when HCAs acquire National Vocational Qualifications (NVQs), creating a sense of grievance about pay levels relative to qualifications. This often arises when HCAs having acquired additional qualifications, find higher graded posts unavailable (Grimshaw and Carroll, 2008). Although public policy has placed a great deal of emphasis on the apprentice role, raising expectations of progression, significant barriers remain for assistants in achieving their career aspirations.

Consequences for professionals and service users

For professionals, the growth of support staff including assistants has altered their jobs, because of the emphasis on team work and the redistribution of tasks, reinforcing a shift away from a legacy of working as autonomous individuals. In the main, professional staff value highly the role of assistants, which enables them to manage their workload more effectively, and to delegate routine tasks to them. In the case of schools, the workload agreement and the growth of support staff has had a marked effect in reducing teacher workload with photocopying, collecting money, chasing absences and other tasks transferred to TAs; contributing to increased job satisfaction (Blatchford et al., 2009b: 123–4). It is when assistants act in a relief role that they are viewed most positively by the professionals with whom they work.

More troubling for professionals is when assistants start encroaching on their work, fulfilling more of a substitute role. This concern about being replaced by cheaper assistants and the threat it may pose to future recruitment has been expressed forcibly in the police service by the Police Federation (Caless, 2007). Across the public services two main issues have arisen. First, professionals have expressed concerns that their own role is being recast in ways that may distance them from front-line service delivery. Although assistants are rarely the primary reason for this shift of emphasis, they represent a visible sign of how their job is altering. Amongst nurses, not only in the UK but also in the USA, concerns have been expressed that they are 'losing nursing' as more direct bedside care is transferred to nursing assistants (Bach et al., in press; Weinberg, 2003). Amongst teachers, there has been strong opposition to leaving TAs in sole charge of classes because this is perceived as an attempt to blur the boundaries between teacher and TA work. Teachers oppose an alteration in the division of labour in which they became primarily responsible for the planning and preparation of lessons that TAs and other support staff have a role in delivering (Bach et al., 2006; Stevenson, 2007).

Second, professionals often feel that their organisations have given insufficient consideration to the management of assistants. This has resulted in professionals not having the requisite training or time to manage support staff effectively (Blatchford et al., 2009b: 133). In the case of nurses this has sometimes led to anxieties about the monitoring of HCAs, because nurses' professional registration makes them accountable for tasks delegated to HCAs. In the police, the rapid expansion of the PCSO workforce led to unsuitable recruitment and subsequent conduct and disciplinary problems amongst some PCSOs (Johnston, 2006). Overall, for the individual practitioner, working with and directing a co-worker is often challenging and there is often insufficient preparation for this type of responsibility.

A final, equally contentious issue relates to the impact of assistants on the experiences of service users and the degree to which assistant staff improve outcomes for the client they support. It may be relatively straightforward for TAs, for example, to deliver a catch-up programme to improve numeracy, but the extent to which this is done effectively requires considerable training and insight into the way children learn, which may be omitted. In health, especially in the USA, there has been some examination of patient outcomes and research indicating that patient outcomes are more favourable with higher levels of registered nursing input, but the focus has been on registered nurse staffing levels rather than the impact of other staff (Gordon et al., 2008).

It is in schools that the contribution of TAs has been examined most fully, although this remains a contested issue. For example, a recent study indicated that increased expenditure on TAs improved student attainment in secondary schools (Brown and Harris, 2010). By contrast, OFSTED, in a report examining provision for children with learning difficulties and disabilities concluded: 'the provision of additional resources to pupils – such as support from teaching assistants – did not ensure good quality intervention or adequate progress by pupils' (OFSTED, 2006: executive summary). Instead OFSTED argued for the importance of specialist teacher input and commitment from school leaders. Blatchford et al. (2009b), focusing on Maths and English, reached similar conclusions, and while highlighting positive effects of TAs in terms of pupil behaviour and relations with peers, concluded that there was generally a negative and statistically significant relationship between support staff contact and pupils' academic progress. They identify a number of possible explanations for these findings relating to: the preparation of TAs and the lack of meaningful discussion with teachers; their subject and pedagogical knowledge; the way in which they are deployed; and the practice of TAs in terms of their more informal and 'chatty' style, which may not have stretched pupils (Blatchford et al., 2009b: 131–40). These findings might be viewed as an indictment of assistants themselves, but in reality they highlight a broader failure to articulate the precise role of assistants, to establish appropriate training and deployment strategies, and to ensure adequate rewards and career development, so that assistants do not remain as low-paid, low-status support staff.

Conclusions

Workforce reforms associated with public service modernisation have emphasised the contribution of assistants to service delivery and highlighted increased training and career opportunities, contributing to enhanced recognition of these roles (Cabinet Office, 2008). The growth of the assistant workforce demonstrates that a state-sponsored programme of workforce change can bring about rapid changes in the composition of the workforce and alter the division of labour between adjacent occupations. Despite the commitment of policymakers, the use of pilots and the elaboration of extensive practical guidance, assistants, while expressing considerable job satisfaction and valuing opportunities to make a difference, have often felt let down by their inability to progress, continuing low pay, and poor recognition of their contribution.

Professional staff certainly appreciate the relief role provided by assistants and their ability to delegate some tasks to support staff. Nonetheless a more prominent role for assistants has implications for the status and professional identities of both professionals and assistants. A sense of unease amongst professionals was reinforced by their distrust of the Labour government and their ambivalence towards the new professionalism (Bach, 2010). It is when a relief role has spilled over into more of substitute role that tensions have arisen. It is no coincidence also that assistants have been able to make greatest inroads where professional status is fragile and uncertain, as is the case amongst nurses, teachers and social workers. These occupations have frequently responded in very traditional ways, scarcely embracing a new professionalism, but seeking to upgrade their credentials (e.g. nursing becoming an all-graduate profession) and reinforcing the boundaries with lower status occupations, notwithstanding a pragmatic interest in delegating mundane tasks to support workers.

The public services have entered a period of sustained austerity accompanied by the shrinkage of the workforce. This fiscal context has created great uncertainty about the future of the assistant workforce. It might be anticipated that the use of assistants would increase as budgetary concerns make the use of cheaper substitute labour more attractive to employers, as has occurred in the past through skill-mix strategies. Such an approach, however, may be constrained by uncertainties about the consequences for service quality, increased emphasis on managing risk, especially in the NHS, the continuing resilience of the professions and the requirement to employ a large professional workforce. There are signs that the centrality of assistants to government policy is waning, with the Labour government replaced by a Coalition Government combining Conservative and Liberal Democratic parties. In autumn 2010 the TDA cancelled the budget for training HLTAs and the planned negotiating machinery for school support staff was also abolished. These policy developments indicate a weakening of support for the development and promotion of assistant roles and the fragility of new institutions established by the Labour government. Despite lengthy debate the government remains reluctant to boost HCA status by regulating them, and recruitment freezes are making it even harder for assistants to move up and progress. Although assistants have forged a more prominent role for themselves over the last decade, they face a highly uncertain future in an era of austerity.

References

Abbott, A. (1988) *The System of Professions: an Essay on the Division of Expert Labor* (Chicago: University).

Bach (2004) *Employment Relations and the Health Service: The Management of Reforms* (London: Routledge).

Bach, S. (2010) 'Public sector industrial relations: the challenge of modernisation', in T. Colling, and M. Terry, (eds) *Industrial Relations: Theory and Practice*, 3rd edn (Chichester: Wiley).

Bach, S., Kessler, I. and Heron, P. (2006) 'Changing job boundaries and workforce reform: the case of teaching assistants', *Industrial Relations Journal*, 37:1, 2–21.

Bach, S., Kessler, I. and Heron, P. (2007) 'The Consequences of Assistant Roles in the Public Services: Degradation or Empowerment?', *Human Relations*, 60:9, 1267–1292.

Bach, S., Kessler, I. and Heron, P. (2008) 'Role redesign in a modernised NHS: the case of health care assistants', *Human Resource Management Journal*, 18:2, 171–187.

Bach, S. Kessler, I. and Heron, P. *'Nursing a Grievance? The Role of Health Care Assistants in a Modernised NHS:' Gender, Work and Organisation* (in press).

Beck, J. (2008) 'Governmental Professionalism: Re-professionalising or De-professionalising Teachers in England?', *British Journal of Educational Studies*, 56:2, 119–143.

Berg, J., Wrzesniewski, A. and Dutton, J. (2010) 'Perceiving and responding to challenges in job crafting at different ranks: when proactivity requires adaptivity', *Journal of Organisational Behaviour*, 31:2, 158–186.

Blair, T. (2002) *The Courage of Our Convictions: Why Reform of the Public Services is the Route to Social Justice* (London: Fabian Society).

Blatchford, P., Bassett, P., Brown, P. and Webster, R. (2009a) 'The effect of support staff on pupil engagement and individual attention', *British Educational Research Journal,* 35:5, 661–686.

Blatchford, P., Bassett, P., Brown, P., Koutsoubou, M., Martin, C., Russell, A., Webster, R. and Rubie-Davies, C. (2009b) *Deployment and Impact of Support Staff in Schools* (London: Institute of Education).

Broadbent, J. and Laughlin, R. (2001) 'Public Service Professionals and the New Public Management: Control of the Professions in the Public Services', in K. McLaughlin and S. Osborne (eds) *New Public Management: Current Trends and Future Prospects* (London: Routledge).

Brown, J. and Harris, A. (2010) *Increased Expenditure on Associate Staff in Schools and Changes in Student Attainment* (London: TDA and SSAT).

Cabinet Office (1999) *Modernising Government*, Cm 4310 (London: The Stationery Office).

Cabinet Office (2008) *Excellence and Fairness: Achieving World Class Public Services* (London: Cabinet Office), online at http://www.fitting-in.com/reports/world_class_public_services%20pdf.pdf.

Caless, B. (2007) '"Numpties in Yellow Jackets": The nature of hostility towards the police community support officer in neighbourhood policing teams', *Policing*, 1:2, 187–195.

Clayton, T. (1993) 'From domestic helper to assistant teacher: the changing role of the British Classroom assistant', *European Journal of Special Needs*, 8:1, 32–44.

Daykin, N. and Clarke, B. (2000) '"They'll still get the bodily care": Discourses of care and relationships between nurses and health care assistants in the NHS', *Sociology of Health and Illness*, 22:3, 349–363.

Department for Education and Skills (2003) *Raising Standards and Tackling Workload: A National Agreement* (London: DfES).

Department for Education and Skills (2005) *Higher Standards, Better Schools for All – More Choice for Parents and Pupils* (London: DfES).

Department for Education (2010) *School Workforce in England* (London: Department for Education).

Dent, M. and Whitehead, S. (2002) *Managing Professional Identities: Knowledge, Performativity and the 'New' Professional* (London: Routledge).

Ducey, A (2009) *Never Good Enough: Health Care Workers and the False Promise of Job Training* (New York: Cornell University Press).

Farrell, C. and Morris, J. (2003) 'The "Neo-Bureaucratic" state: professionals, managers and professional managers in schools, general practices and social work', *Organization*, 10:1, 129–156.

Fitzgerald, J. (2006) *Moving Up in the New Economy: Career Ladders for US Workers* (Ithaca: Cornell University Press).

Gleeson, D. and Knights, D. (2006) 'Challenging dualism: public professionalism in troubled times', *Sociology*, 40:2, 277–295.

Gordon, S., Buchanan, J. and Bretherton, T. (2008) *Safety in Numbers: Nurse-to-Patient Ratios and the Future of Health Care* (Ithaca: ILR Press).

Grimshaw, D. (1999) 'Changes in Skill-Mix and Pay Determination among the Nursing Workforce in the UK', *Work, Employment and Society*, 13:2, 293–326.

Grimshaw, D and Carroll, M. (2008) 'Improving the position of low-wage workers through new coordinating mechanisms: the case of public hospitals', in C. Lloyd, G. Mason and K. Mayhew (eds) *Low Wage Work in the United Kingdom* (New York: Russell Sage Foundation).

HMIC [Her Majesty's Inspectorate of Constabulary] (2004) *Modernising the Police Service: A Thematic Inspection of Workforce Modernisation – The Role, Management and Deployment of Police Staff in the Police Service of England and Wales*, London: HMIC.

Home Affairs Committee (2010) *Police Service Strength*, HC 50 (London: The Stationery Office).

Home Office (2001) *Policing a New Century: A Blueprint for Reform*, Cm5326 (London: Home Office).

Home Office (2004) *Building Communities, Beating Crime: A Better Police Service for the 21st century*, Cm6360, (London: Home Office).

Hutchings, M., Seeds, K., Coleman, N., Harding, C., Mansaray, A., Maylor, U., Minty, S. and Pickering, E. (2009) *Aspects of School Workforce Remodelling: Strategies used and Impact on Workload and Standards*, Research Report 153 (London: DCSF).

Johnston, L. (2006) 'Diversifying police recruitment? The deployment of Police Community Support Officers in London', *The Howard Journal*, 45:4, 388–402.

Kessler, I., Bach, S. and Heron, P. (2006) 'Understanding assistant roles in social care', *Work, Employment and Society*, 20:4, 667–685.

Kessler, I., Bach, S. and Heron, P. (2007) 'Comparing assistant roles in education and social care: backgrounds, behaviours and boundaries', *International Journal of Human Resource Management*, 18:9, 1648–1665.

Kessler, I., Heron, P., Dopson, S., Magee, H., Swain, D. and Askham, J. (2010) *The Nature and Consequences of Support Workers in a Hospital Setting* (London: National Institute for Health Research).

Kirkpatrick, I., Ackroyd, S. and Walker, R. (2005) *The New Managerialism and Public Service Professions* (London: Palgrave Macmillan).

Law, A. and Mooney, G. (2007) 'Strenuous Welfarism: Restructuring the Welfare Labour Process', in G. Mooney and A. Law (eds) *New Labour/Hard Labour? Restructuring and Resistance Inside the Welfare Industry* (Bristol: Policy Press).

Loveday, B., Williams, S. and Scott, P. (2008) 'Workforce Modernisation in the Police Service: Prospects for Reform?' *Personnel Review*, 37:4, 361–374.

Morris, E. (2001) *Trust and Professionalism* (London: Social Market Foundation).

Newman, J. (2001) *Modernising Governace: New Labour Policy and Society* (London: Sage).

NHS Information Centre (2010) *NHS Hospital and Community Health Services Non-Medical Staff England 1999–2009* (Leeds: NHS Information Centre).

NPIA (National Policing Improvement Agency) (2008) *NPIA Neighbourhood Policing Programme: PCSO Review* (London: NPIA).

OFSTED (2006) *Does it Matter Where Pupils are Taught?* (London: OFSTED).

Royal College of Nursing (2005) *The Future Nurse: The RCN Vision* (London: RCN).

Saks, M. and Allsop, J. (2007) 'Social Policy, Professional Regulation and Health Support Work in the UK', *Social Policy and Society*, 6:2, 165–177.

Spilsbury, K. and Meyer, J. (2004) 'Use, misuse and non use of healthcare assistants: understanding the work of healthcare assistants in a hospital setting', *Journal of Nursing Management*, 12:4, 411–418.

Spilsbury, K., Stuttard, L., Adamson, J., Atkin, K., Borglin, G., McCaughan, D., McKenna, H., Wakefield, A. and Carr-Hill, R. (2009) 'Mapping the introduction of Assistant Practitioner Roles in Acute NHS (Hospital) Trusts in England', *Journal of Nursing Management*, 17:5, 615–626.

Stevenson, H. (2007) 'Restructuring Teachers' Work and Trade Union Responses in England: Bargaining for Change?' *American Educational Research Journal*, 44:2, 224–251.

Thornley, C. (1996) 'Segmentation and inequality in the nursing workforce: reevaluating the evaluation of skills', in R. Crompton, D. Gallie and K. Purcell (eds) *Changing Forms of Employment* (London: Routledge).

Thornley, C. (2003) 'What future for Health Care Assistants: high road or low road?' in C. Davies (ed.) *The Future Health Workforce* (Basingstoke: Palgrave Macmillan).

Weinberg, D. (2003) *Code Green: Money-Driven Hospitals and the Dismantling of Nursing* (Ithaca: Cornell University Press).

Wilkinson, G. (2005) 'Workforce remodelling and formal knowledge: the erosion of teachers' professional jurisdiction in English schools', *School Leadership and Management*, 25:5, 421–439.

Worrall, L., Mather, K. and Seifert, R. (2010) 'Solving the labour problem among professional workers in the UK public sector: organisation change and performance management', *Public Organisation Review*, 10, 117–137.

Wrzesniewski, A. and Dutton, J. (2001) 'Crafting a Job: Revisioning employees as active crafters of their work', *Academy of Management Review*, 26, 179–201.

8
The Third Sector's Provision of Public Services: Implications for Mission and Employment Conditions

Ian Cunningham

This chapter is concerned with the expansion of outsourcing public services to third sector organisations under successive Conservative and Labour administrations, investigating the implications for voluntary sector independence and employment conditions. Drawing on research in the sub-sector of social services provision, it will report on findings from a qualitative study of eighteen Scottish-based organisations, presenting data that examine issues including financial dependency, vulnerability to competition and shifts in policy, enhanced audit and how these impact on human resources (HR) policies and practices and terms and conditions of employment. In doing so, it highlights how changes to working conditions and terms and conditions of employment have potentially detrimental effects on employee morale and the missions of voluntary organisations. Moreover, it warns that these tensions in employment relationships in the sector will become more pronounced in an era of government rhetoric that heralds greater voluntary sector activity in public services through the 'Big Society', at the same time as fiscal retrenchment in the public sector takes hold.

The chapter begins by outlining the changing voluntary/state relationship in the UK, highlighting the accompanying fears of loss of independence and mission drift, associated with a growing professional workforce in non-profit organisations. The second section highlights current literature exploring the impact of outsourcing on employment, arguing that the economic crisis from 2008–9 and the subsequent public sector cuts threaten to exacerbate these tensions. The chapter then turns to outline findings of the aforementioned qualitative study, before concluding with some observations regarding the future of voluntary sector employment in an era of public sector austerity.

State–voluntary sector relationships in the UK

There has been a long-standing but recently accelerating tendency in western industrialised countries to contract out public services to the voluntary sector (Kendall, 2003). In the UK, this was accelerated under the Thatcher governments as a consequence of their acceptance of 'New Right' critiques that the welfare state was poorly managed, unaccountable, professionally dominated and lacking client involvement due to an absence of market incentives (Walsh, 1995; Osborne, 1997). To support market-based delivery of public services, Conservative governments created a mixed economy of welfare where local and health authorities changed from being monopoly providers of care to also becoming enablers, contracting out services to non-statutory providers in the private and voluntary sectors (Harris et al., 2001). The enabling role of local and health authorities continued and increased in the period of New Labour rule from 1997–2010. New Labour advanced arguments that 'third sector' organisations possessed virtues that made it desirable to accord them a greater role in the delivery of public services, including their closeness to service users, specialist skills, their expertise and capacity for innovation and reduced cost (Davies, 2007).

These changes have led to significant dependence by the voluntary sector on income from statutory funding. Analysis shows how the sector's income during 2006–7 stood at £33.2bn, a 3.3 per cent increase on the previous year's total. Income from statutory sources accounted for £12bn or one-third of the total. Increasingly, this contribution to voluntary sector income by the state is linked to aforementioned outsourcing of public services by central and local government. The highest proportion of income to the voluntary sector is received by social care organisations totalling £4.2bn in 2006–7. These organisations account for half of all income from local government to the sector. Other areas of the sector receiving significant increases in income include employment and training, health, housing, culture and recreation (Clark et al., 2009).

This increase in resource dependency has led to rising concerns with regard to the threat of 'mission drift'. Mission drift relates to the erosion of independence and autonomy among voluntary organisations when they become dependent on state income. This arises because the priorities of the funder can dictate the type of client receiving a service, to the detriment of other vulnerable groups previously serviced by the sector. In addition, income dependency on state sources can limit resources devoted to other activities, such as advocacy and development work

(Taylor and Lewis, 1997). Such concerns about independence are particularly acute with regard to organisations that have the state as their single source of funding (Wainwright et al., 2006). Moreover, one study has revealed how only twenty-six per cent of charities feel they are free to make decisions without pressure from statutory funders (Charity Commission, 2007).

Further developments in this debate see voluntary organisations becoming hybrids that take on contracts and resources from other sectors and, in turn, adopt the features of private and public sector organisations, leading to mission drift (Billis, 2010). One of the key reasons for mission drift is seen to be when paid staff are the dominant mode of service delivery, rather than volunteers. Management structures and hierarchy, the introduction of the language and practice of business, changes in the way operations are implemented, the structures of job descriptions, managerial accountability and sanctions and reward systems that have become influenced by the priorities of public policy and the commercial world further lead to mission drift (Billis, 2010).

This chapter, however, maintains that it is not the presence of paid staff that accounts for mission drift, but rather how they are managed. There has been a general tendency to adopt private sector management practices in the delivery of public services, reflecting the emerging dominance of the aforementioned New Right ideological perspective that has shaped political and economic policy in industrialised countries. One aspect of these economic and political ideas that has influenced change in social welfare provision has been NPM. NPM assumes that management in organisations, whether profit or non-profit, should be essentially the same (Harris, 2010). The underpinning philosophy of NPM is to encourage professional management, continuous increases in efficiency and to develop a labour force disciplined to improve productivity in the provision of public services (Pollit, 1995).

The introduction of private sector/market values does, however, lead to a difficult balancing act for voluntary organisations in managing paid staff as they will have to introduce policies and practices that fit with their values and mission, but also coordinate these with responses to diverse and contradictory external funding and regulatory pressures (Ridder and McCandless, 2008). These external pressures may call for new ways of working that fit with the priorities of the funder and may imply significant changes to working practices and how services are delivered. Such changes will also fundamentally shape the employment relationship and the attitudes of workers delivering services by focusing on the continual driving down of costs. Both of these pressures, as will be shown, have the potential to distort organisational missions within the sector. It is at this juncture that the chapter turns to explore current research into how the management of staff in voluntary organisations has altered in this climate.

The workforce implications

Employment trends

Voluntary organisations have experienced significant employment growth as state funding has increased. In 2008, UK voluntary sector employment stood at 668,000, just over 2 per cent of the workforce (compared with a headcount of 408,000 employees in 1995). Paid employment within the sector has also increased by nearly one-quarter (23 per cent) or 124,000 employees in the last ten years (Clark and Wilding, forthcoming). The majority of employees in the sector are situated in the larger organisations, with women accounting for over two-thirds (415,000), half of whom are part-timers. These part-timers are also more likely to be found working in smaller voluntary organisations (Wainwright et al., 2006; Wilding et al., 2004).

In focusing on social care, there has also been significant change in workforce numbers over this period. During 1996–2008 the number of voluntary sector workers employed in social work activities grew from 202,000 in 1996 to 374,000 in 2008 – an increase of 85 per cent, reflecting the transfer of social care services from the public sector. Overall, voluntary sector organisations providing social services receive a much larger amount of statutory income than any other sub-sector: £4.2bn in 2006–7 (Clark and Wilding, forthcoming). The voluntary sector workforce now accounts for 26 per cent of total social care employment in the UK (National Council for Voluntary Organisations, 2010).

People management policies and practices

Increased outsourcing under successive Conservative and Labour governments and the influence of NPM have led to greater professionalism in management practices in the voluntary sector. Public bodies have increasingly regulated voluntary organisations with which they had contracts by establishing precise legally binding measurable performance criteria and output controls. As a consequence, studies are increasingly showing how this regulation is manifesting into coercive and mimetic isomorphic pressures (DiMaggio and Powell, 1983) on the sector to conform to commercial private sector practices as the preferred approach to management, with voluntary organisations expected to demonstrate that they are 'business-like' in order to participate in the policy arena (Perri 6 and Kendall, 1997; Tonkiss and Passey, 1999; Harris et al., 2001).

This has, in turn, led to the emergence, growth and expanding influence of the personnel/HR profession that has formalised and modernised human resource policies, practices and procedures within the sector. This formalisation has occurred in direct response to audit and scrutiny from public funding bodies, but has not, in itself, been the cause of mission drift among voluntary organisations. Indeed, studies have indicated how this upgrading of the HR function has contributed to organisational mission by playing a part in securing contracts and growth in services from state sources, which were directly targeted at the very vulnerable groups that voluntary organisations are pledged to serve (Cunningham, 2010; Parry and Kelliher, 2009). To understand how mission drift can emerge through the purchaser–provider relationship, it is necessary to look at other aspects of employment.

Changes to the organisation of work

Mission drift can occur from changes to working practices forced upon voluntary organisations through particular funding streams. For example, the nature of care services under outsourcing can dramatically change for non-profit providers as bureaucratisation and deskilling become features of work organisation. Here, bureaucratisation reflects a general tendency towards audit, monitoring and an increased need for front-line workers to complete paperwork to ensure they fulfil the demands of particular contracts and quality standards imposed by the funder. Another aspect to these tendencies, however, has been to deskill care work. Studies have shown how much of the aforementioned auditing is driven by cost savings where contracts specify the need for workers to provide services to more clients, while fulfiling narrow tasks that focus on menial, domestic care chores thus stripping care work of its capacity to build community links for service users, as well as much of the emotional content (Baines, 2004). In the UK, this dynamic has occurred under the Supporting People funding stream. Here, voluntary organisations benefited from large injections of resources, but their front-line workers have had to deliver services limited to basic domestic tasks and, at the same time, to meet auditing requirements, they have had to complete large amounts of paperwork. This was seen by managers and workers alike to be to the detriment of their organisation's mission, because clients were not provided with services that fully addressed their complex care needs and/or were not offered the facility to build full and independent lives (Cunningham, 2008; Cunningham and James, 2009).

Terms and conditions of employment

Another threat to the mission of voluntary organisations has come from the cost-cutting, efficiency aspects of NPM. Here, the threat to organisational mission comes from the undermining of commitment among the workforce brought about by tensions in the work–effort bargain as cost-cutting affects terms and conditions of employment. This pressure on terms and conditions is within the context of weak unionisation compared to the public sector, with only an estimated 22 per cent of employees being union members (NCVO, 2010).

Outsourcing and the accompanying calls for efficiencies, value for money and cost-cutting have gradually diminished opportunities to mimic public-sector terms and conditions among voluntary organisations. Recent studies drawing from the broader supply chain/inter-organisational literature (*see* Sako, 1992; Marchington et al., 2005; Scarborough, 2000; Bresnen, 1996; Hunter et al., 1996) have identified how cost pressures through the use of arm's-length contracts from public sector commissioners have led to job insecurity, increasing work intensity and reductions in terms and conditions of employment, most notably with regard to pay so that voluntary organisations are increasingly unable to match public sector salary scales (Cunningham and James, 2009; Cunningham, 2008; Barnard et al., 2004).

Moreover, the same studies reveal that where the degradation of terms and conditions are most significant, the dangers to employee morale and therefore organisational mission become most pronounced. Under such conditions, workers have a diminished willingness to engage in organisational citizenship behaviour and even quit their employment. Rises in employee turnover were subsequently responsible for problems in meeting service quality demands and, therefore, jeopardised the mission of voluntary organisations (Cunningham, 2008).

Not all voluntary organisations operate within the same external dynamic, as studies also reflect the complexity of contractual relationships between purchasers and providers (Chew and Osborne, 2009). Voluntary organisations are not always passive recipients of purchaser and market pressures, but at times can actively shape the terms of the contracts they conclude with service commissioners. Because they have a lower level of dependency on public sector funds, or because they have developed a multi-customer base, they occupy a favourable market position stemming from the types of services they provide, and/or have an ability to draw on alternative sources of funding. The overall consequences for employment conditions in the sector are that some organisations have been able to retain the link with public sector pay, while the majority has not (Cunningham, 2008).

Questions of sustainability in an era of public sector austerity

The capacity to retain autonomy and resist cost pressures exist alongside the wider ability in the sector to resist change over time as a result, for example, of shifts in surrounding market conditions (Blois, 2002; Grimshaw and Rubery, 2005). The current era of public sector austerity further threatens terms and conditions of employment, employee morale and organisational missions of employers, as the economic crisis of 2008–09 is likely to serve to increase the pressure on commissioners to 'obtain more for less' when contracting for the delivery of services.

Other pressures include the removal of ring-fencing from such funding streams as Supporting People, the Mental Health Specific Grant and the Changing Children's Services fund. This means that these sources of funding will be more vulnerable to shifts in the priorities of individual local authorities, a potential vulnerability that is only reinforced by a study indicating that since the removal of ring-fencing a majority of organisations (74 per cent) had seen their budgets frozen (Harrow, 2009).

In addition, evidence indicates that following the implementation of the Public Contracts Regulations 2006 and Public Contracts (Scotland Regulations 2006), introduced to transpose the Public Contracts Directive 2004/18/EC, there has been an increase in re-tendering of contracts delivered by voluntary organisations. An increase in re-tendering clearly carries the risk of contracts moving from one provider to another, along with the potential loss of previously well-established inter-personal relationships between providers and commissioners, and increased opportunities for service commissioners to obtain competitively generated reductions in contract prices (Cunningham and Nickson, 2009).

There is also anticipation that pressure will not just be on pay, but other terms and conditions. Recent reports have highlighted how Britain's largest voluntary organisations face pensions deficits of £1bn (Ramesh, 2010). This situation has been caused by what has been labelled a 'recession double whammy' brought about by falls in statutory and non-statutory income. The sector is also seen as anticipating a further impact from public spending cuts and losses of income on its contracts with the state. This has led to the closure of final salary schemes (e.g. the National Society for the Prevention of Cruelty to Children (NSPCC)) and an increase in contributions among employees (Ramesh, 2010). Moreover, the issue of pensions also has significant implications if governments aspire further to outsource public services to the non-profit sector to cut costs. In particular, if voluntary organisations take on staff previously employed by local authorities, then they are potentially liable for their pensions (Dearden-Phillips, 2010).

In the light of the above summary, this chapter now turns to provide an overview of findings from a qualitative study of eighteen voluntary organisations undertaken in 2008–09 that specifically focused on the issues of financial dependency, vulnerability to competition and shifts in policy, enhanced audit and how these have had an impact on the workforce and terms and conditions.

Method

The research (twenty-eight interviews), was undertaken in 2008–09 and involved interviews within eighteen voluntary sector organisations. Interviews were conducted with HR respondents (17 cases) or managers with responsibility for HR (one case). In addition, interviews were conducted with 10 managers who were responsible for negotiating or dealing with tenders and re-tendering with local authorities. Their service activities covered the areas of children and young people (three cases); services to young people and adults with disabilities/special needs (two cases); the elderly (one case) and the remainder cited adults with disabilities/special needs (12 cases).

Findings

People management practices

The data revealed the influence of private sector people management practices in voluntary organisations. For example, seven HR respondents identified how, to varying degrees, they were moving towards developing a HR function that was more strategic in its outlook, and which adopted something akin to a 'business partnership model', as part of moves to a more professional, private sector and NPM-inspired organisational culture.

> I think a lot of our core values remain the same, but the one that probably has come aboard is this notion of being businesslike ... we need to start thinking about, not just the quality of the service we

deliver, but how do we deliver that quality of service in a value for money cost effective way.

(HR Director, children's services)

To help manage newly emerging approaches to people management in their organisations, several of these HR respondents added that they had been specifically recruited from the private sector through the influence of newly appointed CEOs. Others had been established in post, but had experienced a change in status, for example, promotion to HR Director with a specific remit to add value to achieve the organisation's mission.

We had a new Chief Exec and he wanted to make his mark. So he advertised for a Director of HR. So it was very difficult and it was outside competition as well. So I managed to secure my post. It was a strategy that the Chief Exec had to make sure that HR was at the top table.

(HR Director, adult services)

In these new cultures, managers were seen as 'customers – we are there to provide them with a service and if we are not doing it well enough, they have a right to express that' (HR Manager, children's services). This respondent further added how newly qualified graduates in HR had been appointed to further professionalise their function.

A key part of the role across all HR respondents was to respond to intensifying scrutiny and audit from government funders and regulators.

I have noticed a change in my role and there is a lot more in terms of the policy side of things. They are far more insistent that we have up-to-date policies on x, y and z... so it's virtually every policy, or every kind of issue regarding the legal aspects of terms and conditions of employment or providing a service and they will check dates and when you last reviewed it.

(HR Manager, adult physical disabilities)

Local authorities scrutinised policies around health and safety, equality, discipline and grievance and the requirements of the Working Time Directive. Requirements and scrutiny of information concerning health and safety could be quite detailed and include how organisations conducted risk assessments. Equality issues would include respondents having to report on issues such as management training in diversity. In the case of discipline and grievance, for some organisations this scrutiny involved inquiries into the numbers of staff disciplined and employment tribunal claims. The impact of this upgrading of HR policies was not perceived as a way to undermine organisational missions, rather the consensus among respondents was that local authorities were largely screening out risky providers in tender or re-tender processes to minimise their own risks associated with outsourcing.

Respondents also reported increased scrutiny and audit requirements from the Care Commission. A minority of respondents felt the auditing by the Commission intrusive, inflexible, repetitive and bureaucratic. Most HR respondents in this study, however, welcomed Care Commission inspections.

> The Care Commission I would say is probably the most thorough out of them at the moment. We have to do detailed self-assessment, send that in and then they come out and inspect and they are fairly rigorous. They no longer just look at your policies and procedures because they've done that. They are going to dig below that and look at new things.
>
> (HR respondent, adult services)

Respondents also argued that such audits could be useful in emphasising the need for continuous improvements in care and performance among front-line staff, as well as such audits bolstering their new approaches to people management. One organisation, for example, had received several poor inspection reports by the Commission. HR saw this as an opportunity to emphasise the need for proper performance management in order to retain the organisation's reputation. In doing so, the organisation saw an increase in numbers of low-level discipline cases and the dismissal of two staff.

Changes to terms and conditions of employment

Respondents reported the emergence of several new dimensions to the traditional funding insecurity and competition in the sector that were increasingly impacting on terms and conditions of employment. The first related to the impact of the aforementioned EU measures on re-tendering with some local authorities using these regulations to re-tender services to push down the costs of services provided by the voluntary sector through increasing the number of providers in the market. This increase in competition included organisations from the private sector, and respondents indicated that the move to e-procurementin tendering and re-tendering was a major factor in encouraging increasing numbers of organisations (in some cases from overseas) to compete. The second dimension was linked to the emerging financial climate of recession and crisis within local authorities, where some were holding investments in Icelandic banks, while others were struggling because of having to meet the financial consequences of successful equal value claims among their own staff.

These conditions were impacting on pay and other terms and conditions. Among the eighteen organisations, prior to the study eight had already moved away from using Scottish Joint Council (SJC) collective agreements that covered local authority workers. The remaining ten aligned their reward packages to these public sector conditions, but were undergoing a potentially significant transformation, as all reported that they were considering changing their approach to pay in the forthcoming years. With regard to the former group, the move away from public sector pay scales had not fully resolved financial tensions with local authorities. These organisations were still left with the reality of some local authorities continuing to refuse to provide cost of living increases to funding packages. In the years preceding the study, these organisations had found the money to fund inflationary pay rises to their staff from their own resources, for example, efficiencies or organisational reserves. Upon the onset of recession, the common response to further funding cuts was to introduce pay freezes.

In focusing on the second group of organisations, that is, those that still adhered to local authority pay rates, it was clear that the internal debates about the future of pay and conditions were driven by cost considerations. The Business Development Manager (BDM) from one organisation providing services to vulnerable adults and young people for twenty-nine of Scotland's thirty-two local authorities, reported how, due to the financial crisis facing some funders, the organisation was less likely to be approached to form a partnership to develop new business. Rather, the organisation increasingly was asked to respond to open tenders, along with other private and voluntary providers, where cost considerations were high on the agenda. The respondent illustrated this by citing a local authority that outlined in its re-tender document a new scoring matrix (10% of possible marks) that requested providers to indicate what 'additional service we can actually provide to XXX council for no additional cost' (BDM, Adult and Children's services).

The HR respondent and BDM outlined how her organisation had the strategic aim of being 'a good employer' that embraced union recognition and public sector pay scales, but she feared that over the next two years the continuation of the public sector salary link was unsustainable. A further complication related to the fact that a minority of the organisation's staff were teachers with pay firmly tied to public sector scales. The HR respondent reported how the organisation would be unable to recruit or retain teachers on anything less than these scales, suggesting that any reform of pay may lead to some employees losing their public sector comparators, while others retained them.

Disruption and inconsistency in pay systems was emerging in other organisations due to the growth of re-tendering of services by local authorities. Several organisations that had won re-tenders would take on staff from other organisations. The protections guaranteed through the TUPE led to these organisations bringing in staff with terms and conditions superior to existing employees despite being on the same grade, with one respondent noting that they currently operated six different types of terms and conditions.

These pay anomalies led to several problems. On the one hand, some respondents reported that they struggled to control discontent among existing workers on poorer terms and conditions, leading to several refusing to bid for re-tenders because of the risk of taking on staff on higher pay. On the other hand, a proportion of respondents also reported difficulties in efforts to harmonise these terms and conditions, because of the potential implications for employee morale among workers that transferred in. Here, respondents reported how they were hoping staff turnover would gradually erode pay anomalies created as a result of transfers, as new starts were hired on the organisation's own terms and conditions. Some, however, were looking for more rapid change, with the HR Director from the aforementioned organisation that had six different sets of terms and conditions stating:

> It's a nightmare. You could have one manager in one service managing three different sets of terms and conditions. So there is going to have to be a time when we say we can't continue. We're going to let it run and assess it in the next year or so.

This prospective change did not augur well for employees, as the BDM in this organisation reported how, as part of this process, new starts were being recruited on £13,600 per annum, whereas in the past they would have been paid between £14–15,000 on entry.

In terms of changes to pension entitlement, three organisations had recently made changes to current provision through moving to a stakeholder pension for new employees, in place of a final salary scheme. Another HR respondent reported how her workforce pension scheme was matched directly to a local authority model of three times the employee contribution. This respondent was planning changes whereby new employees would have to join a reduced scheme. At the same time, the organisation was aiming to sweeten the change; part of the savings on the employer pension contribution were being channelled into offering employees the ability to exercise choices (cafeteria style) in the type of employment benefits they could receive, for example, more holidays, health benefits, or sabbatical leave.

A new approach to sickness absence was also emerging. Changes to sick pay entitlement occurred within 12 organisations, including a more robust application of current absence management policy, or the removal for all staff of entitlement that mirrored the public sector. The more robust approach was best illustrated by a HR manager from a children's services organisation who stated:

> The preferred position of many of our managers is to be a social worker rather than a manager. Managers were inclined on some occasions to not dig too deeply into the factors that lay behind poor attendance – almost as if this was a service user. Forgetting that there is an employment relationship there and that the balance needs to be met between what the organisation needs and the individual needs. These are issues that managers need to deal with, and now the Business Partners sit alongside them to deal with them but also encourage them to fulfil their role, because they are after all, paid as managers.

Cost considerations were the key factor in persuading organisations to move away from aligning their approach to sickness absence with the public sector. One organisation, for example, had moved away from public sector pay scales as early as 2001, but offered other aspects of its employment package in line with local authority conditions, including sick pay. The ability to offer these hybrid market and public sector packages is diminishing in the worsening financial climate.

> We have just got through a new sickness policy… and so there's a part about managing and doing some training on return to work meetings, bOut there's a part about our terms and conditions reflecting the council's, and we can't afford to pay out the way we've been paying out, and sickness absence being so high.
>
> (HR Manager, adult services)

The organisation's response to this pressure was typical of most of the other organisations, in that it stopped paying sick pay for the first three days of absence and offered no occupational sick pay for new starts for the first six months of their employment. For long-term sickness, the organisation moved from twenty-six weeks' full pay and twenty-six weeks' half pay, to seventeen weeks' full pay and seventeen weeks' half pay, accompanied by a greater emphasis on home visits and return to work – 'we need to be sharper about saying, "Well, you know, if you can't get back in a few months, we need to look at what that means for your job"' (HR Manager, adult services).

Industrial relations

Within the above context, although ten respondents recognised trade unions, there were limited opportunities for workers to express discontent through collective bargaining because of low membership. In all but a few of these workplaces unions struggled to make an impact with reports of membership not reaching higher than 10–15 per cent, or collective strength was confined to pockets of workers. Reasons for this included problems recruiting shop stewards and a geographically dispersed workforce. There were also examples of anti-unionism, with one respondent considering de-recognition. Another, a traditionally non-union organisation, had TUPEd in a union agreement during a successful re-tender, but the HR Director admitted the organisation was waiting for numbers of union members in the particular project to diminish through natural wastage, rather than encourage further growth.

Tensions were apparent between management and unions, with one of the organisations experiencing two strikes between 2007 and 2009 over pay and changes to contracts and sick pay respectively. Each of these examples of industrial action led to concessions by management, but not without reports of a great deal of strain and tensions with union representatives and workers, the latter fearing the impact of their action on service users. Another organisation had experienced a ballot for industrial action over pay in late 2008, but this did not lead to a strike.

The emerging climate of economic recession at the time of the interviews saw unions in some organisations make compromises to save jobs. In the case of the organisation mentioned in the previous section that undertook changes to its sickness absence arrangements, the first effort to introduce these changes failed because of union resistance. The second effort was introduced in the context of a wholesale re-tendering of the organisation's services, where funders were reportedly scrutinising absence statistics and their associated costs. The HR Manager reported how, as a consequence, union officials reluctantly accepted the aforementioned changes in order to retain contracts and save jobs.

Responding to market changes

Voluntary organisations faced a dilemma of responding to cost pressures, but also maintaining staff morale. In response, the majority of organisations attempted to sustain their funding by participating in the market for new and existing contracts. Some organisations (five cases) had also begun to invest in the recruitment of BDMs to improve their prospects in tenders. As one stated – 'They have set a target for growth in care support services and they knew they couldn't deliver it without an entrepreneur coming to help do it.' These BDMs were recruited to grow and diversify income so that organisations were to a degree immunised from changing priorities or budgets from existing funders. Thus falls in income from specific funders would not have a dramatic effect, nor necessitate restructuring that might have a detrimental impact on services and/or pay and other terms and conditions.

At the same time, several of the respondents undertaking such a role reported how they lacked the resources (especially administration help) to undertake their function adequately. Other organisations (six cases) had devolved responsibility for gaining additional business to regional service managers/directors, but with added training in financial, negotiation and presentation skills, as well as active interventions from specialists in the HR and finance functions. Respondents also reported how some organisations were beginning to respond to re-tenders and tenders through consortiums with other voluntary providers. Another organisation was attempting to attract income through establishing a cafeteria/restaurant facility, and employing service users on incomes that reflected market rates for catering and hospitality, rather than the public sector. There was also evidence of respondents adopting a more hard-line business approach to the funding of projects, with the newly appointed CEO of one organisation that specialised in services for the elderly refusing to subsidise services through dipping into organisational reserves.

Others were becoming more discerning in their choice of bids for re-tenders because of fears concerning the transfer of new staff with different pension rights. Here, several of the BDMs reported how they were reluctant to get involved in certain re-tenders, because they could involve staff who had previously been employed in the public sector and, therefore, the organisation would have to take on responsibility for pension liabilities. This was exacerbated by the lack of information provided during the re-tendering process, and two respondents had backed out of re-tenders because of potential pension liabilities – 'if we have to take council staff with all their pension rights and salary scales, we can't deliver the service for that price' (BDM, adult services).

Discussion and conclusion

This chapter has explored the impact on the independence and mission and terms and conditions of employment of voluntary organisations that have taken on the delivery of public services through outsourcing. These two issues are inter-related as the voluntary sector literature has indicated how the risk of mission drift arises with the move towards relying increasingly on paid staff to deliver services (Billis, 2010).

This chapter adds to this debate by showing that it is not just the increased presence of paid staff under outsourcing alone that risks the mission of voluntary organisations providing public services, but rather how this vital resource is managed. In doing so, the sections revealed how NPM-inspired cost pressures present a significant threat to missions through the imposition of changes to working practices that bureaucratise and deskill work, and significantly, cut terms and conditions. These pressures, in their different ways, have a deleterious impact on service quality and therefore organisational missions.

The data from this study suggests that the state–voluntary sector relationship remains one characterised by a heavy emphasis on audit and scrutiny, with the HR function playing its part. The threat to organisational missions, however, stems *principally* from the fall-out of the financial crisis of 2008–09, which is forcing voluntary sector employers to cut any links with public sector employment terms and conditions. Here, organisations that clung to public sector pay scales were unanimously being forced to reconsider this approach to reward and respondents were also moving from comparability with regard to sickness absence or pensions.

The future for the sector and its employees looks more uncertain and precarious under the UK's Coalition Government between the Conservative and Liberal Democrat parties. Part of their programme includes the development of the 'Big Society', advocating greater participation and voice to civil society, enhancing opportunities for volunteering and transferring power to local communities, principles that arguably favour further growth of voluntary organisations in the provision of public services (NCVO, 2010). This policy, however, is in parallel with a commitment by the Coalition Government to accelerate cuts in public expenditure to reduce the fiscal deficit. As a start, in June 2010, the coalition announced £1.2bn cuts in local government grants. At the time of writing, reports from the sector indicate that pressure for cuts from funders were already beginning to emerge as a consequence of this reduction in central government support (NCVO, 2010). This raises the question of whether we will witness the emergence of a 'perfect storm' for those employed in delivering public services in voluntary organisations. There is likely to be enhanced threats to job security through, perhaps, greater reliance on volunteers and/or as local authorities re-tender and re-prioritise their provision of services to protect their own workforces from the forthcoming cuts. For those that remain employed in the sector, they risk a steady diminution in their terms and conditions of employment so that the link with public sector terms and conditions evaporates. These threats, in turn, come back to and undermine the missions of voluntary sector organisations as morale among the workforce is affected adversely. Overall, policymakers in their haste to make cuts through reducing employment costs may be sacrificing the very attributes that attracted them to the voluntary sector as a provider of public services.

References

Baines, D. (2004) 'Caring for nothing: work organisation and unwaged labour in social services', *Work, Employment and Society*, 18:2, 267–295.

Barnard, J., Broach, S. and Wakefield, V. (2004) *Social Care: The Growing Crisis: Report on Recruitment and Retention Issues in the Voluntary Sector* (London: Social Care Employers Consortium).

Billis, D. (2010) 'From welfare bureaucracies to welfare hybrids', in D. Billis (ed.) *Hybrid Organizations and the Third Sector: Challenges for Theory, Practice and Policy* (Basingstoke: Palgrave Macmillan).

Blois, K. (2002) 'Business to business exchanges: a rich descriptive apparatus derived from MacNeil's and Menger's analyses', *Journal of Management Studies*, 39:4, 523–551.

Bresnen, M. (1996) 'An Organisational Perspective on Changing Buyer-Supplier Relations: A Critical Review of the Evidence', *Organization*, 3, 1, 121–46.

Charity Commission (2007) *Stand and Deliver: The Future for Charities Providing Public Services* (London: Charity Commission).

Chew, C. and Osborne, S. (2009) 'Exploring strategic positioning in the UK charitable sector: emerging evidence from charitable organizations that provide public services', *British Journal of Management*, 20:3, 90–105.

Clark, J., Dobbs, J., Kane, P. and Wilding, K. (2009) *The State and Voluntary Sector: Recent Trends in Government Funding and Public Service Delivery* (London: NCVO).

Clark, J., and Wilding, S. (forthcoming) 'Trends in voluntary sector employment', in I. Cunningham, and P. James (eds) *Voluntary Organisations and Public Service Delivery: the Employment Outcomes of Government Outsourcing and their Implications* (London: Routledge).

Cunningham, I. (2008) *Employment Relations in the Voluntary Sector* (London: Routledge).

Cunningham, I. and James, P. (2009) 'The outsourcing of social care in Britain: what does it mean for the voluntary sector workers?' *Work, Employment and Society*, 23:2, 363–375.

Cunningham, I. and Nickson, D. (2009) *A Gathering Storm? Procurement, Re-tendering and the Voluntary Sector Social Care Workforce* (Glasgow: Scottish Centre for Employment Research).

Cunningham, I (2010) 'The HR Function in purchaser – provider relationships: insights from the UK voluntary sector', *Human Resource Management Journal*, 20, 2, 189–205.

Davies, S. (2007) *Third Sector Provision of Local Government and Health Services: A Report for UNISON* (London: UNISON).

Dearden-Phillips, C. (2010) 'Time to cull a mammoth pensions problem', Guardian Society – *The Guardian*, 22 February: 6.

DiMaggio, P. J. and Powell, W. W. (1983) 'The Iron Cage Revisited: Institutional isomorphism and collective rationality in organisational fields', *American Sociological Review*, 35, 147–60.

Grimshaw, D. and Rubery, J. (2005) 'Inter-capital relations and network organization: redefining the work and employment nexus', *Cambridge Journal of Economics*, 29, 1027–51.

Harris, M. (2010) 'Third sector organizations in a contradictory policy environment', in D. Billis (ed.) *Hybrid Organizations and the Third Sector: Challenges for Theory, Practice and Policy* (Basingstoke: Palgrave Macmillan).

Harris, M., Rochester, C. and Halfpenny, P. (2001) 'Voluntary organisations and social policy: twenty years of change', in M. Harris and C. Rochester (eds) *Voluntary Organisations and Social Policy in Britain: Perspectives on Change and Choice* (Basingstoke: Palgrave Macmillan).

Harrow, J. (2009) 'Thistles, roses, thorns: some reflections on third sector/government relations and policy expectations in economic downturn', paper to *ESRC/ SCVO Public Policy Seminar Series – Recession and the Third Sector*, Edinburgh, November.

Hunter, L., Beaumont, P. and Sinclair, D. (1996) "A Partnership Route to HRM", *Journal of Management Studies*, 33:2, 235–257.

Kendall, J. (2003) *The Voluntary Sector* (London: Routledge).

Marchington, M., Grimshaw, D., Rubery, J. and Wilmott, H. (2005) *Fragmenting Work: Blurring Organizational Boundaries and Disordering Hierarchies* (Oxford: Oxford University Press).

National Council for Voluntary Organizations (NCVO) (2010) *The UK Civil Society Almanac 2010* (London: NCVO Publications).

Osborne, S. (1997) 'Managing the coordination of social services in the mixed economy of welfare: competition, cooperation or common cause?' *British Journal of Management*, 8:4, 317–328.

Parry, E. and Kelliher, C. (2009) 'Voluntary sector responses to increased resourcing challenges', *Employee Relations*, 31:1, 9–24.

Perri 6 and Kendall, J. (1997) 'Introduction', in Perri 6 and J. Kendall (eds) *The Contract Culture in Public Services* (Aldershot: Ashgate).

Pollit, C. (1995) *Managerialism and Public Services* (Oxford: Blackwell).

Ramesh, R. (2010) 'Charities face pensions crisis with shortfall of more than £1bn', *The Guardian*, 16 February: 4.

Ridder, H. G. and McCandless, A. (2008) 'Influences on the architecture of Human Resource Management in nonprofit organisations: an analytical framework', *Nonprofit and Voluntary Sector Quarterly*, 20:10, 1–18.

Scarborough, H. (2000) 'The HR implications of supply chain relationships', *Human Resource Management Journal*, 10:1, 5–17.

Sako, M. (1992) *Prices, Quality and Trust: Inter-firm Relations in Britain and Japan* (Cambridge: Cambridge University Press).

Taylor, M. and Lewis, J. (1997) 'Contracting: What does it do to voluntary and non-profit organisations?' in Perri 6 and J. Kendall (eds) *The Contract Culture in Public Services* (Aldershot: Ashgate).

Tonkiss, F. and Passey, A. (1999) 'Trust, confidence and voluntary organisations: between values and institutions', *Sociology*, 33:2, 257–274.

Wainwright, S., Clark, J., Griffith, M., Jochum, V. and Wilding, K. (2006) *The UK Voluntary Sector Almanac 2006* (London: NCVO publications).

Walsh, K. (1995) *Public Services and Market Mechanisms* (Basingstoke: Palgrave Macmillan).

Wilding, K., Collins, G., Jochum, V. and Wainright, S. (2004), *The UK Voluntary Sector Almanac 2004* (London: NCVO Publications).

9
Leaders in Public Service Organisations

Patrick McGurk

Introduction

Questions of leadership in public service organisations (PSOs) have become central to the 'modernisation' agenda (Alimo-Metcalfe and Alban-Metcalfe, 2004; O'Reilly and Reed, 2010). While political and academic interest in how PSOs are managed and led is not new (Denis et al., 2005: 447), the latter years of public service reform have seen a particular concern with the management of people (Ingraham, 2005), especially in terms of the processes by which managers bring about change and innovation (Milner and Joyce, 2005). Such preoccupations have brought about 'a veritable rush to leadership' (Gold et al., 2003: 2, cited in Lawler 2008: 23).

Within the academic and policy-related literature on leaders and leadership, in spite of a recurrent recognition of the specificities of the public service context, scant attention has been paid to how leadership concepts have been manifested and experienced by managers at organisational level. The key argument of this chapter is that the extent to which different managers in PSOs have the opportunity to 'lead', and therefore to practice leadership, is primarily shaped by organisational context. Contemporary PSOs face some similar management issues in terms of securing staff commitment and responding to the pressures of adaptation. But the diversity of managerial work and organisational types in the public services means that managers experience quite different opportunities and incentives to practice the motivational and change-oriented elements of managing that have become associated with leadership (c.f. Mintzberg, 2009).

The chapter has five parts. The first part analyses the formation of leadership concepts in the modernisation phase of public service reform. The second part discusses three competing perspectives on leadership that have been most relevant for policy articulations. The third part demonstrates how policy has been manifested in attempts to promote leadership in the public services. The fourth part presents empirical data that illustrate managers' experiences of such attempts in three quite different PSOs – a traditional public bureaucracy, a professional bureaucracy and a commercialised bureaucracy – and how experiences are shaped by organisational contingencies. The final part concludes that our understanding of 'leaders' in PSOs therefore requires greater contextualisation according to different types of organisational types and their directions of change.

Formation: from management to leadership in public service reform

The theoretical distinction between managers and leaders (Kotter, 1990; Zaleznik, 1992), while disputed, is valuable for understanding how priorities have changed in public service reform in the last twenty years (Storey, 2004b: 7; Milner and Joyce, 2005: 71; Lawler, 2008: 22; O'Reilly and Reed, 2010). The asserted differences between managers and leaders are worth reviewing and are summarised in Figure 9.1.

The concept of the management-leadership distinction has had a significant impact on policymakers. A 2001 report by the UK government's Performance and Innovation Unit (PIU) provides an insight into how

Managers	Leaders
are transactional	are transformational
seek to operate and maintain current systems	seek to challenge and change systems
accept given objectives and meanings	create new visions and new meanings
control and monitor	empower
trade on exchange relationships	seek to inspire and transcend
have a short-term focus	have a long-term focus
focus on detail and procedure	focus on the big strategic picture

Figure 9.1 Managers versus leaders
Source: Storey, 2004a.

the public service environment was seen as having shifted with the new millennium:

> public organisations face new pressures to adapt, learn, innovate and keep up with the best performers. Amongst these new pressures are:
> - more rapid technological and other change, creating new opportunities and threats and allowing greater integration across a range of organisational boundaries...;
> - greater organisational complexity, as new technology and organisational forms combine to promote new ways of organising service delivery; and
> - increased consumer expectations of service delivery, together with a more complex array of other demanding stakeholders.
>
> (PIU, 2001: 10)

Another report for the UK government in 2006, by management consultants Ernst and Young, heralded the new priorities of public service reform as a step change from 'management and competition' towards 'leadership and plurality' (Ernst and Young, 2006). Such a change in emphasis echoed wider trends observed by academics, in which the efficiency-driven measures of the NPM of the late 1980s and mid-1990s were giving way to modernisation policies designed to improve service quality, user-satisfaction and involvement, governance and partnership working (Newman, 2002; Dunleavy et al., 2006; Osborne 2006).

A slightly different analysis was advanced by the OECD in 2001 to describe the changing landscape of public service reform across advanced industrial democracies. Recognising that '[i]n all countries, structural and management reform in the public sector had been used to better align public services with the needs of contemporary society', the OECD went on to argue that 'something was missing', namely 'a lack of dedication to the underlying values of public service cultures and the public interest' (OECD, 2001: 12). This 'something' was to be 'fixed' through leadership (ibid.).

The specific challenges facing managers in contemporary PSOs appear to be fourfold: i) coping with an increasingly fast pace of change; ii) managing greater organisational complexity; iii) motivating staff to deliver higher quality and more personalised public services; and iv) attending to the emotions and the psychological wellbeing of staff, due to the stress of change and new sources of employment insecurity in PSOs (c.f. especially Alimo-Metcalfe and Alban-Metcalfe 2004: 175–6 on this last point). Given this changing and more demanding environment, it is not surprising that policymakers should have been drawn to the solutions offered by models of leadership and the more attractive figure of the public service leader, rather than the more mundane and predictable alternative of management and the public sector manager (or, worse still, the senior bureaucrat) (c.f. Salaman 2004: 76; Storey 2004a: 30). Arguments about the management/leadership dichotomy, and the supposed superiority of leadership for achieving motivation and change, have admittedly become less important in theoretical discussions, with even the most ardent advocates of leadership recognising that both managers and leaders are needed in organisations (Storey, 2004a). With specific regard to public service reform, Hughes (2007) identifies the underlying reasons for recent political interest in organisational leadership as opposed to management, and clarifies their interrelationship:

> The emergence of concepts of leadership in the public sector should be seen as a reassertion of individual and personal attributes in management, and, as a corollary, a reduction in the emphasis on management by formal rules. Giving a manager real responsibility to achieve results means that he or she must then deliver and their part of the organization must also deliver. The staff involved need to achieve and the manager needs to lead them. A good manager must not only deliver results, but somehow get subordinates to agree with the general parameters of the vision and to be inspired to achieve themselves, for the overall benefit of the organisation.
>
> (2007: 320–21)

Hughes' down-to-earth depiction of the leader as a 'good manager' is close to Mintzberg's later definition of leadership as simply 'management practised well' (2009: 9). Moreover, Hughes' description of the practice of leading as 'somehow getting subordinates to agree' sits comfortably with Shackleton's widely quoted definition of leadership as 'the process in which an individual influences other group members towards the attainment of group or organizational goals' (1995: 2).

This basic grasp of what leadership actually involves is important to keep well above the surface when navigating the complex theoretical terrain. Despite the academic consensus that both management and leadership are required in organisations as integrated and mutually reinforcing practices, radically different interpretations of leadership persist. These different interpretations have informed the various ways in which public service reforms have been articulated.

Articulations of leadership in the public services

Academic commentators have long complained of the problems in successfully defining leadership. The various competing definitions and theories need not be rehearsed here. (For a comprehensive overview, *see* Storey 2004a: 14ff.) It is more important to point out the three main competing interpretations of organisational leadership in the public services from which policy articulations tend to be derived. The main dividing line is between the 'entrepreneurial' view and the 'stewardship' view of public service leadership (c.f. Denis et al., 2005; and Hughes 2007: 335). However, a third theme of 'distributed leadership', has emerged more recently as important in discussions of public service reform (Gold et al., 2003: 14, cited in Lawler 2008: 31; Storey, 2004a: 13).

The entrepreneurial view of leadership of PSOs contends that 'the achievement of effective public services depends on the creativity and dynamism of strong leaders who do not feel constrained by the weight of tradition or formal rules' (Denis et al., 2005: 450). This individualistic perspective is heavily influenced by transformational leadership theory (Burns, 1978; Bass, 1985). In such a view, rather than manage transactional exchanges with staff to achieve objectives, leaders act as inspirational role-models, forming motivational relationships with staff to stimulate and develop them to go beyond their self-interest and contribute to the whole organisational effort.

The entrepreneurial view of public service leadership has been most influential in the United States, notably articulated in Osborne and Gaebler's Reinventing Government (1992) and in the rhetoric of the first Clinton administration. In the UK, although great disagreement about what constitutes effective public service leadership has been acknowledged by the government (PIU 2001: 1, cited in Alimo-Metcalfe and Alban-Metcalfe, 2004: 173), the transformational rhetoric of the entrepreneurial view has also tended to predominate (Currie and Lockett, 2007). For example, in response to a commissioned report by the Centre for Excellence in Management and Leadership in 2002, the government proclaimed: 'By tackling our management and leadership deficit with real vigour, we will unlock the doors ...and create the conditions for a radical transformation of public services' (DfES/DTI, 2002). Despite the ambitious rhetoric of many politicians and policymakers, however, and in spite of some examples of inspirational leaders temporarily 'turning round' PSOs, the empirical evidence makes it 'difficult to argue that managers, workplaces and organisations are being transformed either into or by leaders' (Grugulis, 2007: 149).

The stewardship view of public service leadership is less concerned with the transformation of PSOs; instead it emphasises the role of public leaders as 'guardians of public goods and values' (Denis et al., 2005: 451). This is closer to the traditional administrative model in which '[c]onformity to bureaucratic rules is not an impediment to the delivery of effective public services, but the means by which public leaders ensure democratic accountability for their decisions and actions' (ibid.). The stewardship view of public service leadership therefore has a stronger association with the mainland European tradition of public administration than with the 'high-NPM' Anglo-Saxon models operating in the UK, US, Australia and New Zealand (c.f. Pollitt, 2002; Pollitt and Bouckaert, 2004; Proeller and Schedler, 2005).

Certainly in the UK, the stewardship view has not featured strongly in the rhetoric of policymakers and its articulation has tended to be confined to academic critiques of the entrepreneurial view and the 'new managerialism' in the public services (c.f. Clarke and Newman, 1997; Clarke et al., 2000). Such analyses point out how the increased powers afforded to senior managers in PSOs, in the name of 'giving managers the freedom to manage', have in turn reduced the powers of public service professionals and democratically elected politicians (Milner and Joyce, 2005: 7–9). Nevertheless, the stewardship view has not been entirely absent in policy rhetoric. For example, in his 2002 vision of the twenty-first century civil service, the Head of the Civil Service, Sir Andrew Turnbull, declared the need for leaders not only to 'think creatively and operate strategically', but also to 'be identified with the traditional values of integrity and trust, impartiality and readiness to serve all citizens and governments' (Turnbull 2002, cited in Horton 2007: 4).

Distributed leadership represents to some extent a mid-way position between the entrepreneurial and stewardship perspectives. Yet it also provides a new theoretical departure and is becoming increasingly articulated in policy in the UK. In this perspective, leadership is defined not as a product of enterprising individuals, nor a stewardship responsibility attached to one's official position, but as a collective practice dispersed throughout the organisation and its complex, professional networks (c.f. Denis et al., 2005: 449, 452ff; MacBeath 2005). In particular, Alimo-Metcalfe and Alban-Metcalfe have promoted the view that leadership occurs in more democratic and collegiate ways through the day-to-day interactions of senior, middle, front-line and project managers with staff at various levels in the organisation; it 'is fundamentally about engaging others as partners in developing and achieving the vision' (2004: 179). Their research in the UK public sector (2001, 2004) has demonstrated the relevance of a 'nearby transformational leadership model', that is less individualistic, 'heroic' and North American in its orientation, and less reliant on white, male senior managers for its evidence base.

Alimo-Metcalfe and Alban-Metcalfe's alternative model of transformational leadership has been influential in recent years in informing visions and models of multi-levelled leadership in various parts of the UK public services. The most important examples are in the NHS and local government (c.f. Alimo-Metcalfe and Alban-Metcalfe, 2004), the Fire Service (ODPM, 2005) and the Police Service (Dobby et al., 2004). The concept of distributed leadership has also been explicitly developed in the education sector. This is most notable in the model of the 'middle leader', referring to those mid-hierarchy teaching staff within schools, who initiate and effect innovation while practising alongside their professional colleagues (c.f. Glatter, 2004; Busher, 2005; MacBeath, 2005). Together with ideas deriving from the entrepreneurial view, models of distributed leadership have influenced a variety of interventions that have sought to identify, promote and develop leadership behaviour in PSOs.

Manifestations: attempts to promote leadership in the public services

The general response to the perceived new public service environment has been a surge in international interest in leadership and leadership development (Raffel et al., 2009), accompanied by a burgeoning private sector management consultancy and training industry (Storey, 2004a: 13). In the UK, there has been a wave of public investment to promote more effective leadership in PSOs, notably in the creation of the National College for School Leadership, the NHS Leadership Centre and the Leadership Centre for Local Government (Storey, 2004b: 4–6; Guest and King, 2005: 248–249; Lawler, 2008: 22). More specifically, interventions to promote leadership in the public services have centred on: (i) the recruitment of senior executives; (ii) the identification of leadership competences for all managers in PSOs; and (iii) leadership development.

Recruitment of senior executives

Earlier leadership interventions tended to be concerned with the recruitment of exceptional and inspirational individuals to head up, and help transform, bureaucratic PSOs. This was clearly influenced by the entrepreneurial view of leadership. However, the 'parachuting in' of temporary chief executives from the private sector to transform health trusts or civil service departments, or 'superheads' to turn around 'failing schools', appears to have subsided somewhat (Storey, 2004b: 30). There is a lack of precise data on the extent and effect of external recruitment of senior executives in the public services. The nearest approximation seems to be Boyne et al.'s research on leadership in English local government, which reports that 47 out of 148 authorities saw at least two changes of chief executive between 1998–99 and 2005–6 (2008b: 270), but concludes that external recruitment appears to have made either no difference, or even have had a negative impact on an authority's performance (2008a: 11).

Notwithstanding the lack of firm evidence of success in the appointment of senior executives, the cooling of enthusiasm in this area can also be understood in the context of some ethical unease about entrepreneurism in a public services context (c.f. Borins, 2000, cited by Currie and Lockett, 2007: 345) and more general criticisms of US-derived transformational leadership theory. For many, theories of leadership that emphasise the importance of the charismatic and maverick individual leader have played a role in encouraging and excusing narcissistic, manipulative and even corrupt behaviour by senior executives, as exemplified by the imprisonment of Enron's CEO Jeff Skilling in 2001 (c.f. Storey, 2004a: 32; Mintzberg, 2009: 222).

Recent accounts of organisational transformation and renewal in PSOs tend to tell a more nuanced story, in which leaders in PSOs have demonstrated the importance of adapting to the demands of specific professional and political contexts and navigating complex networks of social relationships, while promoting and implementing their personal vision (c.f. Milner and Joyce, 2005). Nevertheless, in such accounts considerable emphasis continues to be placed on the critical importance of the exceptional personal qualities of individual figureheads. Although effective leadership in the public services is increasingly being recast as 'adaptive' (Milner and Joyce, 2005: 166) or 'network leadership' (Hall and Janmen, 2010: 38), the preoccupation with the experience of senior executives and the underlying individualism of the entrepreneurial view have not been entirely shaken off.

Leadership competences

In recent years, the main policy emphasis in the UK has been on the identification and development of leadership behaviours for all managers, and situating this within broader frameworks of professional competence and performance. Rooted in the distributed leadership view is the notion that middle and front-line managers can also be leaders, and this has become subsumed to a large extent by the 'competence movement' in the public services (Burgoyne, 1993; Horton, 2002; *c.f.* also Salaman 2004). The competence movement involves widespread and detailed attempts across the public sector to identify the leadership behaviours that any effective manager should display, whatever his or her level in the organisation.

The basis of the competence movement in the UK is in the National Occupational Standards (NOS) in Leadership and Management, revised in 1997, 2004 and 2008 and adapted for various vocational and professional groups. Close examination of some of these standards provides an insight into the detailed way in which leadership concepts have manifested. The latest version of the NOS organises over 70 competences into six 'skill clusters', the first three of which are concerned with the leadership-orientated activities of 'managing self and personal skills', 'providing direction' and 'facilitating change' (MSC, 2008). The skill cluster most explicitly concerned with the basic leadership process of influencing others towards organisational goals is that of 'providing direction'. The 'behaviours which underpin effective performance' in providing direction, are specified at four different levels of management, for team leaders, first-line managers, middle managers and senior managers. Whereas team leaders are, amongst other things, expected to 'create a sense of common purpose', first-line and middle managers are expected to do not only this, but also to 'articulate a vision that generates excitement, enthusiasm and commitment', 'make complex things simple for the benefit of others' and 'encourage and support others to make the best use of their abilities'. Senior managers are expected to do all of this (except the last part), as well as to 'present information clearly, concisely, accurately and in ways that promote understanding' (MSC, 2008).

In stating exactly what managers should do and how they should behave at various levels of management, rather mechanical formulations such as these have led to much criticism of leadership competences for reductionism and their over-simplifying of managerial work (Bolden and Gosling, 2004: 3–4; Salaman, 2004). However, as Burgoyne et al. point out, competence-based approaches have proved remarkably resistant (2004: 14–16) and continue to underpin many selection, development, reward and performance management frameworks in large organisations. Moreover, in the public services, competence-based approaches provide HR practitioners with unified frameworks to integrate not only desired management and leadership behaviours, but also specific professional behaviours that help safeguard and promote public service values (*see* Skills for Care, 2008 for a specific example).

Leadership development

Most leadership development activity in the UK public sector seems to follow the general trend of integrating leadership development as part of long-term, competence-based management development programmes (Burgoyne et al., 2004: 22). However, the role of the competence movement in taking out some of the 'mystique' of leadership may help to explain why many PSOs also continue to invest in more personalised and informal leadership development interventions.

Investment in long-term competence-based development programmes, particularly for front-line and middle managers, is reflected in the increased take-up of qualifications such as the Certificate and Diploma in Management from the Chartered Management Institute, or sector-specific derivations thereof (*c.f.* Mabey, 2005). Such programmes tend to include classroom-based learning of leadership theory, combined with the compilation of individual evidence portfolios that are intended to demonstrate the achievement of specific NOS-related competences. This latter type of development is often delivered as a bureaucratic rather than a learning exercise (*c.f.* Grugulis, 1997). However, the more personalised content in such learning programmes, concerned with discovering and developing one's leadership style, increasingly makes use of more individualised development methods, such as 360-degree feedback, coaching, mentoring, personal development planning.

Such individualised leadership development activities are also found as stand-alone interventions and, after the longer-term management development programmes, are the next most popular type of leadership development (*c.f.* Gold et al., 2003: 10). However these methods are resource-intensive and require considerable expertise on the part of HR practitioners if they are to be implemented effectively (c.f. Van Velsor and McCauley, 2004). This is perhaps why individualised development is more commonly found amongst the smaller group of senior managers than amongst front-line and middle managers (c.f. Burgoyne et al., 2004: 23).

A popular alternative to longer-term development programmes and expensive individualised interventions seems to be the running of in-house workshops, designed to help managers in PSOs discover their leadership qualities and inspire them to innovate and initiate change. The precise amount and frequency of these less formal interventions in PSOs is hard to measure. However, there are numerous reports of PSOs investing in this type of activity. For example, in recent years private consultants Devas have been contracted by the fire brigades of Leicester, Avon, Cleveland and London to run a 'values-centred' leadership course for all managers called 'The Wow Factor' (Devas Group, 2010). The course uses introspective, small group discussions to explore and share the emotional side of managerial work so that managers become more aware of their own attitudes towards colleagues and the organisation's mission. Other examples include a three-day leadership course entitled 'From Good to Great' and a series of workshops entitled 'Inspirational Leadership' in one of England's largest local authorities (McGurk, 2010).

The influence of transformational leadership ideas on such interventions is clear. More closely derived from a distributed leadership perspective, however, are collective leadership development activities such as special team assignments and 'action learning sets'. These types of interventions bring together groups of managers to engage in learning exercises that also seek to solve workplace problems of common interest, thereby helping to build a 'community of practice' amongst managers (*c.f.* Brown and Duguid, 1991). Again, the extent of investment in such development activity in PSOs is hard to gauge, but Gold et al. (2003: 10) suggest that more collective and open-ended methods of leadership development are relatively rare.

Managers' experiences of leadership development

Given the pervasiveness of leadership concepts and rhetoric in the contemporary public services, but also the diversity of its different manifestations, it remains to be asked how the phenomenon has been experienced on the ground. The different types of organisations in the public services, and the various management groups within them, broaden the potential for a very diverse set of experiences. As observed above, 'leaders' in PSOs might include anyone from senior executives, to middle, front-line and project managers. Similarly, PSOs, which provide the organisational context in which leadership is practised, range from fully publicly owned public sector bodies, to privately owned providers of public services, to public–private partnerships (Grout and Stevens, 2003; Flynn, 2007: 210). While policy interventions around leadership have affected public sector bodies most directly, the underlying thinking has also been influential in privatised organisations, indeed integral to the franchising out of some services to the private sector (Currie and Lockett, 2007: 346).

This section of the chapter presents accounts of middle managers' experiences of leadership development during organisational change in three contrasting types of PSOs, including two public sector organisations and one private provider of a public service (The evidence is taken from McGurk 2009, 2010 and some unpublished interview notes). The first case organisation is a fire brigade, a traditional public sector bureaucracy that implemented a new set of management and leadership competences as part of modernisation. The second is a local authority adult social services department, a professional bureaucracy that used leadership development to address staff retention problems and encourage managers to advance a new set of strategic priorities. The third is a privatised train operating company, a commercialised bureaucracy, although publicly regulated and subsidised and, thus, according to European Union law an 'emanation of the state', that sought to promote a customer service culture amongst its managers.

The traditional public sector bureaucracy: fire brigade

The UK regional fire brigade in this first case study pioneered its own management and leadership competence statements in the mid-1990s. These were used for the purposes of selection and promotion to senior officer grades, and this process was supported by leadership development workshops, classroom instruction and individual evidence portfolios. The competence-based approach to development and promotion was then formalised for all uniformed roles and across all fire brigades in England and Wales in 2001 through the introduction of the Integrated Personal Development System (IPDS). This became the 'cornerstone of the Government's reform of the human resource management of the fire and rescue service' (ODPM, 2003: 57) in the wake of a prolonged and acrimonious industrial dispute in 2002–4.

IPDS underpinned the shift from 'rank to role', in which the military-like rank structure was officially abolished and replaced with a smaller set of 'modernised' roles. Each new role had a 'role map' of various competences, including leadership competences at the senior levels that staff were required to demonstrate before being considered for promotion. The middle officer rank of 'station commander', for example, was replaced with role of 'station manager' to reflect greater responsibility for the development of the station's resources and its staff, rather than overseeing fire incidents. Development interventions were then used to promote the new strategic agenda in the fire service, which was principally concerned with increasing transparency and diversity in the selection and promotion process, and eradicating the command-and-control management culture in favour of a more empowering approach. This was to involve developing and encouraging firefighters to take greater responsibility for decisions at fire incidents, and to spend more time in the community promoting fire safety and prevention.

Official attempts to promote leaders and leadership at all levels in the fire service in the early 2000s were therefore inextricably linked with the highly politicised and contested modernisation reforms. This was reflected in the experiences of station commanders in the case study brigade, most of whom dismissed the new system at best as irrelevant to their 'real' work and at worst as dangerous bureaucratic interference by non-specialists in the business of firefighting. As one station commander commented of his experience of classroom instruction on leadership: 'It was refreshing to see that the Fire Service did such training, [but] less refreshing to realise that it was never implemented .... [T]he Fire Service just didn't run like that'. And, as another viewed IPDS: 'It's like the King's New Clothes. We will believe we have better people, because it says so on paper'.

But away from classrooms and evidence portfolios, station commanders were more accepting and enthusiastic about the empowering and developmental approach to management, even if they did not express it in these terms. Learning that took place in a more practical and specialist setting was far more successful in promoting the type of leadership behaviour that modernisation reformers wished to see. As one station commander related from a simulated fire incident on the training ground:

> One day, on the last couple of days of the ... course, they said 'Right, on this drill... we want you to assess the next officer in charge ...where do you think [he] should be standing?' I said, 'Where I am'. And it was like the heavens opened and I suddenly realised that, as a manager, you need to see the big picture, you need to step away ... It was just changed overnight.... For me, it was just an amazing experience.
>
> (Interview with station commander, 2005)

The experiences of these managers in the fire service illustrate the dangers of attempting to extricate leadership from its professional, political and organisational setting in the public services. Senior staff often identify closely with their subordinates and their professional colleagues, and are reluctant to commit to the changing strategic priorities of senior management (*c.f.* Scase and Goffee, 1989). It cannot be assumed that managers in PSOs will be readily convinced of the need to demonstrate leadership behaviour in the ways in which they are articulated in official competence statements. However, if managers are more directly involved in identifying and agreeing what constitutes leadership in their own specialist and organisational context, then leadership development is likely to be more effective.

The professional bureaucracy: local adult social services department

The second case organisation is the adult social services department of a large English local authority, which also responded to an employment relations crisis by introducing a package of HR measures, including investment in management and leadership development. Radical national reforms to social care management from the mid-1990s to the mid-2000s, combined with problems of staff recruitment and retention, particularly among social workers, presented social security departments with a range of strategic and HR challenges. In this authority, however, between 1998 and 2007, local government and social services inspectors noted significant improvements in leadership and management, which they believed contributed to large increases in staff retention and the transformation of services from 'poor' to 'excellent'.

The most important investment in management and leadership development was the provision of a suite of nationally recognised management qualifications, run in-house by the authority's corporate HR function. This took the form of sponsorship of individual managers to study for qualifications such as a Diploma in Management (DM), which included a significant leadership development component. Crucially, however, the learning activities in the diploma were closely related to the strategic plans of the authority and the social services department and the reference points provided by the government's social care quality standards. This enabled individual managers to apply their leadership skills with a clear sense of strategic purpose. As one manager saw it:

> I'm not that far away from being a teamster myself to have forgotten what it's like to be in the team room and to be asked to do things that are not connected to anything – it's just a task. Now at the other side of the fence I can see all of the connections, and the DM [Diploma in Management] has made me try hard to try and sell those.
>
> (Interview with social care manager, 2007)

As an alternative to the longer-term management qualifications, the authority's HR function also provided a series of shorter-term leadership development workshops for its middle managers. These interventions included the aforementioned residential workshops in 2006–7 entitled 'From Good to Great'. Some individual managers felt changed by the workshop, but it was rare that they could identify how this might have changed their practice in any substantial way. In some cases, the transformational rhetoric of the programme was echoed in managers' own accounts of personal change. For example, one manager related her realisation that she was so 'strong' and 'powerful', and described the course as 'very, very freeing' in helping her adapt to the fact that her staff 'don't have my energy'. In contrast, however, another participant admitted to a type of 'leadership development fatigue', explaining that:

> I have to be honest… I am incredibly busy in my job and I use these [courses] to reflect. So even if they sat there and played nursery rhymes, it would be something that would be good for work.
> (Interview with social care manager, 2007)

In terms of a concrete contribution to strategic change, the most effective leadership development intervention was a series of leadership workshops in 2006–7 called 'Inspirational Leadership', organised locally in the adult social services directorate. The workshops followed a period of organisational restructuring and national and local reforms, in which the authority began to personalise care services for clients and make greater use of partnerships with organisations in the health, employment, housing services and voluntary sector. Over a period of several months, all middle managers in the directorate participated in workshops and action learning sets facilitated by an external trainer to help prepare for, and make sense of, the new adult care management environment.

The reception of the workshop activities by the trainees was mixed. However, after a few sessions, the action learning set members decided to dispense with the services of the trainer, and the meetings were converted into a semi-formal 'County District Managers Group'. This new group convened regularly and was enthusiastically attended by middle managers and other interested parties. Discussions centred on how to implement organisational strategic objectives, such as receiving electronic payments for personalised care plans. One manager explained the value of the new group as follows:

> [W]e [the district managers] kept saying this [the new strategy] isn't going to work, and then …we get an email from HQ saying 'You have to make this work'… [W]e need it, because that's the future. But the

actual practicalities of it, the detail, they don't want to hear. ...You want the good ideas, ...but you want some time and space and some understanding of how we deliver them, really.

(Interview with social care manager, 2007)

The local authority social services example illustrates how leadership development can be most positively experienced by managers and most effective in organisational terms when there is a clear and well-communicated set of strategic priorities and terms of reference within which to apply one's leadership learning. But the case also illustrates that in a professional environment, in which there is significant operational uncertainty and need for managerial discretion, the promotion of leadership requires the allowing of 'time and space' for managers to identify the organisational issues collectively and for common solutions to emerge.

The commercialised bureaucracy: train operating company

In the final case study, the organisation was created as an independent franchise in the British Rail privatisation of 1996. It experienced a series of industrial disputes and fines from the government regulator for poor performance in its first five years, with employment relations problems coming to a head with a strike by station staff in 2002. This prompted the board of directors to introduce a new 'employee-centred strategy', which was principally designed to reduce staff absence and improve customer service on the front line, and included heavy investment in management and leadership development.

The first major investment in leadership development was the two-day 'Wow factor' course, as referred to above, for all of the company's some five hundred managers in 2003. The course divided opinion and took many managers – responsible mainly for drivers, stations and fleet – 'out of their comfort zones'. Although described by one as 'excellent', 'brave' and 'radical', another found the Wow course 'appalling' and 'diabolical'. As she explained:

A lot of that course, I found, was about making people feel on the spot, opening up things that people may have not wanted to share at work ... I really did walk away from those two days thinking '... [H]ave I learnt anything that is going to make me a more effective manager? No'. And feeling frustrated that I knew all my managers were going to be released for the same two days and thinking 'what a waste of time'.

(Interview with guards manager, 2006)

The company's second main leadership development intervention was in 2005, in the form of a talent management programme for fifty selected 'high-performing' managers. It included a 360-degree exercise, psychometric testing and personal development planning. Most managers welcomed the opportunity to be singled out for such individualised attention and the insights gained into their personal leadership style. However, the intervention was relatively inconsequential in terms of changing individual leadership practices. As one driver manager said of the difficulties of setting meaningful objectives in his personal development plan: 'It was quite difficult for me to find anything that I felt I couldn't do that related to the job'.

The lack of obvious opportunities for managers to put their newfound insights into practice was related to the highly regulated work environment and the constraints of managerial job roles, particularly in the driving and fleet areas of the operation. However, the talent management programme did appear to succeed in making managers more reflective about how they related to their staff. In particular, several realised the importance of softening their communication styles. As one station manager learnt from his 360-degree feedback exercise:

> [S]ome of my managers actually really appreciate the direct, blunt approach, because they know where they stand. But I had to adapt myself for some of my team, because they obviously didn't react to that particular way of management.
>
> (Interview with station manager, 2006)

Indeed, the results of staff and customer satisfaction surveys indicated that the whole package of HR measures implemented as a result of the employee-centred strategy had led to significant improvement in staff attendance, motivation and the quality of customer service.

Yet it is important to observe that specific opportunities for individual managers to apply their learning in terms of contributing to service innovations or organisational change were effectively limited to those managers in customer-facing environments. Notably station managers had access to detailed and frequent customer service performance data that could be attributed to their particular station or group of stations. They could then use this data to go beyond issues of absence and behaviour in their discussions with staff, and have wider consultations about how to achieve better business performance. As one station manager related as a consequence of his leadership development:

> I was out with a guy, one of my managers, last week, just going round his group of stations and helping him see what I see, and

telling him how I approach addressing looking at a station ...Just getting him to see how I approach looking at stuff, and then getting him to tell me how he approaches it and just giving him some pointers about what he could do differently.

(Interview with station manager, 2006)

Like the fire brigade case study, therefore, the train operating company example illustrates how attempts to promote leadership behaviour in standardised public service work environments are at their most effective when grounded in contexts where managers have meaningful opportunities to practice motivation and change strategies with their staff. Yet in addition, this case illustrates how such opportunities might vary within the organisation itself, and how even in commercialised, customer-orientated PSOs, opportunities for individual managers to practice leadership may be constrained.

Conclusions

The experiences reported above show that there is clearly a place for promoting leadership in PSOs in the sense of improving how individual managers interrelate with and develop their staff (*c.f.* also Lawler, 2008: 31). But opportunities to contribute to innovation and organisational change are strongly influenced, and often constrained, by the organisational context. Especially in the standardised work environments of many PSOs, the changes with which the promotion of leadership is associated may be politically contested or contingent on managerial involvement in a particular part of the organisation. Opportunities for making concrete contributions to strategic change are more likely in professionalised environments, where managers tend towards developing solutions to organisational problems in ways that remain consistent with shared values and norms (*c.f.* Currie and Procter, 2005).

The reality is that PSOs tend to be large and rule-bound organisations, so opportunities even for more senior managers to initiate strategic changes and innovations may be few and far between. As Pollitt puts it:

Occasionally, reformers may be able to jump through a 'window of opportunity' (and it is part of the skill of a reform leader to recognize one), but for the most part they would well advised to 'go with the grain'.

(2003)

At the more extreme end, machine-like bureaucracies are still widespread in the contemporary public services, in transport (such as train and bus companies), distribution (such as postal services) and parts of local government and the civil service that specialise in routine administration (*c.f.* Mintzberg, 1973, 2009: 50). The perceived need for transformation and cultural change may sharpen the focus on leadership in some of these cases, such as the soon-to-be-privatised Royal Mail (*Financial Times*, 10 September 2010). Nevertheless, without a huge leap in automation, the core operational and management tasks will remain fundamentally unaltered.

Insights from distributed leadership perspectives that draw on theories of organisational networks and complexity theory (such as in Denis et al., 2005) represent an important step forward in painting a more realistic picture of leadership practice in PSOs, especially in professional environments such as in health and social care and where governance arrangements are very complex. However, the overall effect may be to overstate the importance of decentralised organisational forms in the public services. As Hales (2002) demonstrates, despite the recent wave of restructuring of organisations to make them flatter and less bureaucratic, there is little evidence that, for the typical manager, network forms of coordination have become more significant than hierarchical forms. Leadership for most managers therefore becomes largely a question of a judicious use of one's initiative, interacting constructively with colleagues, and building positive relationships with staff. While these are important, they are but normal parts of effective management practice.

In the aftermath of a global financial crisis hangs the inevitable question of the future of leadership 'in an age of austerity' (*c.f.* Leslie and Canwell, 2010). In the UK, plans for unprecedented public spending cuts, as well as greater decentralisation of public services to include more provision by private and voluntary sector organisations (*Financial Times*, 20 October 2010), can be expected to have significant implications for leadership in PSOs. On the one hand, the imperative of achieving greater financial efficiencies will almost certainly reduce the number of managers and could bring tighter centralised controls, resulting in a more restrictive, less participatory type of management. On the other hand, greater organisational decentralisation could increase the complexity of public service provision and governance arrangements, and therefore provide greater scope for managers to innovate. Faced with these potentially contradictory pressures, it remains to be seen which kind of leaders and leadership will prevail.

References

Alimo-Metcalfe, B. and Alban-Metcalfe, J. (2001) 'The development of a new Transformational Leadership Questionnaire', *Journal of Occupational and Organizational Psychology*, 74, 1–27.

Alimo-Metcalfe, B. and Alban-Metcalfe, J. (2004) 'Leadership in public sector organizations', in J. Storey (ed.) *Leadership in Organizations: Current Issues and Key Trends* (London: Routledge).

Bass, B. M. (1985) *Leadership and Performance Beyond Expectations* (Cambridge, MA: Harvard University Press).

Bolden, R. and Gosling, J. (2004) 'Leadership and management competencies: lessons from the National Occupational Standards', *SAM/IFSAM VIIth World Congress: Management in a World of Diversity and Change*, 5–7 July (Göteborg, Sweden).

Borins, S. (2000) 'Loose cannons and rule breakers? Some evidence about innovative public managers', *Public Administration Review*, 60:6; 498–507.

Boyne, G. A., James, O., John, P. and Petrovsky, N. (2008a) 'Does chief executive succession affect public service performance?' paper prepared for presentation at the *Thirteenth Annual Association for Public Policy Analysis and Management Research Conference*, 8 November (Los Angeles, CA).

Boyne, G. A., James, O., John, P. and Petrovsky, N. (2008b) 'Executive sucession in English local government', *Public Money and Management*, 28:5, 267–74.

Brown, J. S. and Duguid, P. (1991) 'Organizational learning and communities-of-practice: toward a unified view of working, learning, and innovation', *Organization Science*, 2:1; 40–57.

Burgoyne, J. (1993) 'The Competence Movement: issues, stakeholders and prospects', *Personnel Review*, 22:6; 6–11.

Burgoyne, J., Hirsh, W. and Williams, S. (2004) *The Development of Management and Leadership Capability and its Contribution to Performance: the Evidence, the Prospects and the Research Need* (London: Department for Education and Skills/ Lancaster University).

Burns, J. (1978) *Leadership* (New York: Harper and Row).

Busher, H. (2005) 'Being a middle leader: exploring professional identities', *School Leadership and Management*, 25:2; 137–153.

Clarke, J., Gewirtz, S. and McLaughlin, E. (2000) *New Managerialism, New Welfare?* (London: Sage).

Clarke, J. and Newman, J. (1997) *The Managerial State* (London: Sage).

Currie, G. and Lockett, A. (2007) 'A critique of transformational leadership: moral, professional and contingent dimensions of leadership within public services organizations', *Human Relations*, 60:2; 341–370.

Currie, G. and Procter, S. (2005) 'The antecedents of middle managers' strategic contribution: the case of a professional bureaucracy', *Journal of Management Studies*, 42:7; 1325–1356.

Denis, J.-L., Langley, A. and Rouleau, L. (2005) 'Rethinking leadership in public organizations', in E. Ferlie, L. E. Lynn and C. Pollitt, (eds) *The Oxford Handbook of Public Management* (Oxford: Oxford University Press).

Devas Group (2010) *Our Clients* (London: Devas Group), online at http:// devasgroup.com/ourClients.html [accessed 21 November 2010].

DfES/DTI (2002) *Managers and Leaders: Raising our Game. Government Response to the Report of the Council for Excellence in Management and Leadership* (London: Department for Education and Skills/Department for Trade and Industry).

Dobby, J., Anscombe, J. and Tuffin, R. (2004) *Police Leadership: Expectations and Impact* (Home Office Online Report 20/04) (London: Home Office), online at http://webarchive.nationalarchives.gov.uk/+/http://www.homeoffice.gov.uk/rds/pdfs04/rdsolr2004.pdf [accessed 2 December 2010].

Dunleavy, P., Margetts, H., Bastow, S. and Tinkler, J. (2006) 'New Public Management is dead: long live Digital-Era Governance', *Journal of Public Administration Research and Theory*, 16, 467–494.

Ernst and Young (2006) *Good Britain to Great Britain* (Government Services report series). (London: Ernst and Young LLP).

Financial Times (2010) 'Coalition to press on with Royal Mail privatisation', 10 September.

Financial Times (2010) 'Osborne enters unknown and cuts £81bn', 20 October.

Flynn, N. (2007) *Public Sector Management* (London: Sage).

Glatter, R. (2004) 'Leadership and leadership development in education', in J. Storey (ed.) *Leadership in Organizations: Current Issues and Key Trends* (London: Routledge).

Gold, J., Rodgers, H., Frearson, M. and Holden, R. (2003) 'Leadership development: a new typology', *Working Paper* (Leeds Business School and Learning and Skills Research Centre).

Grout, P. A. and Stevens, M. (2003) 'The assessment: financing and managing public services', *Oxford Review of Economic Policy*, 19:2; 215–234.

Grugulis, I. (1997) 'The consequences of competence: a critical assessment of the Management NVQ', *Personnel Review*, 26:6; 428–444.

Grugulis, I. (2007) *Skills, Training and Human Resource Development: A Critical Text* (London: Palgrave Macmillan).

Guest, D. and King, Z. (2005) 'Management Development and Career Development', in S. Bach (ed.) *Managing Human Resources* (Oxford: Blackwell).

Hales, C. (2002) 'Bureaucracy-lite' and continuities in managerial work', *British Journal of Management*, 13:1; 51–66.

Hall, T. and Janmen, K. (2010) *The Leadership Illusion: The Importance of Context and Connections* (Basingstoke: Palgrave Macmillan).

Horton, S. (2002) 'The competency movement', in S. Horton, A. Hondeghem and D. Farnham, (eds) *Competency Management in the Public Sector: European Variations on a Theme* (Amsterdam: IOS Press).

Horton, S. (2007) 'Leading the Civil Service in the 21st Century: A case study of the senior civil service top leadership programme', paper presented at the *2007 Public Administration Conference*, (University of Ulster, Northern Ireland).

Hughes, O. E. (2007) 'Leadership in a managerial context', in R. Koch and J. Dixon (eds) *Public Governance and Leadership* (Wiesbaden: Deutscher Universitaets-Verlag).

Ingraham, P. W. (2005) 'Striving for balance: reforms in Human Resource Management', in E. Ferlie, L. E. Lynn, and C. Pollitt (eds) *The Oxford Handbook of Public Management*, (Oxford: Oxford University Press).

Kotter, J. (1990) *A Force for Change: How Leadership Differs from Management* (New York: Free Press).

Lawler, J. (2008) 'Individualization and public sector leadership', *Public Administration*, 86:1; 21–34.

Leslie, K. and Canwell, A. (2010) 'Leadership at all levels: leading public sector organisations in an age of austerity', *European Management Journal*, 28:4; 297–305.

Mabey, C. (2005) 'Management development works: the evidence', *Achieving Management Excellence Research Series 1996–2005* (London: Chartered Management Institute).

MacBeath, J. (2005) 'Leadership as distributed: a matter of practice', *School Leadership and Management*, 25:4; 349–366.

McGurk, P. (2009) 'Developing 'middle leaders' in the public services? The realities of management and leadership development for public managers', *International Journal of Public Sector Management*, 22: 6; 464–477.

McGurk, P. (2010) 'Outcomes of management and leadership development', *Journal of Management Development*, 29:5; 457–470.

Milner, E. and Joyce, P. (2005) *Lessons in Leadership: Meeting the Challenges of Public Services Management* (Routledge, London).

Mintzberg, H. (1973) *The Nature of Managerial Work* (London: Harper and Row).

Mintzberg, H. (2009) *Managing* (Harlow: FT Prentice Hall).

Management Standards Centre (MSC) (2008) *National Occupational Standards in Leadership and Management* (London: MSC), online at www.management-standards.org [accessed 23 October 2009].

Newman, J. (2002) 'The New Public Management, modernization and institutional change: disruptions, dijunctures and dilemmas', in K. McLaughlin, S. P. Osborne and E. Ferlie (eds) *New Public Management: Current Trends and Future Prospects* (London: Routledge).

O'Reilly, D. and Reed, M. (2010) ''Leaderism': an evolution of managerialism in UK public service reform', *Public Administration*, 88:4; 960–978.

Office of the Deputy Prime Minister (ODPM) (2003) *Our Fire and Rescue Service*, White Paper, June (London: ODPM/HMSO).

ODPM (2005) *Leadership and Development in the Fire and Rescue Service: Consultation Paper* (London: ODPM).

OECD (2001) *Public Sector Leadership for the 21st Century* (Paris: OECD).

Osborne, D. and Gaebler, T. (1992) *Reinventing Government: How the Enterpreneurial Spirit is Transforming the Public Sector* (Reading, MA: Addison-Wesley).

Osborne, S. P. (2006) 'Editorial. The New Public Governance?', *Public Management Review*, 8:3; 377–387.

Performance and Information Unit (2001) *Strengthening Leadership in the Public Sector: A Research Study by the PIU* (London: Cabinet Office).

Pollitt, C. (2002) 'Clarifying convergence. striking similarities and durable differences in public management reform', *Public Management Review*, 4:1; 471–492.

Pollitt, C. (2003) *The Essential Public Manager* (Maidenhead: Open University Press).

Pollitt, C. and Bouckaert, G. (2004) *Public Management Reform. A Comparative Analysis* (Oxford: Oxford University Press).

Proeller, I. and Schedler, K. (2005) 'Change and continuity in the continental tradition of public management', in E. Ferlie, L. E. Lynn, and C. Pollitt (eds) *The Oxford Handbook of Public Sector Management* (Oxford: Oxford University Press).

Raffel, J., Leisink, P. and Middlebrooks, A. (2009) 'Introduction', in J. Raffel, P.Leisink and A. Middlebrooks (eds) *Public Sector Leadership: International Challenges and Perspectives* (Cheltenham: Edward Elgar).

Salaman, G. (2004) 'Competences of managers, competences of leaders', in J. Storey (ed.) *Leadership in Organizations* (Abingdon: Routledge).

Scase, R. and Goffee, R. (1989) *Reluctant Managers: Their Work and Lifestyles* (London: Unwin Hyman).

Shackleton, V. (1995) *Business Leadership* (London: Routledge).

Skills for Care (2008) *Leadership and Management for Care Services*, online at http://www.skillsforcare.org.uk/developing_skills/National_Occupational_Standards/LeadershipandManagementforCareServices.aspx [accessed 3 March 2009].

Storey, J. (2004a) 'Changing theories of leadership', in J. Storey (ed.) *Leadership in Organizations: Current Issues and Key Trends* (Abingdon: Routledge).

Storey, J. (2004b) 'Signs of change: "damned rascals" and beyond', in Storey, J. (ed.) *Leadership in Organizations: Current Issues and Key Trends* (Abingdon: Routledge).

Turnbull, A. (2002) *Delivery and Reform Agenda* (London: Cabinet Office).

Van Velsor, E. and McCauley, C. D. (2004) 'Introduction: our view of leadership development', in Van Velsor, E. and McCauley, C. D. (eds) *The Center for Creative Leadership Handbook of Leadership Development*, 2nd edn (San Francisco: Jossey Bass).

Zaleznik, A. (1992) 'Managers and leaders: are they different?' *Harvard Business Review*, March–April, 126–36.

10
Organised Labour and State Employment

Graham Symon

Introduction

The extent of the collective organisation of workers is both a crucial distinguishing feature of employment in the public sector and a focus for modernising critiques. In the UK and most of the industrialised world, the contrast between the fortunes of unions in the public and private sector can be illustrated by the fact that not only does union density in the public sector generally dwarf that of the private sector, but the actual numbers of union members in the public sector tends to be greater than that in the private sector (*see* Bryson and Forth, 2010). This is despite typically around a quarter of the aggregate workforce being employed by the state (Fredman and Morris, 1989; Matthews, 2010). It should be stressed that the resilience is relative, as both, membership levels and density are arguably on a negative trajectory; the union movement in the public sector has faced considerable challenges in the past three decades, which it has not managed to counter with unqualified success. These challenges are complex and stem from both tendencies in the wider milieu of work organisation and more specifically from the restructuring of state apparatus that has been ongoing since 1979. It is argued that, unless the unions can put in place sophisticated and coordinated strategies of organisation and campaigning, unions' future prospects are more bleak than many decision makers in the movement have fully acknowledged (*see* Bryson and Forth, 2010).

This chapter provides an analytical overview of the nature and activities of public sector trade unions. In doing so, it will feature the landscape of and trends in public sector trade union organisation and activity and fortunes of unions since 1997. It will assess the strategies that unions are implementing to reinvigorate their capacity to represent workers' interests and ultimately consider the prospects for unions in the light of the fiscal restraint and reorganisation of the Conservative–Liberal Democrat Coalition Government elected in May 2010.

The chapter starts by establishing the nature and dynamics of public sector trade unions; in doing so there will be a brief historical account in order to provide context, an overview of the organisation, structure and membership dynamics (including an acknowledgement of the heterogeneity of unions in size, shape and form). The initial discussion will also consider the forces the unions have been subject to and the consequences of this for their capacity to act. Although public sector unions have fared better in maintaining membership levels and influence than their counterparts in the private sector (NB: many unions straddle both sectors), they have faced considerable challenges from changes in the industrial relations and public policy environments attributable both to ideology and structural, political and economic forces.

The election of the Blair administration in 1997 gave rise to considerable discussion about the prospects for organised labour (in general and in the public sector particularly) (*see* Corby & White, 1999). Although some amelioration after eighteen years of New Right hostility was identified (particularly in the face of considerable fiscal investment and improved economic circumstances), it was only the naive who anticipated a golden era for unions. Numerous challenges from before lingered and numerous new challenges emerged. Aspects of individual employment rights, and to a lesser extent collective frameworks, have been enhanced. However, managerialism has remained the dominant paradigm in the public sector with the centralising of targets and control, but the devolution of delivery. Privatisation and outsourcing have remained on the policy agenda with associated impact on industrial relations at workplace and national levels.

The landscape of public sector union organisation and activity

As discussed in chapter 1 of this volume, the nature and form of state employment can be seen as a product of the historical development of the state in an industrialised democracy such as the UK. The isomorphic effects of the wider development of capitalism, class relations, the institutions of state and those of production have been central to the shaping of state apparatus and thus the mores of the distribution and disposal of public goods including personnel (*see* DiMaggio and Powell, 1983; Polanyi, 1944). It follows that we must see the development and trajectories of the institutions of industrial relations (e.g. trade unions, employers' associations, collective bargaining, other forms of representation) as being shaped and conditioned by these forces. A detailed historical analysis lies beyond the remit of this chapter and the author's expertise; however, it is worth acknowledging that these institutions of industrial relations in the public sector have been shaped by a complex interplay of forces perpetuated by the imperatives of driving and sustaining a mass production/consumption economy and the ideological espousals of policymakers (Kirkpatrick, 2006).

From the origins of the modern state in the nineteenth century, trade union organisation and collective bargaining in municipal and central government organisations was somewhat sporadic and piecemeal. In the early years of the twentieth century moves towards the formalisation of public sector industrial relations had already begun, but it was only in 1919 in the wake of the Great War of 1914–1918 that the government of Lloyd George made a commitment to the consolidation of state apparatus and the aspiration for the state to set a 'good example' as a model employer. This aspiration included commitments to job security, pensions and benefits and that employees should be represented by independent trade unions with the right to bargain and, through frameworks such as the recently convened 'Whitley Councils', participate in policymaking and service delivery The promotion of worker rights and labour standards were also encouraged through the government's procurement processes and in other organisations under the influence although not directly under the control of the state (see Fredman and Morris, 1989).

In the interwar years industrial relations became more formalised, collective bargaining (for pay, at least) more centralised and union density increased. After WWII (1939–45), the reforming and mandated Labour administration of Attlee and his colleagues not only greatly expanded the provision of the welfare state – most notably with the formation of the NHS – but also brought a number of corporations into public ownership thus greatly increasing the numbers of workers employed by the state and joining the trade unions that represented them in the by-now highly formalised frameworks of national and local collective bargaining (Winchester and Bach, 1995). Often overlooked during this period is the extent to which the professions in the public sector – particularly in health care and education – were given voice in shaping delivery through their representative bodies. For instance teaching unions in Scotland, England and Wales were viewed as being part of a tri-partite system of administration with local authorities and the respective central education departments (Briault, 1976; Seifert and Ironside, 1995; *c.f.* Carter, 2004; Edwards, 2009).

Despite the symbiosis with Fordism that many highly plausible commentators have identified in the public sector in the period 1945–1979 (*see* Kirkpatrick, 2006), there was nothing monolithic or standard about the organisation or behaviour of the myriad trade unions. Public sector employers found themselves bargaining with a complex array of often competing and ideologically divided unions of varying size and resources (Fryer, 1989); even today an NHS Trust or unitary local authority typically bargains with ten or more unions (Bach, 2004; Richardson et al., 2005). Some unions straddled both public and private sectors in the composition of their memberships, for example, GMB, whereas some were – and continue to be – exclusive to the public sector and frequently the sub-sector, for example, National Union of Teachers (NUT), a phenomenon that remains the case to this day. Also, some unions are general and have ostensibly 'open' membership criteria whereas some are exclusive to particular groups of employees. Furthermore, despite the role of these institutions in representing employee interests and as bargaining agents, some were apparently reluctant to be regarded as orthodox unions; the NUT and the Educational Institute of Scotland (EIS), the two biggest teaching unions south and north of the border only affiliated with the Trades Union Congress (TUC) as recently as 1972 (Seifert and Ironside, 1995; Ross, 1986). The Royal College of Nursing (RCN) and the Police Federation – in common with a number of other notable organisations – are representative bodies that continue to operate outside of the umbrella of the TUC.

Although the period 1919–79 cannot be regarded as stable or homogenous by any stretch of the imagination for industrial relations or any other aspect of history, it is remarkable for the enduring consensus that unionisation and collective bargaining were constructive means by which to administer public sector employment and that it ultimately provided stability and various other social externalities associated in particular with post-1945 social democracy (Fryer, 1989; Kirkpatrick, 2006). Thus, according to regulation theorists in particular, class conflict could be institutionalised in order to enable the stable growth of the capitalist economy (*see* Jessop, 2002). During the period 1945–1979 both public sector employment and union membership grew considerably, as did that of the industrial sector. This system of industrial relations arguably delivered relative stability; although not entirely immune from union militancy, the public sector tended to enjoy more stable and cooperative industrial relations than the industrial sector. Indeed, when one considers the dispute and stoppage figures for the period 1945–1979, a significant proportion of the days lost to strikes are in the state-owned industrial corporations such as the mines and automotive industry rather in the core public sector (*see* Fryer, 1989; Kelly, 1998).

Invoking a reworking of the standard Marxian thesis the aforementioned regulation commentators have identified the late 1970s as an era of crisis for the Fordist social democratic model of economic governance (Kirkpatrick, 2006). Thus the breakdown of the economic system led to industrial conflict and widespread strikes in the public sector culminating in the notorious 'Winter of Discontent'. The disrupting of public services in 1978–1979 coincided with particularly bad weather and consequently the public felt aggrieved and the unions became the subject of negative public opinion (Hay, 1996). It should be noted that there was a ready-formed remedy to this crisis of social democratic capitalism in the form of the New Right, a neoliberal-inspired intellectual movement of economic liberals who offered a critique of social democracy whose time had come. At its figurehead was Margaret Thatcher who was elected Prime Minister in 1979 with a mandate to not only cure the 'British Disease' of militant unions, but to significantly re-engineer the state and the relationship between citizen and state.

The reforms of the Thatcher years (1979–1990) have been well documented (*see* Hay, 1996). Not only was a programme of anti-union legislation implemented curtailing industrial action and regulating internal democracy, but a new culture was established where employers could be less 'indulgent' of unions and impose their will with confidence. Just as profound throughout the 1980s and into the 1990s was the restructuring of the state through retrenchment of social welfare, privatisation of state organisations, contracting-out, de-centralisation of organisational structures and the marginalisation of local government. More generally, recession and neoliberal economic restructuring led to an increase in unemployment to levels not seen since the 1930s. The result for the union movement was that union influence and membership – which had been at its zenith in 1979 (*see* Figure 10.1) – fell considerably (Achur, 2010). However, this phenomenon was relatively slight in the public sector where density remained high (*see* Figure 10.2); but organisational restructuring and a more sophisticated application of managerial techniques, developed in the private sector, meant that unions were put on the defensive as they struggled to defend the interests of their membership (Winchester and Bach, 1995). During the 1980s there were numerous high-profile and lengthy strikes, including strikes by miners and school teachers to which the government decided not to yield.

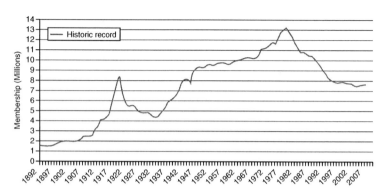

Figure 10.1   Trade union membership, 1892–present
Source: Achur (2010) from Labour Force Survey, Office for National Statistics, Department for Employment (1892–1974); Certification Office (1974–2008).

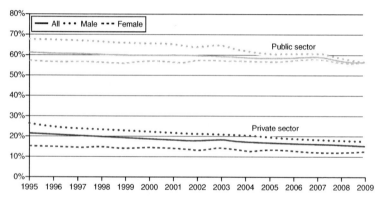

Figure 10.2   Trade union density by sector and gender, 1995–2009
Source: Achur (2010) from Labour Force Survey, Office for National Statistics.

Many commentators caution overplaying the agency of the Thatcher government in engineering the emasculation of collective labour generally and the restructuring of the state. Some more determinist scholars point to global competitive and technological forces ushering in a 'Post-Fordist' era of decentralised production, diminished manufacturing, individualisation of social relations and the need for more flexible consumer relationships (*see* Jessop, 2002; Kirkpatrick, 2006). Thus Thatcher's administration was one of many neoliberal regimes across the industrialised world that instituted economic and social reforms in response to the prevailing forces of market capitalism (Harvey, 2007). Similarly, the fortunes of unions have broadly been on a downward trajectory across the developed world, albeit to different degrees depending on the institutional dynamics in any particular system (Kelly, 1998).

The 1980s also saw the identification and emergence of the phenomenon of the NPM (Hood, 1991; Pollitt, 1990), which has been identified as the tendency whereby the public sector, by evolution or design, apparently began to behave more like the private sector. Managers adopted industrial techniques such as quality management and systems of performance management (including performance-related pay; *see* White, this volume) and reforms encouraged marketisation and competition within services; again, unions struggled to cope as collective agreements were compromised and terms and conditions eroded. Thus the unions found themselves struggling to respond to undermined – and frequently abolished – national bargaining arrangements (e.g. with the creation of pay review bodies). Administrative reforms in the NHS and local government sought to encourage 'opt-outs' from national arrangements in the name of flexibility (Winchester and Bach, 1995); however, this strategy was not an unqualified success as national bargaining broadly endured.

By the 1990s, the trade union movement as a whole had begun to give serious practical consideration to how they might adapt to changing circumstances. The merger has throughout its history been a noticeable phenomenon. Particularly in the post-1945 period this was the case for the public sector unions in particular as many smaller and esoteric associations were either swallowed by bigger institutions or merged with a number of similar-sized ones (*see* Mathieson and Corby, 1999). However, the most symbolically (and organisationally) significant merger came in 1993 when the three largest exclusively public sector unions (COHSE, NALGO, NUPE) joined to form Unison, an undertaking that was not without its controversies, but which has ultimately sustained what was for fourteen years the UK's biggest union. Subsequently in 2007, two other unions that have a significant – although not exclusive – public sector membership – the TGWU and Amicus – merged to form Unite (*see* Table 10.1).

During the period 1990–1997, John Major's less radical but no more union-friendly administration continued the programme of privatisation – most notably of British Rail, a bastion of unionisation – and the decentralisation of the delivery of public services, thus enhancing the capacity of managers to deliver changes and in doing so counter resistance from unions. However, by the mid-1990s, the Conservative government had become very unpopular; a new political force had emerged

Table 10.1 An overview of the most significant public sector unions (membership over 100,000)

Name of Union	Scope/Membership composition	Membership 2009
Unite	General union formed in 2007 by the merger of the TGWU (general membership) and Amicus (skilled, technical and managerial). Significant minority of membership works in the public sector.	1,572,995
Unison	Formed in 1993 by the merger of three unions with membership base in the NHS and local government; 'open' membership, primarily administrative, manual and some management grades	1,374,500
General, Municipal and Boilermakers' Union (GMB)	General union, around 50 per cent of membership works in public sector.	601,730
National Union of Teachers (NUT)	Union exclusively for qualified teachers.	376,797
Royal College of Nursing (RCN)	Union for nursing professionals, registered and non-registered. Not affiliated to TUC. Chooses not to strike.	400,716
NAS/UWT	Union exclusively for qualified teachers; competes with NUT for members.	326,659
Public and Commercial Services Union (PCS)	Primarily Civil Service, formed in 1998 by the merger of two unions.	301,562
Communications Workers' Union (CWU)	Majority of members work as postal workers for Royal Mail. Remainder in the previously state-owned British Telecom.	217,807
Police Federation	Exclusively for police officers. Legally prohibited from taking strike action. Not affiliated to TUC.	164,000 (Combined UK total)
Prospect	Managerial and technical membership base. Incorporated Connect union in 2010.	103,0611

Source: Certification Office, Police Federations of England & Wales, Scotland and Northern Ireland.

in the form of New Labour and the union movement and advocates of comprehensive public services looked to Tony Blair's 'Third Way' administration of 1997 with considerable optimism.

The fortunes of unions since 1997

'New Labour', a reformed and 'electable' party with mass appeal and more of a centrist orientation espoused the Third Way, an apparent reconciliation of economic dynamism and social justice (Hall, 2003). New Labour was elected with a mandate to redress the erosion of the public sector and the years 1997–2008 have borne witness to considerable investment in infrastructure and capacity as levels of public sector employment have increased. Greater taxation revenues from a growing economy enabled investment in schools and hospitals. In particular, resources have been targeted at areas that are seen as being in the most need, for example through 'Action Zones' for health, education and so on. However, the post-1997 Government was determined that this increased investment be accompanied by a 'modernisation' agenda that, despite less hostile rhetoric, had resonance with the Thatcherite reforms of the previous decade. Indeed, it became clear that New Labour wished to maintain much of the momentum of reforms that sought to decentralise, 'managerialise' and marketise public service provision. Thus any optimism on the part of the trade union movement that the status quo ante would be restored was found to be misplaced. However, although New Labour did not actively restore the position of public sector unions, a more sympathetic operating climate did develop, due in no small measure to the improved fiscal context (*see* Shaoul, this volume).

New Labour did not embark on a programme of abolition of the anti-union legislation of the 1980s; however, they did introduce various pieces of employment rights legislation – albeit primarily with an individual orientation (e.g. statutory minimum wage, bolstering of equal opportunities regulation) – that mitigated some of the erosion of the 1980s and complied with the requirements of a more substantial embracing of the European Social agenda. The Employment Relations Act 1999 gave some rights to unions to represent employees but reports of its efficacy were mixed to say the least (*see* Ewing, 2001). However, some symbolic gestures were made in the shape of reinstating collective bargaining (complete with 'no-strike' clause) at GCHQ where it had been banned on 'security' grounds in 1984 and the diffident suggestion by the Cabinet Office that government departments seek to encourage collective bargaining in their sphere of influence (Corby, 2000). Also, Best Value replaced CCT: the Conservative policy of outsourcing various services; although the principle of value-for-money remained, commissioning authorities were charged with taking into account a broader range of 'value-added' criteria. Thus employment practices could, and occasionally did, influence decision-making and lead to improved industrial relations (Richardson et al., 2005).

A key rhetorical device of New Labour was 'partnership', which was used in a number of public policy areas, for example, in local economic development and regeneration and in the contracting out of services. In industrial relations terms, the notion of workplace and 'social' partnerships – that is, the forging of cooperative, performance-orientated agreements between managements and unions – preceded New Labour (*see* Kelly, 1998), but the progressive yet utilitarian tone of the construct had resonance with the Third Way. Furthermore, the union movement in the form of the TUC and the larger unions gave their endorsement to this agenda (Symon, 2004). Thus numerous public sector employers – principally local authorities and NHS Trusts – were able to forge partnership agreements; some accounts report their success in bringing about favourable or 'fair' industrial relations outcomes (*see* Stuart and Martinez Lucio, 2005). Some prominent critics remain not merely sceptical to partnership but downright hostile (e.g. Kelly, 1998) seeing it as a means of pacifying union militancy and enabling managers to exploit industrial relations engagements with the complicity of the unions, which should be safeguarding against such liberties. Whether they are good for unions or not, partnership remains entirely voluntary in the UK (unlike in much of continental Europe. (*See* chapter 2, this volume.)

Regional devolution – of Scotland, Wales, Northern Ireland and, to a certain extent, London – will endure as a legacy of the New Labour era and it has already started to impact upon industrial relations and therefore the experiences of unions. With the administrations in these regions able to make more policy decisions locally and, in the case of the more progressive regimes, resist Whitehall-driven reform, some evidence suggests that unions in Scotland in particular have enjoyed more influence (Adams and Robinson, 2002). However, any assessment of these circumstances should be qualified by the fact that Scotland enjoys significantly higher per capita public expenditure enabling public sector employers to maintain staffing levels that keep public employment as a proportion of the labour market higher than in England (Matthews, 2010).

Despite the more benign rhetoric, the content of much of New Labour's modernisation agenda was potentially threatening to unions.

Martinez Lucio (2007) identifies a number of trends in policymaking in the first decade of the twenty-first century that continue to present particular challenges to organised labour and put pressure on collective bargaining in the UK (and, indeed across much of the industrialised world):

- Privatisation: New Labour has shown considerable appetite for further outsourcing of many services, thus fragmenting services and exposing workers to the sorts of market pressures that public sector unions have had difficulty coping with. Often the subcontractors are not unionised (Cunningham and James, 2010).
- Decentralisation: the creation of 'cost centres' at devolved levels putting pressure on managers to deliver services efficiently. Also, as with the point above, the fragmentation makes it difficult for unions to co-ordinate activity. However, it has also been suggested that with the right strategies, fragmentation could work in the favour of unions as managers may also find it difficult to co-ordinate their responses.
- Marketisation: bringing pressures to deliver in response to externally imposed or competitive targets and linking reward and output. The sanction for underperformance might be replacing of 'in-house' services with an external agency.
- Targets: under the influence of Gordon Brown – Chancellor of the Exchequer (1997–2007) and then Prime Minister (2007–10) – central government has subjected the units responsible for the delivery of public sector (most notably the NHS, local government and the police) to a regime of 'targets' that have often proved particularly problematic for managers, employees and public service users. Thus managers and unions have found themselves constrained in the industrial relations choices they can make at a local level (*see* Bach, 2004). In an intriguing piece of politicking, the new Coalition Government has pledged to end the 'culture' of targets, replacing it, as per their 'localism' agenda, with enhanced accountability at a local level. How this will play out in reality is at the time of writing a matter of some uncertainty.
- Individualisation: although the fetish of the individual is primarily associated with the Conservative Government of 1979–1997 (*see* Mathieson and Corby, 1999) the trend appears to have continued. Martinez Lucio (2007) makes specific reference to the use of more flexible forms of labour. Also, unions have been significantly unsuccessful in recruiting new – and by implication younger – workers; Bryson and

Forth (2010) identify a generation of workers who have never been a member of a union as a particular matter of concern for unions. Also, more individualised rewards strategies have also contributed to this phenomenon (*see* White's chapter, this volume).

(adapted from Martinez Lucio, 2007: 7–8)

Although unions have sought to innovate and adapt (*see* the initiatives discussed below) the New Labour era can either be seen as one of missed opportunities for the union movement or, more worryingly, evidence that there is little place for them in the new 'Post-Fordist' public sector. After all as Figure 10.2 illustrates, density continues to decline despite continued – relatively – comprehensive collective bargaining coverage (Bryson and Forth, 2010). However, one must take into account the diverse and heterogeneous nature of the public sector where change has occurred at different rates in different ways. Also, in many well-documented instances unions have rediscovered their confidence for militancy; Monger (2004) draws attention to the increase in numbers of days lost in the earlier part of the last decade, rises almost exclusively due to public sector disputes. More recent figures illustrate spikes in working days lost in 2007 and 2008 similarly attributable to public sector strikes (Hale, 2010; *see* Table 10.2). However, militancy cannot be solely relied upon as a vehicle for union revitalisation; especially as employers have become more sophisticated in their efforts to manipulate the regulatory environment to avert strike action (see Gall, 2010). Rather unions have been pursuing a range of more sophisticated strategies and it is to these initiatives our discussion now turns.

Table 10.2   Working days lost, 2000–9, by sector

Year	Working days lost ('000s)	
	Private sector	Public sector
2000	136	363
2001	128	397
2002	200	1,123
2003	130	369
2004	163	742
2005	59	99
2006	98	656
2007	39	1,002
2008	48	711
2009	88	368

Source: Hale (2010); ONS Labour Market Statistics.

Union strategies of development and renewal

It is worth reiterating the point raised at several times throughout this volume that reform and change in the public sector has not been uniform across all functional areas of the public sectors or even geographically even across the UK. Some unions such as the major teaching unions and the RCN have seen significant rises. The RCN's membership in particular has risen from 282,000 in 1989 to 401,000 today (Certification Office, 2009; Mathieson and Corby, 1999). As such, the impact of these changes on the fortunes of unions is similarly uneven and varied; the wider political and economic challenges facing the labour movement as a whole notwithstanding. However, the imperative for effective response to these challenges has been acknowledged across the union movement and by commentators in the wider sphere. Furthermore, contrary to charges of crude self-interest levied at the unions, a case can be made whereby union challenges to arbitrary management authority in the public sector might be an important means of safeguarding the integrity of public goods and vital services that redress social injustice (Bach, 2004; Symon and Crawshaw, 2009).

The traditional formal medium of union workplace activity is through collective bargaining and as observed above, despite change and erosion it has been resilient in the public sector by comparison to the private. It is perfectly understandable that unions continue to concentrate a significant amount of effort around the bargaining table. However, although collective bargaining has never by any means been the exclusive activity of unions, it is reasonable to suggest that due to the challenges and changes outlined above, the unions will continually need to seek more innovative and imaginative means of protecting worker interests (*see* Hyman, 1999). A number of broad strategies for 'renewal' have emerged in the movement in the UK public sector (mirrored in some respects by developments in other sectors and also in other national systems). However, accounts of these strategies of renewal suggest a number of tensions and ambiguities as to their wisdom and impact.

From the literature on union renewal generally and that specifically relating to the public sector, there appears to be four principal strategies that are employed by unions as part of programmes of renewal, which we will consider in turn:

- Organising
- Managerial servicing

- Partnership and learning
- Community Unionism

Organising

The 'organising model' of trade unionism has been discussed at length and has caused considerable controversy among industrial relations commentators and trade unionists as to its impact and appropriateness (*see* Heery, 2003 for a review of debates). The organising thesis suggests that union revitalisation can come from enhanced activity in recruiting and mobilising membership and support in the workplace in an organic 'bottom-up' fashion (Waddington and Kerr, 2009). In the more Marxian accounts, writers suggest that with the right approach and under the right circumstances unions can appeal to class sensibilities and invoke a spirit of solidarity and cohesiveness that will enable greater influencing capacity in the industrial relations arena (Kelly, 1998). The activities of local union officers – voluntary and salaried – are seen to be central to these strategies. This form of activity can be put to use both in the furthering of interests in the workplace and also in wider social justice-cum-political campaigning such as against service curtailment, privatisation and pension reform.

Empirical studies of organising activity explain how unions such as Unison have been seeking to devise initiatives such as the National Organizing and Recruitment Strategy which, although centrally planned, seeks implementation at the 'grass roots'. This is done primarily through the provision of training and resources for local representatives. In their survey of Unison branches, Waddington and Kerr (2009) found mixed results, concluding that success was dependent on the agency of local activists and to local circumstances. These results have resonance on earlier studies by geographers: by Painter (1991) of UK union responses to privatisation; and by Rhee and Zabin (2009) of efforts in the US to organise 'spatially atomised' care workers.

Ultimately the age-old tension of central vs. local – or top-down vs. bottom-up – in the organisation of unions rears its head. Drawing such dualisms is unwise in the contemporary social sciences, but unions do appear to suffer from a general inability to reconcile the needs and activities of their elites and their local activists. This is evident in a number of instances in the UK public sector. There are two notable pieces of research from the education sector that appear to support this with Carter (2004) and Edwards (2009) both explaining how local organising initiatives by the NUT have to some extent been confounded by the central bureaucracy.

Managerial servicing

Heery's (2003) managerial serving unionism is the quintessential 'top-down' renewal initiatives and typically contrasted with the organising model. This model seeks to appeal to members' – and potential members' – instrumental needs, primarily as individuals. The focus is not so much on collective action but on the provision of services to members. The major public sector unions display characteristics of this with advertised benefits for members ranging from legal advice to discounted financial services.

Heery points out that the model goes beyond the mere prosaic offering of inducements. It encompasses a range of centrally co-ordinated strategies leading to campaigns on various issues: the protection of professional boundaries, flexible working practices and 'family-friendly' policies and the interests of minority groups (where there may be some overlap with the organising model). However, many are sceptical that the managerial model has the strength to be the principal force behind any programme of renewal.

Partnership and learning

As discussed above partnership was a key rhetorical device of the New Labour era where in the spirit of Third Way and 'stakeholding', capital and labour could put aside any archaic animosities and work together for mutual gains and, if the spirit of Europe could be invoked, this co-operation would yield social externalities (*see* Stuart and Martinez Lucio, 2005). More pragmatically, and with some congruity with the managerial servicing model discussed above, unions have sought to exert influence through a 'can't beat 'em, join 'em' mindset. In the UK, partnership in practice perhaps owes more to the US mutual gains 'integrative' model than the European social model. Numerous partnership agreements have been forged at the level of NHS trusts and local authorities where the parties agree to work together to enhance performance. Convincing evidence exists of enhanced industrial relations being fostered through these media. Indeed, particularly in professional contexts there is a long history of cooperative industrial relations – not necessarily labelled as partnership – in large sections of the public sector at central and local levels, health care and education being prime examples (Bach, 2004; Briault, 1976). However partnership also has highly vocal critics (e.g. Kelly, 1998) as noted above.

One aspect of partnership that has apparently yielded qualified success for unions is the lifelong learning agenda whereby unions have

bargained and campaigned for and indeed, with state assistance, provided education and training (McIlroy, 2008; Symon, 2004). The lifelong
learning agenda is particularly strong in the public sector unions with
Unison, Unite and the GMB among others very active in this area.
This can take the form of providing workers in low-pay low-skill jobs
with elementary skills training or campaigning for resources for more
skilled workers to undertake higher-level career development. Union
involvement in skill formation is at the heart of the social models of
industrial relations that have been so successful on continental Europe,
for instance. Also, with partnership in mind, a mutual-gains scenario is
evident whereby the enhanced human capital might provide benefits for
both employer and employee. However, as with most things in industrial relations it is rarely this straightforward, with critical commentators
such as McIlroy (2008) cautioning against any self-congratulation in
the movement. The spectre of incorporation is ever-present, even to the
extent of the unions being used as a wing of the state. It is naive to see
lifelong learning as a purely co-operative issue. Learning can be seen as
part of the 'contested terrain' of the labour process and as such, employers may be reluctant to provide resources for the sort of skilling opportunities that workers might actually want and need (Symon, 2004).

Community unionism

With the apparent shortcomings of unions' strategies in respect of
organising in the workplace, the focus of recent research has been the
activities of unions outside the workplace. Unions, normally in the
form of coalitions of multiple unions and other civil society organisations such as churches and citizens' groups have rediscovered the
value of seeking to mobilise in the community, spatially rather than by
workplace (Symon and Crawshaw, 2009). Wills (2004) has researched
community union activity in London in particular depth and her findings point to numerous successes of campaigns undertaken under the
umbrella of the London Citizens organisation and its affiliates (including various unions) to apply pressure on public sector organisations
to pay (or to force their sub-contractors to pay) the 'living wage', a
voluntary supplement to the statutory minimum wage to compensate
for higher living costs in London. Elsewhere, community groups have
been successfully mobilised to campaign for improved public services
(*see* Symon and Crawshaw, 2009).

Community unionism has been regarded with some ambivalence
by union hierarchies. On the one hand, the successes give cause for
encouragement. However, community initiatives, despite rhetorical

endorsement at strategic levels, have been primarily organic and driven by 'maverick' local activists who operate outside of the sphere of influence of union bureaucracies. However, on balance the phenomenon of community unionism gives some cause for optimism that, even at local levels, innovative activities are paying dividends.

Prospects for unions for the foreseeable future

At the time of writing, severe cuts to public expenditure have been announced that will lead to the curtailment of services and the loss of jobs from the public payroll. The cuts have been presented by the Coalition as a reaction to the apparent fiscal mismanagement of the previous New Labour regime. However, the policy agenda appears to go beyond mere thrift to an aspiration to 'roll-back' the state and open up opportunities for more private and voluntary sector involvement in the delivery and co-ordination of services from health care to 'welfare-to-work' to the creation of 'free schools' (*see* Lethbridge, this volume). This presents the obvious challenge to unions in the form of disaggregation and the complexities of organising across fragmented boundaries, particularly in dealing with a potentially union-hostile employer with a tacit license to be hostile from the commissioning authorities. However as suggested above, if unions can innovate and adapt, they could find opportunities for local campaigning and action as has been witnessed in North America in particular (Rhee and Zabin, 2009).

Also at the time of writing there have been a number of demonstrations on the streets at the cuts in which the public sector unions have participated. While this ostensible show of solidarity is encouraging, the underperforming capacity of the public sector unions to present a sufficiently robust united front means they are not making sufficient impact on the agenda to counter government action. France, with an industrial relations system with far lower union density than the UK, seems better equipped to mobilise mass action that is taken seriously. Similarly, anecdotal accounts suggest that public support for unions in their efforts to resist the potentially damaging reform of the public sector is lukewarm at best. Thus it is imperative that the unions better articulate their case to the public in order to generate support (*see* Ross, 1986).

Conclusion

Union membership and the coverage of collective agreements in the public sector remain strong. Also, despite numerous union mergers,

206 Organised Labour and State Employment

the public sector recognises a varied array of unions and of bargaining purposes and these individual unions differ widely in membership base and strategy. There is little evidence of increased militancy, although over the past decade, almost all high profile disputes have been in the public sector (e.g. Fire, Post, Transport). However, a significant preoccupation of many unions has been the resisting of what they present as harmful reform to public service delivery, which has inevitable consequences for employment.

A rhetorical mantra of the New Labour era has been 'partnership' and this has influenced the tone of industrial relations with partnership agreements being forged between unions and employers; accounts of the efficacy of these agreements are mixed (McIlroy, 2008). Away from the bargaining table, unions have been pursing strategies of 'servicing' of members' interests and also organising around constructive issues like skilling, lifelong learning, equality and 'family-friendly'/flexible employment practices.

The formation of the Conservative–Liberal Democrat Coalition Government in the wake of the May 2010 general election has produced further challenges for the trade union movement. This is not merely an administration with a historical antipathy to collective labour that is in government, but in the months after taking office the Coalition has launched comprehensive and severe cuts in public expenditure as an apparent response to the fiscal deficit, without having any electoral mandate for that course of action (*see* Shaoul, this volume). However the continuing reform not only of the structure of the public sector but of the very nature of social welfare and how it is provided arguably constitutes the taking of an opportunity that will potentially nullify organised labour as an institutional force unless the movement undergoes radical repositioning. To end on a more optimistic note, as we have discussed, if the union movement does position itself effectively, it might be able to turn these scenarios associated with malevolent forces into opportunities for renewal.

References

Achur, J. (2010) *Trade Union Membership 2009* (London: Department for Business Innovation and Skills/Office for National Statistics).
Adams, J. and Robinson, P. (eds) (2002) *Devolution in Practice: Public Policy Differences within the UK* (London: IPPR).
Bach, S. (2004) *Employment Relations and the Health Service: the Management of Reforms* (London: Routledge).
Briault, E. (1976) 'A distributed system of educational administration: an international viewpoint', *International Review of Education*, 22:4; 429–439.

Bryson, A. and Forth, J. (2010) *Trade union membership and influence 1999–2009*, Discussion Paper No 62 (London: National Institute for Social and Economic Research (NIESR)).

Carter, B. (2004) 'State restructuring and union renewal: the case of the National Union of Teachers', *Work, Employment and Society*, 18:1; 137–156.

Certification Office (2009) *Annual Report 2009* (London: Certification Office).

Corby, S. (2000) 'Employee relations in the public services: a paradigm shift?' *Public Policy and Administration*, 15:3; 60–74.

Corby, S. and White, G. (eds) (1999) *Employee Relations in the Public Services* (London: Routledge).

Cunningham, I. and James, P. (2010) 'Strategies of union renewal in the context of public sector outsourcing', *Economic and Industrial Democracy*, 31:1; 34–61.

DiMaggio, P. J. and Powell, W. (1983) 'The iron cage revisited: institutional isomorphism and collective rationality in organizational fields', *American Sociological Review*, 48, 147–160.

Edwards, G. (2009) 'Public sector trade unionism in the UK: strategic challenges in the face of colonisation', *Work, Employment and Society*, 23:3; 442–459.

Ewing, K. (ed.) (2001) *Employment Rights at Work: Reviewing the Employment Relations Act 1999* (London: Institute of Employment Rights).

Fredman, S. and Morris, G. (1989) *State as Employer: Labour Law in the Public Services* (London: Mansell).

Fryer, R. (1989) 'Public service trade unionism in the twentieth century', in R. Mailly, S. Dimmock and A. Sethi (eds) *Industrial Relations in the Public Services* (London: Routledge).

Gall, G. (2010) 'Blocking RMT strike solves nothing', guardian.co.uk ('Comment is Free'), online at http://www.guardian.co.uk/commentisfree/2010/apr/02/rmt-strike-balloting-trade-unions [accessed 2 April 2010].

Hale, D. (2010) 'Labour Disputes in 2009', *Economic and Labour Market Review*, 4:6; 47–59.

Hall, S. (2003) 'New Labour's double shuffle', *Soundings*, 24, 10–24.

Harvey, D. (2007) *Spaces of Global Development: Towards a Theory of Uneven Geographical Development* (London: Verso).

Hay, C. (1996) *Re-stating Social and Political Change* (Buckingham: Open University Press).

Heery, E. (2003) 'Trade unions and industrial relations', in P. Ackers and A. Wilkinson (eds) *Understanding work and Employment: Industrial Relations in Transition* (Oxford: Oxford University Press).

Hood, C. (1991) 'A public management for all seasons', *Public Administration*, 69:1; 3–19.

Hyman, R. (1999) 'Imagined solidarities: can trade unions resist globalization?' in P. Leisink (ed.) *Globalization and Labour Relations* (Cheltenham: Edward Elgar).

Jessop, B. (2002) *The Future of the Capitalist State* (Cambridge: Polity).

Kelly, J. (1998) *Rethinking Industrial Relations: Mobilisation, Collectivisation and Long Waves* (London: Routledge).

Kirkpatrick, I. (2006) 'Post-Fordism and organizational change in state administration', in L. Enrique-Alonso and M. Martinez Lucio (eds) *Employment Relations in a Changing Society: Assessing the Post-Fordist Paradigm* (Basingstoke: Palgrave Macmillan).

Mathieson, H. and Corby, S. (1999) 'Trade unions: the challenge of individualism?' in Corby, S. and White, G. (eds) *Employee Relations in the Public Services* (Routledge: London).

Matthews, D. (2010) 'The changing face of public sector employment 1999–2009', *Economic & Labour Market Review*, 4:7; 28–35.

McIlroy, J. (2008) 'Ten years of New Labour: workplace learning, social partnership and union revitalisation in Britain', *British Journal of Industrial Relations*, 46:2; 283–313.

Monger, J. (2004) 'Labour disputes in 2003', *Labour Market Trends*, June, 235–247.

Martinez Lucio, M. (2007) 'Trade unions and employment relations in the context of public sector change: the public sector, "old welfare states" and the politics of managerialism', *International Journal of Public Sector Management*, 20:1; 5–15.

Painter, J. (1991) 'The geography of trade union responses to local government privatization', *Transactions of the Institute of British Geographers*, 16:2; 214–226.

Pollitt, C. (1990) *Managerialism and the Public Services: The Anglo-American Experience* (London: Routledge).

Polanyi, K. (1944) *The Great Transformation* (Beacon Hill, MA: Beacon Press).

Rhee, N. and Zabin, C. (2009) 'Aggregating dispersed workers: union organizing in the "care" industries', *Geoforum*, 40, 969–979.

Richardson, M., Tailby, S., Danford, A., Stewart, P. and Upchurch, M. (2005) 'Best value and workplace partnership in local government', *Personnel Review*, 34:6; 713–728.

Ross, D. (1986) *An Unlikely Anger: Scottish Teachers in Action* (Edinburgh: Mainstream).

Seifert, R. and Ironside M. (1995) *Industrial Relations in Schools* (London: Routledge).

Stuart, M. and Martinez Lucio, M. (eds) (2005) *Partnership and the Modernisation of Employment Relations* (London: Routledge).

Symon, G. (2004) 'Lifelong learning and workplace relations: singing from the same hymn sheet, worshipping different gods?' in C. Warhurst, I. Grugulis and E. Keep (eds) *The Skills that Matter* (Basingstoke: Palgrave Macmillan).

Symon, G. and Crawshaw, J. (2009) 'Urban labour, voice and legitimacy: economic development and the emergence of community unionism', *Industrial Relations Journal*, 40:2; 140–155.

Waddington, J. and Kerr, A. (2009) 'Transforming a trade union? An assessment of the introduction of an organizing initiative', *British Journal of Industrial Relations*, 47:1; 27–54.

Wills, J. (2004) 'Organising the low paid: East London's living wage campaign', E. Heery, P. Taylor and W. Brown (eds) *The Future of Worker Representation*, (Basingstoke: Palgrave Macmillan).

Winchester, D. and Bach S. (1995), 'The state: the public sector', in P. Edwards (ed.) *Industrial Relations: Theory and Practice in Britain* (Oxford: Blackwell).

11
Consultants in Government: A Necessary Evil?

Peter Graham

'With their pre-packaged solutions they go in search of confused, anxious clients'. Jackall, 1988

Introduction

The above quotation seems to encapsulate the suspicion that surrounds the activity of consultants in government. They seem to be the 'folk devils' of modern business and their activity frequently attracts criticism in the media and also in some academic journals. Although on the face of it, it may seem reasonable that government should access specific expertise to improve its operations, critical commentators express a number of concerns (*see* Clark and Fincham, 2002). The concerns seem to fall into two areas. The first is that in the perception of the public and the media, government's spending on consultancy seems to be too high and has got out of control (*see also* Accountants for Business, 2010). The second centres on an uneasy feeling that consultants are not acting in the public interest and do not seem to be accountable. More generally there is a similarly vague suspicion that they have acquired a power and influence out of all proportion to the amount of work that they do.

Having sketched the background, this chapter unpacks several of these issues and assesses the validity of these charges. In order to do this, the underlying models and rationale of consultancy are first examined. This helps us to understand the frequently polarised views of the activity. The chapter then turns to spending and effectiveness/value for money. It next examines the client–consultant relationship and the barriers to change and finally, the possible future of consulting in government is considered.

Background

The use of consultants by government is not at all new. There is a long history stretching back to the 1960s when McKinsey, the American firm, was enlisted to look at the organisation of the BBC and the Post Office amongst others. In discussing this trend, the *Times* newspaper asked how many other public agencies were to be 'McKinseyed' (*see* McKenna, 2006). This was at a stage when the big American consulting firms were making significant efforts to internationalise and the UK government was keen to draw on their methods of management. In its annual report for 1966, the Management Consultancies Association (MCA) commented that a significant proportion of its members' work came from the public sector and that there was a great deal more potential in this market (Kipping and Saint-Martin, 2005). One of the biggest UK firms of management consultants in the 1960s claimed to have worked with 220 local authorities. The majority of this work was focused on organisational improvement, making better use of manpower, materials and money, as well as some cost-benefit studies on public programmes.

In the 1980s and early 1990s there was a surge of consulting activity due to the UK government's commitment to privatisation, efficiency studies and competitive tendering. Derek Rayner was appointed by the then Prime Minister, Margaret Thatcher, to head an 'Efficiency Unit' and to bring market discipline and commercial management techniques to the public sector. Out of this came the Financial Management Unit within central government, containing six civil servants and eight consultants, all from the big firms of the time (Metcalfe and Richards, 1990). Articles appearing in issues of trade periodicals such as *Management Consultancy* in the early 1990s would make frequent, bold pronouncements to the effect that 'public sector consultancy is big business'. Indeed during the 1990s close to £200m was spent annually. The change of government in 1997 intensified this trend and the Labour government is estimated to have spent close to £15bn in the last ten years on consulting fees (Muzio et al., 2010).

Models of consultancy

The word 'consultancy' may be frequently used, but is poorly understood (Werr and Styhre, 2003) and there are two main contrasting views of consulting and how it operates These two views also help us understand the polarised viewpoints from which consulting is commented

	Traditional	Critical model
Key metaphor	Medical doctor	Witchdoctor
Expertise	Lies with the consultant – in subject, process and x industry knowledge.	Consultant has no truly exclusive knowledge. Rhetoric, drama and fashion are used.
Power	Client is in charge – controls key elements and evaluates quality – can stop payment.	Consultant is in control. Manages the anxiety of an uncertain and dependent client
Client relation	Informed client – mutual respect – provision of business service	Client is the secondary partner. Consultant defines problem and supplies solution.
Criteria of value	Objective measures – performance improvement	Objective measures take a back seat. Subjective ones used and whether 'client feels better'.

Figure 11.1   Two opposing views of consulting

upon (*see* Figure 11.1). We shall call them the 'traditional' and the 'critical' viewpoints.

The traditional view

This is the view that sees the consultant as an 'expert business helper'. The client has a need for expertise that they do not possess and therefore need to seek this externally. For example, an organisation seeks to review its reward arrangements for all of its employees. A reward consulting firm is chosen to assist because it is perceived to have considerable experience and competence in successfully conducting such reviews and will be able to advise the client on the most effective course of action. The client specifies the problem, the objectives of the work and expects the consultant to carry this out to successful conclusion resulting in agreed payment as per the contract. The implications of this model are that the consultant supplies expertise but client is clearly in control and a competent partner in the project. Even within this apparently straightforward model, however, there are some important variations. Edgar Schein (1987) defines three distinct roles within this model.

1. Expert: This is where the client articulates a problem and the consultant uses their specialist knowledge to identify a solution.
2. Doctor–patient: This involves expertise, but the consultant also takes responsibility for diagnosing the problem in the first place. The client expresses a vague uneasiness and some initial symptoms but is unclear about what exactly is wrong.
3. Process consultation: This is different from the first two. Rather like a psychotherapy relationship, the client is seen as the only one who can truly understand and fix the problem. The consultant does not impose but works with the client in order to diagnose the problem and discover a solution. The consultant is a facilitator of change.

Role number 3 – 'process consultation' – is the undoubted favourite of many management consultants and particularly those working on organisational change projects of which there have been a significant number in the public sector (Muzio et al., 2010). The idea is that the consultant acts as a 'trusted advisor'. This idea has been popularised by various 'gurus', particularly the feted David Maister who is a consultant to the consulting firms as well as many professional service firms (*see* Maister et al., 2000).

The critical view

The critical view has emerged since the early 1990s. The authors tend to be mostly career academics who are far from convinced by the traditional model. Many of these writers, such as Clark (1995), Alvesson (1993) and Sturdy (1997), challenge the legitimacy of consulting as an activity and its claimed professional status. In the critical viewpoint, consultancy is seen as an almost dramatic performance (Clark and Salaman, 1997), where consultants use stories, rhetoric and current fashion to create the appearance of value because they have no solid base of expertise (Sturdy, 1997). In these relationships, the client changes from informed buyer to confused, naive victim who is deceived by the 'smoke and mirrors' of the persuasive consultant. Two joint authors even titled their book *The Witchdoctors* (Micklethwait and Wooldridge, 1996). The rise of Business Process Reengineering (BPR) in the 1990s is seen as one example of this fashion effect (Legge, 1995). We might also think of the legendary Tom Peters – co-author of the biggest selling management text of all time (Peters and Waterman, 1982) – and his carefully orchestrated seminars (Micklethwait and Wooldridge, 1996). Consultants are seen as part of wider networks of power, including government, which operate to transmit and legitimise ideas and activity (Clarke and Newman, 1997).

The traditional model – from its functionalist perspective – views consulting as a useful activity with tangible benefits, in contrast to the critical view, which is based on a social constructionist epistemology and questions both the legitimacy and effectiveness of consulting. In short, according to the critical view, consulting is an activity that provokes a degree of suspicion for its opaque pervasiveness and implied unaccountable power. On a superficial level, the critical model is apparently affirmed by frequent reports in the media of large sums spent on questionable consulting projects that did not deliver the expected results; however, the more articulate proponents of management consultancy are quick to challenge and refute such reports (see Accountants for Business, 2010).

This becomes particularly relevant in respect of the public sector. A great deal of the reform seen since the late 1980s has been allied to commercial practice and ideas spread by the major consulting firms. The implication, voiced by academics and journalists, is that the public sector is being changed, not for the benefit of citizens but to serve other managerial interests and many methods are inherently undemocratic or at odds with a public service ethos (Clarke and Newman, 1997). Finally, perhaps the most concerning accusation is that the consultants, in league with public decision makers and leading business schools, have grown fat on all of this work (see Muzio et al., 2010).

Spending on consultants

How much exactly is spent by public agencies on consultancy support? The Government's own figures admit to £1.8bn being spent in 2009 according to the recently released 'COIN' database of public expenditure (*see* ft.com, 2010). The figure is similar in magnitude to the past 6 years or so where between £1.4bn and £2.5bn has been spent. The point worth noting is that this is far greater than the MCA estimate of under £200m (*see* Muzio et al., 2010). The MCA membership is estimated to account for around 70 per cent of the total of consulting activity in the UK. Even factoring in this information, however, it is clear that consulting spend has achieved a step change between the two decades. Moreover, the figures from different sources do not agree and, indeed, even the official ones (unbiased) mask a multitude of discrepancies. The MCA puts the spend figure for 2009 at £540m, so if this is about 70 per cent of the actual total, this gives a sum of about £800m. Nevertheless, this still falls short of the government COIN figure of £1.8bn; a big difference.

Part of the explanation lies in the fact that the COIN figure actually includes a number of additional categories that are not normally classed as management consulting. For example, the COIN figure includes legal fees and fees paid to public relations firms. Perhaps the reality is probably £1–1.2bn or thereabouts, which is sufficiently large to support the claim that consulting has grown significantly since the last decade in terms of actual spend.

Effectiveness and value

Consultancy firms and government agencies justify this increase with the argument that significant reforms were required in order to improve public sector organisations so as to meet the expectations of a more demanding citizenry and achieve targets promised by the Labour government since 1997. The permanent secretaries claim that the objectives and timescales could not have been achieved without the assistance of consulting firms. This is both in terms of expertise and sheer manpower to boost these programmes.

Consulting is an intangible service and so does present some problems in terms of quality and results (Clark, 1995). It is paid for when it is consumed and sometimes the experience may be slightly disappointing. In terms of outputs from consulting projects, organisations typically seek an improvement of some kind, (key operational or service metrics) and/or increased organisational capability to solve future problems.

A comprehensive report by the National Audit Office (NAO, 2006) details some of the apparent successes of consultancy interventions in the public sector:

- In 2005–6 McKinsey was brought in by Her Majesty's Revenue and Customs (HMRC) to apply lean manufacturing techniques in order to improve a range of performance indicators, such as speed of tax calculation and error rates. In terms of these metrics the work was broadly successful.
- Accenture has worked with a number of government departments to move away from expensive form filling to online transactions. For

the Department of Work and Pensions time taken to process a new pension dropped from two weeks to a 20 minute phone-call.

- PricewaterhouseCoopers worked with the Ministry of Justice recently to assess costs and benefits for a range of bought-in services to manage offenders. The project was judged a success by the client, who believed they now had a clear view of where money was spent and what the outcomes were achieved.
- The Defence Logistics Operation spent about £2m on McKinsey in 2005 and felt they gained future savings of over 20 times this spend.

The principal difficulty when considering the impact of consultants is establishing whether the results are indeed due to the consulting intervention or some other factor. Projects do not happen in a vacuum and, indeed, many organisational reforms have several interrelated elements that need to combine in order to achieve overall improvement. In the case of HMRC the consulting project, was the main organisational change initiative and so the improved figures do imply good 'value for money'. Much of their work (and that of PA consultants) was introducing 'lean' techniques (common in manufacturing). Nevertheless, it is possible to achieve improvement in key metrics and still not necessarily improve the organisation's capability. Yet capability is notoriously difficult to actually measure and to achieve. Research by Hope Hailey et al. (2006) suggested that managers in HMRC suffered a significant degree of 'change fatigue' and, while 'lean techniques' were implemented, they were not owned by the staff who felt it was done to them, and the extent of knowledge transfer was questionable.

The consultant–client relationship

The last section starts to hint at a series of issues about how the consulting engagement is understood and managed. The main mechanism through which this is accomplished is the consultant–client relationship. The traditional view implies that there is a fully informed client and an expert consultant; this is overly simplistic. Usually there will be a team of people on both sides. Furthermore, on the client side, as well as the main in-house team, there will be other parties with an interest in the project, its objectives and outcomes. This all creates a complex internal web within the client organisation and the consultant is, unwittingly, automatically a part of that web (Fincham, 1999). The extent to which these complexities are understood and carefully managed depends upon the sophistication of the client.

Recent research (e.g. Graham, 2010) indicates that this issue of 'client sophistication' is a major stumbling block to effective consulting engagements. The concept has two elements. First, there is a technical understanding of the work to be done, whether it is supply chains or employee reward, and this is often limited to a few in-house managers' own limited experience. Second, there is the more subtle, but crucial understanding of how to work, or collaborate, in the most effective way, with an external consulting firm. Consultants often claim that even if the former is present, the latter is invariably poor (Graham, 2010).

The problem is that this second skill is subtle, complex and rarely taught outside of the consulting firms themselves. For example, there are important considerations such as:

- what exactly are the respective roles of consulting firm and client;
- who has knowledge/expertise and is this to be transferred;
- who has lead ownership at what stages; and
- the balance between technical and process consulting.

Lippitt and Lippitt (1978) produced a model of consultant client interaction that shows the relative involvement of consultants with the client in the form of a continuum that runs from 'objective detached observer' at one end through to 'in-house advocate' at the other. The model offers the possibility of understanding what role the consultant is playing at any time and, therefore, the implications for the client. However the reality in most sizeable consulting projects (above £100,000) is that at different stages the consultants will be playing different roles, sometimes simultaneously (Graham, 2010). It is easy to see how clients become confused as to who exactly is 'in charge' or is shaping the project at any given moment. This is exacerbated by the fact that it is common in government projects for a senior civil servant to handle the initial negotiations and then pass the project on to a much more junior colleague who may have very little experience of consultants. This often results in difficulties on both sides and a client unable to control what is happening (Clark and Salaman, 1997).

Even if the client ultimately has ownership of outcomes, it may make sense for the consultant to lead at certain times, particularly in the initial stages (training of client staff, initial analysis). The problem as Pellegrinelli (2002) points out, having looked at several case studies, is that all of this creates confusion and tension in a relationship that may not have been easy to start with. If public agencies rarely carry out large consulting engagements then it is unlikely that their project managers will have much experience/competence in this crucial role. Furthermore, attitudes towards the consultants amongst most staff may be less than welcoming.

In a project for the HMRC in 2005–6 (implementing lean techniques), managers and staff had a sense that even though they were not entirely happy with the consultants and what they were doing (and this included the head of HMRC), the project had the backing of the Cabinet Office and was part of a reform agenda from the Prime Minister. So there was some confusion over the role of the consultants and whether they were helping or implementing. This seriously affected the degree of collaboration and also client ownership of the work (Hope Hailey et al., 2006).

Edgar Schein (1987), distinguishes between whether the consultant is diagnosing and finding cures (doctor–patient relationship), or whether he/she is enhancing the client's own problem-solving ability (process consulting) as noted above. Two Australian academics Kitay and Wright (2004) talk about whether the consultant is being used as advisor, partner, implementer or provider. These four categories are about the knowledge and nature of the consultant use. Knowledge transfer and enhanced client capability may be part of an initial proposal but then mid-project, with deadlines and other priorities, the mechanism for this to happen may not be implemented. Furthermore, client staff may have limited interest and/or commitment to this element because it may involve unwelcome job and skill changes. This was true of the HMRC case mentioned already. Also one case, the Metropolitan Police project (Graham, 2010), resulted in wider discussions about what roles were appropriate for non-police officers to perform. Clearly this kind of question starts to encroach on strategic issues of public sector provision that should perhaps be open to a wider debate in a democratic context.

Linked with consultant–client relationships is the extent to which boundaries become blurred and consultants on large projects are insiders (part of the client) or still outsiders (clearly external advisors). It is a concept highlighted by Kitay and Wright (2004) who researched what happens when consultants become involved in longer projects with clients.

Those holding critical views of consultants tend to be concerned that commercial ideas inappropriate for the public sector are foisted on it by external advisors. For example, a major Department of Work & Pensions (DWP) transformation project in 2005–6 had a director of the change project who was an ex-partner of IBM, the main consulting firm engaged to assist. The author, who was an independent consultant on this project, witnessed very few DWP managers involved and the use of a lot of short-term interim human resources managers, while every aspect of the programme seemed centrally driven by IBM. There was a strong sense that with the constant presence of IBM, the change was being 'done' to the majority of DWP staff and that there was little joint working (*see* NAO, 2006).

Yet while in some cases, consultants can be classed as outsiders, in others they become insiders. Kitay and Wright (2004) discovered that on large projects, the individual consultants would often work for up to two years immersed in client teams. They often felt a 'stranger' back in their own consulting firm and, unsurprisingly, often 'went native'. Interviews with consultants (Graham, 2010) often reveal value statements about why they specifically chose to carry out public sector assignments and how it matched their personal value set. Graham (2010) also found consultants were trying very hard to achieve the best for the public agency they worked for, and this led them sometimes to argue with their own firm. This would indicate a positive benefit for the public sector of the consultant 'insider'.

It can, however, lead to tensions from the consultants themselves. Sturdy (1997) has shown how insecure consulting can be and that individual consultants on large projects are often adrift from their own firm and yet expected to maintain the firm's strict commercial criteria. This tension is exacerbated by the fact that the consultant on a client project is part of a wider operational and career structure in their own firm and sometimes these demands conflict with client service.

So the consultant on a longer term project is often caught in the middle, in a whole series of conflicts. Kitay and Wright create a picture of sincere, public-minded consultants being abused by both a client that resents their intrusion and a home firm that wishes to maintain control over them. When you add the inevitable long hours and heavy demands of this kind of work, it does not seem like the glamorous job that business school graduates crave (McKenna, 2006).

The critical viewpoint would claim that it is precisely by such insidious infiltration techniques that consultants get their methods accepted and, for instance, discover further problems, which extend the project. Again, Sturdy (1997) comments that consultants, once on a project, are expected to 'sell on' to create further work with the client that may not be strictly necessary. So the consultant can lose objectivity for the project, which is clearly not good for the client. In addition, if a consultant is working very closely with the client then their ability to recognise poor practice and challenge it, may also be diminished.

On the one hand, as noted above, it has been argued that the consultant goes native and becomes an insider. On the other hand is the view that the consultant uses his/her power and/or influence to manipulate the client. In a classic definition, Dahl (1957: 214) talks about power as 'getting people to do something they would not otherwise do'. This is substantive or executive power, the ability to cause something to happen, whereas influence is the ability to encourage decisions in a particular direction, but not actually take them (Pettigrew, 1973).

So do consultants have power? The traditional model already discussed (*see* Figure 11.1) would say clearly no, and that only the client has genuine decision-making power over key aspects of a consulting assignment. Having said this, the possession of expertise would allow significant influence over issues of scope, method and timescale in projects, if not actual decisions, and the critical view would argue for a very significant degree of influence. According to this latter view, consultants use rhetoric and persuasion to convince confused and anxious clients (Clark and Salaman, 1997).

Consultants are also able to exploit the fact that organisations are becoming more internally complex (Pellegrinelli, 2002) and it is often not clear how managers should respond. Pfeffer (1981) argues that consultants accrue power due to their ability to handle uncertainty and convince managers to accept their version of what is real and valid. The way that managers accepted Business Process Re-engineering in the 1990s would seem to support this (Legge, 1995). A study by Danieli and Bloomfield (1998), however, concluded simply that the consultants' technical and political skills seemed inseparable in their operation and many consultants themselves feel they have influence, but not power (Graham, 2010). It is not just influence/power over particular decisions that the critics of consultants fear, but a seamless involvement in the process at an even earlier stage. They argue that there is a network of senior contacts in government, business and academia that support this (Kipping and Saint-Martin, 2005).

Readiness to change

One of the essential ingredients in a good consulting project is the client's openness to new ideas and willingness to change, but even though senior management engage a consulting firm, it does not mean that all staff are keen to adopt new practices or agree with the ideas put forward by the consultants. Also, the organisation's systems and bureaucracies are structured to perform today's business, rather than to be changed (Kipping and Saint-Martin, 2005).

The reality of 'change projects' is that the organisation's staff need to work with external consultants and then at some point the consultants leave, and the staff are left to continue. If the rationale of change is not well communicated then staff may not understand and/or resent the consulting input. This will affect the realisation of any benefits from the work. This may also include the senior civil servants. Already, this chapter has referred to a change project for the DWP in 2005 involving IBM. In that project, the consultants remarked on the overlapping nature of a number of very senior roles leading to possible duplication, confusion and lack of accountability. Clarity and clearer performance had been one of the aims of the project and yet little or nothing was done to prevent role confusion. The consultants were thanked for their insightful comments but more or less ignored (Graham, 2010).

In the HMRC example that this chapter previously referred, the new system required a different philosophy of tax collection and some risk management. The long-serving staff had built up a culture of 'not letting anyone get away with it' and this was hard to change and affected the effectiveness of the new 'lean and efficient' process.

In terms of an organisation's systems there are also barriers to change. Government is a succession of bureaucracies in individual competing departments and departments may not always easily cooperate. This last point was strongly made in the NAO (2006) report on government consulting projects pointing out a number of failings in the management of projects, concluding that a large part of the value was often lost due to the client's own poor ability.

The Coalition

The Coalition Government has said that its 'most urgent task ... is to tackle our record debts' (Cabinet Office, 2010: 7). Against that background the Treasury has indicated its intention significantly to cut consulting spend on public projects (*Guardian*, 2010). In the second quarter of 2010, anecdotal evidence (from the author's conversations) indicated that two of the large consulting firms experienced a 15 per cent drop in revenues and it seems likely that this might extend to other firms. There has also been a total block placed on all new consulting projects. A large number of projects already started, however, such as major IT projects, will have to be continued in order to avoid penalties and also to achieve promised service objectives.

What the public sector economic crisis may do is to focus effort and thinking. Key projects will probably still take place, but it is likely that tougher, better justified business cases will be expected before money is granted. There will be a greater focus on value gained and how this will actually be realised. This matches what was recommended by the NAO (2006) but is now much more likely to actually happen. There will probably be a range of measures implemented, as the NAO suggested, to achieve 'intelligent buying', for example, much greater cooperation between procurement functions and the specific client. Also, there is likely to be more sharing of work across government departments and greater focus on transfer of expertise and capability.

In addition, there is likely to be greater consideration of contingency fees (payment for results) and performance monitoring. A recent MCA survey of their members indicate that government clients are not overly keen on these kind of contracts (less than 10% of contracts are on this basis), the problem being that it is much easier to judge performance in terms of input (costs) than outputs or value gained (mixed measures) (MCA, 2010). To do this properly also requires a much more sophisticated client and measurement processes, than the Government has.

Nevertheless, given the continuing rate of change in the public sector and the focus on improved capability, consulting expertise is likely to be even more relevant than before. The desire to use external input to achieve value and the need to meet demanding timescales may encourage spending similar to that in previous years. Therefore, as with all the organisations that supply services to central government, there may be a tendency to re-categorise spending in ways that are less apparent and to use words such as 'project management support' or 'short term contractors', to cloak the fact that consultants are being used.

Conclusion

So what have we learned? First, consulting seems to provoke polarised views and a great deal of criticism from those outside government. Second, spending on consultants has clearly increased significantly from the early 1990s. Third, there is evidence of positive improvements as a result of consultants' interventions if metrics are used as the basis for evaluation. Nevertheless, there are still barriers to change, as identified fifty years ago by Tilles (1961) as well as more recently by the NAO (2006).

Fourth, there seems little doubt that consultants have influence, but their actual power is much more questionable. The real question perhaps is about the competence and sophistication of government departments effectively to manage consulting interventions and gain value from the expense. What is required, in the author's opinion, is an increased sophistication and capability on the part of government clients so that more effective collaboration can occur. Clients need to be much more sophisticated and competent and consider not only price and measurement, but also the more intangible benefits. This is the route to getting 'value for money'. The consultants, for their part, need to support their clients' objectives and public values and not just try to commercialise them. To start this process, we need to stop treating consultants as 'devils' and adopt a more nuanced approach.

References

Accountants for Business (2010) *Management Consultants and Public Sector Transformation* (London: ACCA).

Alvesson, M. (1993) 'Organizations as rhetoric: knowledge-intensive firms and the struggle with ambiguity', *Journal of Management Studies*, 30:6; 997–1015.

Cabinet Office (2010) *The Coalition: Our Programme for Government* (London: Cabinet Office).

Clark, T. (1995) *Managing Consultants* (Buckingham: Open University Press).

Clark, T. and Fincham, R. (eds) (2002) *Critical Consulting: New Perspectives on the Management Advice Industry* (Oxford: Blackwell).

Clark, T. and Salaman, G. (1997) 'The management guru as organizational witch-doctor', *Organization*, 31:1; 85–107.

Clarke, J. and Newman, J. (1997) *The Managerial State* (London: Sage).

Dahl, R. (1957) 'The concept of power', *Behavioral Science*, 2:3; 201–215.

Danieli, A., Bloomfield, B. (1998) 'Management consultants: systems development, power and the translation of problems', in J. Bryson and P. Daniels (eds) *Service Industries in the Global Economy* (Cheltenham: Edward Elgar).

Fincham, R. (1999) 'Rhetorical narratives and the consultancy process', paper presented at *British Academy of Management (BAM) Conference* (Manchester, 1–3 September).

ft.com (*Financial Times Online*) (2010) 'Welcome to the Whitehall data sausage factory', online at http://blogs.ft.com/westminster/2010/06/welcome-to-the-whitehall-data-sausage-factory/ [accessed 4 June 2010].

Graham, P. (2010) 'Whores in pinstripes? Consultants in the public sector: a necessary evil', paper presented at the *WERU Symposium* (University of Greenwich, London, 22 July).

Guardian (2010) 'Q&A: the 2010 spending review', *The Guardian*, 21 October.

Hope Hailey V. R., Farndale, E., Clarke, C., Kelliher, C., Balogun, J., Abbotson, S. and Rees Jones, T. (2006) 'HMRC: a longitudinal study of the merger of Inland Revenue and Customs and Excise in the UK', in *Change Management Consortium Report No. 9* (London: Cass Business School, City University).

Jackall, R. (1988) *Moral Mazes: The World of Corporate Managers* (New York: Oxford University Press).

Kipping, M. and Saint-Martin, D. (2005) 'Between regulation, promotion and consumption: government and management consultancy in Britain', *Business History,* 47:3; 449–465.

Kitay, J. and Wright, C. (2004) 'Take the money and run? Organisational boundaries and consultants', *The Service Industries Journal,* 24:3; 1–19.

Legge, K. (1995) *Human Resource Management: Rhetorics and Realities,* Basingstoke: Palgrave Macmillan.

Lippitt, G. and Lippitt, R. (1978) *The Consulting Process in Action* (LaJolla, CA: University Associates).

Maister, D., Green, C. and Galford, R. (2000) *The Trusted Advisor* (New York: The Free Press).

MCA (Management Consultancies Association) (2010) *Annual Report* (London: MCA).

McKenna, C. (2006) *The World's Newest Profession: Management Consulting in the Twentieth Century* (Cambridge: Cambridge University Press).

Metcalfe, L. and Richards, S. (1990) *Improving Public Management* (London: Sage).

Micklethwait, J. and Wooldridge, A. (1996) *The Witch Doctors: Making Sense of the Management Gurus* (New York: Times Books and Random House).

Muzio, D., Kirkpatrick, I., and Kipping, M. (2010) 'Professionalism without professions: the case of management consultancy in the UK', *CERIC Working Paper (No. 8)* (Leeds: University of Leeds).

NAO (National Audit Office) (2006) *Central Government's Use of Consultants* (London: NAO).

Pellegrinelli, S. (2002) 'Managing the interplay and tensions of consulting interventions: the consultant-client relationship as mediation and reconciliation', *Journal of Management Development,* 21:5; 343–365.

Peters, T. and Waterman, R. (1982) *In Search of Excellence: Lessons from America's Best-run Companies* (New York: Haper & Row).

Pettigrew, A. (1973) *The Politics of Organizational Decision Making* (London: Tavistock).

Pfeffer, J. (1981) *Power in Organizations* (Marshfield, MA: Pitman).

Schein, E. (1987) *The Clinical Perspective in Fieldwork* (Newbury Park, CA: Sage).

Sturdy, A. (1997) 'The consultancy process: an insecure business?' *Journal of Management Studies,* 34:3; 389–413.

Tilles, S. (1961) 'Understanding the consultant's role', *Harvard Business Review,* 39: Nov–Dec, 87–99.

Werr, A. and Styhre, A. (2003) 'Management consultants – friend or foe? Understanding the ambiguous client–consultant relationship', *International Studies of Management and Organization,* 32:4; 43–66.

Part V
Conclusions

12
Making Sense of Public Sector Employment Relations in a Time of Crisis

Graham Symon and Susan Corby

Introduction

The purpose of this book has been thematically to illuminate and analyse an aspect of our society that is in the midst of a particularly turbulent phase of reform and transition: the public sector and more specifically the experiences of its many millions of workers. From Plato through Hobbes and Mill to Hayek and (Ralph) Miliband, the role, function and ideal extent of the State has been debated and contested. To some, a strong, democratic, redistributive state is the hallmark of a civilised society. To others, it is a constraining authority and the taxation it requires to operate is, an unjustifiable imposition. Nevertheless in the modern era, the world's industrialised democracies have found themselves with a significant proportion of the workforce employed in the delivery of the State's various activities. Yet the scope and nature of the public sector workforce have become more contested than ever over the last three decades as the influence of the 'neoliberal turn' has come to dominate policy discourses (Harvey, 2007). This has been driven by crisis and the shifting forces and relations of production, which have in turn impacted on the political economy of the State and the citizens' relationship to it.

The symbiotic relationship between State and economy has been well established, as has the logic of the State establishing the best 'fit' to support the prevailing production imperatives. Thus we had Victorian paternalists bringing sanitation to our industrial cities to provide a healthy labour supply (*see* Hunt, 2004); the Fordism of the mid-twentieth century catering for mass production and consumption (*see* Kirkpatrick, 2006); and today the aspiration for a leaner, more flexible post-Fordist state to underpin the demands of volatile and unforgiving global markets (Harvey, 2007). Consequently we have seen attempts to 'modernise' the public sector so that it is fit for purpose with associated discourses of making it more efficient and responsive to the consumer. In parallel, according to some sections of the media, the organisation and composition of the public sector workforce has been presented as a key barrier to modernisation; a workforce that is, inter alia, bloated, cosseted, hyper-unionised and the place where the whimsy of self-interested bureaucrats and professionals prevails (*see* Du Gay, 2000; Le Grand, 2003).

The chapters in this volume have presented more sophisticated and circumspect analyses of the changing public sector and its workforce in particularly challenging circumstances. We have discussed how the parlous economics of the public sector have exerted pressure on numbers of personnel and their terms, conditions and status (Shaoul, Chapter 3; White, Chapter 5; Bach, Chapter 7 – in this volume) and how this scenario has played out across Europe (Gold and Veersma, Chapter 2, in this volume). In this context, notions of justice that are associated with the democratic state have suffered (see Lethbridge, Chapter 4; Corby, Chapter 6 – in this volume). Furthermore, we have considered how the actors have struggled to cope with these rapidly changing agendas, both from the perspectives of employee representatives (Symon, Chapter 10, in this volume) and managers (McGurk, Chapter 9, in this volume). We have looked at accounts of a particular bone of contention, the involvement of the private sector and the outsourcing of services in the shape of Cunningham's analysis of employment relations in third sector providers (Chapter 8, in this volume) and Graham's novel consideration of the role and experiences of – often maligned – management consultants in the machinery of the State (Chapter 11, in this volume). Drawing from this, we will outline some broad conclusions about the position of state employment and its prospects.

Tracking trajectories

In the past two decades, the more considered literature on public policy and administration (e.g. Dibben et al., 2007; Marsh and Rhodes, 1992) has cautioned against making any sweeping or reductionist judgements about ideological zeal, change or decay. Similarly, industrial relations analysts have pointed to the complexity of change with regard to collective organisation, labour processes, conditions and patterns of work inter alia (*see* Kersley et al., 2006; Wood and James, 2006). The analyses in this volume are intentionally eclectic in their subject matter and the authors' approaches are not uniform, reflecting their various views and stances. Nevertheless, this volume also aspires to present a degree of coherence and, without seeking to generalise, identifies broad threads and trajectories as follows:

1. Crisis and decline
2. Fragmentation
3. Managerialism

Crisis and decline

The populist polemical position of 'declinology' – that is, the belief that one's society is in a state of moral and material decline (Harkin, 2008) – is frequently taken by commentators with regard to the institutions of state and public services. From the right, it is contended that any apparent decline or crisis is the inevitable consequence of an overloaded and overbearing state, stifling individual liberty and free enterprise. From the left, the counter argument is that common goods and the welfare state have been subordinated to the needs of capital and as a consequence have been starved and the state's redistributive capacity has been sabotaged with the vulnerable suffering (*see* Hutton, 2010a for an overview).

More circumspect investigations of the nature and robustness of the state and the public sector present a range of theoretical and empirical accounts. The influential notion of crisis, supported by neo-Marxian and regulation theorists (*see* Kirkpatrick, 2006), maintains that because modes of capitalism (e.g. Fordism) have crisis tendencies, the state must intervene to mitigate these crises and in doing so may itself suffer what Habermas termed 'legitimation crisis' (Habermas, 1975). A rough illustration of this process can be drawn from the 1970s in the UK where economic crisis – with associated symptoms in finance and industrial relations – precipitated a crisis of the state and led to an apparent ideological and structural 'turn' from social democracy to neoliberalism (Harvey, 2007).

The Conservative administration of Thatcher (1979–90) set in train the restructuring of the UK state, which encompassed retrenchment (for example, privatisation, curtailment of welfare) and marketisation and the desire to create a more 'business-friendly' environment (counterpoised with the seemingly unsympathetic state). However, further pressures on the state were to follow, possibly as a result of neoliberalism (*see* Harvey, 2007) as the world economy became more 'globalised' and therefore competitive and risky (Hay, 2005). Thus, even when economies and incomes were growing in the industrialised world, the public sector continued to be restructured. (This should be considered in the light of wider restructuring of work and economic activity, for example, the shift away from mass-production to services and the 'knowledge economy' (*see* Wood and James, 2006)). Despite increasing prosperity and consumer spending power, sociological accounts have complained of the degradation of experiences of people in the workplace (e.g. Braverman and the 'labour process' school; *see* Thompson and McHugh, 2009) and in civil society (e.g. with the erosion of social capital identified by Putnam, 2000).

Certainly Shaoul (Chapter 3, in this volume) provides a detailed critique of trends in UK public expenditure both under the Conservatives (1979–1997) and New Labour (1997–2010) and trenchantly comments on the conduct of the Treasury during and after the financial crisis of 2008, when several failed banks – or rather their liabilities – had to be nationalised on an emergency basis. This resulted in the spending cuts of the October 2010 review, the ramifications of which are yet to be fully realised at the time of writing, but are likely to result in job losses, erosion of terms and conditions for existing workers and curtailment of services for the public. Shaoul also suggests we look more closely at the manner in which public money is distributed and accounted for and how finance is raised and particularly at the Private Finance Initiative/ Public Private Partnership about which she expresses concerns in relation to the high costs incurred by the state and thus the taxpayer and the impact on the experiences and conditions of the workers.

Without wishing to romanticise state provision, Lethbridge's (Chapter 4, in this volume) discussion presents convincing evidence of what have historically been the dividends of the public service 'ethos': a sense of professional integrity and an interest in the common good. With privatisation and other developments such as the Coalition's so-called free schools, however, that 'ethos' appears to be under threat. Even when, as Cunningham (Chapter 8, in this volume) discusses, the voluntary sector is commissioned to deliver services, with the expectation that particular charities will bring their own esprit de corps to that delivery, the obstacles of downward pressure on resources and conditions of employment inhibit this. Furthermore, the severe nature of the contracts that commissioning public sector bodies form with charities appears to inhibit the flourishing of the sort of trust and confidence that is consistent with the espoused missions of these organisations.

We must be cautious of defaulting to pessimism without a thorough and balanced scrutiny of the research data. Nevertheless, the picture of state employment in the UK and across Europe (*see* Gold and Veersma, Chapter 2, in this volume) is less than encouraging. Fiscal and managerial pressures are leading to the erosion of worker rights, pay and conditions and the declining robustness of union representation; and this has implications for justice in the public sector workplace and the capacity of public services to deliver, particularly to those most in need. The Coalition Government's austerity measures put obvious pressure on resources; however, in parallel with these cuts are a series of organisational changes (e.g. changes to the structure of the NHS) and cultural shifts (e.g. shifting the raison d'être of the social security function from welfare to workfare) will have similarly serious consequences for the nature and future of the public sector.

Fragmentation

The notion of the post-1945 welfare state as being a paternalistic, monolithic behemoth is something of a caricature, although it has served critics well (Du Gay, 2000). The more informed accounts that draw on regulation theory and the symbiosis of the state with Fordist production – with its characteristic economies of scale and rigidities – have been exposed as having limitations, principally stemming from the idea that the state was not as monolithic as assumed and that the association with Fordism was based on a flawed premise (Kirkpatrick, 2006). However, there can be little dispute that disaggregation has been a prominent aspect of recent developments in the UK public sector. This is supported by the commentaries in this volume.

Of course, the observation that organisational structures in the public sector have become dissaggregated, decentralised and devolved is not a new one and indeed has been made vociferously for at least twenty years (Hoggett, 1996; Hood, 1991). The more nuanced and somewhat paradoxical analysis of this scenario sees the decentralisation of administrative and financial responsibility concurrent with strict performance management controls. Be that as it may, successive privatisations and outsourcing result in more and more of the workforce being effectively displaced from public sector employment. The consequences of these developments for collective representation and bargaining (Symon, Chapter 10, in this volume); pay and conditions (White, Chapter 5, in this volume); equality in the workplace (Corby, Chapter 6, in this volume); and 'ethos' (Lethbridge, Chapter 4, in this volume) are likely to be adverse, despite the rhetorical espousals of policymakers to the contrary.

Managerialism

The development of managerialism in the public sector is not a new one and has been widely discussed previously, both in terms of its impact on systems, structures and the policy process (Hood, 1991) and the culture of the public sector and welfare provision (Clarke and Newman, 1997). Notions of a particular ideology and technocratic framework for effective performance have become embedded through various sources, including the influence of a business ethos at a policymaking level and the intervention of management development initiatives and management consultants. The work in this volume has highlighted some interesting phenomena in the managerialist debate that both enhance and challenge established accounts of New Public Management (NPM).

The first contribution of this volume to the managerialism debate is that the contributors appear to indicate the presence of an ongoing trajectory from the New Right NPM of the 1980s and early 1990s through the rhetorically amended – but in many ways similarly controversial – New Labour Third Way Modernisation project to a phase beyond, as yet – at the time of writing – without an established label but with distinct characteristics. At the end of the Thatcher period (1979–1990), Marsh and Rhodes (1992) controversially suggested that the New Right project had been unfinished and indeed characterised by policy failure. Harvey (2007) appears to concur, explaining that the neoliberal agenda was unable to achieve all that its philosophical underpinnings suggested was possible and desirable. Marsh and Rhodes (and the contributors to their volume, 1992) attribute this to poor implementation. Harvey's Marxian analysis cites more abstract philosophical contradictions in neoliberalism. However, it also seems likely that a certain degree of resistance to managerialism was encountered from the workforce institutionally, collectively and also from the service-using public (*see* Burrows and Loader, 1994; Symon and Crawshaw, 2009). This is not to say, however, that profound changes were not enacted and similarly profound effects were not felt by the workforce and public alike.

In terms of clues as to how this 'new' managerial phase (for want of a better term) is evolving and impacting on employment matters, we must consider the forces that are acting on the public sector in promoting this spirit of managerialism. Shaoul (Chapter 3, in this volume) discusses how systems and structures of finance and expenditure in the public sector have been allocated, explaining how policymakers and managers can accordingly gain leverage through particular governance and budgetary systems and structures. Similarly Lethbridge (Chapter 4, in this volume) as noted above, indicates how managerialism threatens the public sector 'ethos'. Additionally, she explains how large private sector corporations, where managerialist discourses are embedded, are seeking greater involvement in state provision.

In particular, however, discussions of the continuing and developing influence of managerial ideology in the delivery of public services is illuminated in McGurk's discussion (Chapter 9, in this volume). In that chapter he charts the establishment and legitimation of a particular conceptualisation of leadership (as opposed to mere management). He demonstrates the means by which the discourse of leadership has become embedded so that it is seen as part of the natural fabric of organisational life in the twenty-first century public sector (with reference to a privatised service for comparison) and how those in managerial positions are socialised into a set of behavioural expectations and how they respond to the message. Although a substantial critique of leadership is offered in McGurk's chapter, he demonstrates the apparent success of the leadership agenda in becoming established and naturalised in organisational mindsets.

A related phenomenon is the role and influence of management consultants in disseminating and perpetuating a managerial agenda. Graham's contribution (Chapter 11, in this volume) provides an account of what the management consultant does in the public sector. There can be little doubt that considerable sums of money are spent on consultants (although Graham cautions against any superficial analyses of the figures in the public domain) and, more importantly for the purposes of our discussion at this juncture, their influence on decision making and policy development. At a benign level, Graham explains how consultants can have a constructive impact on the way public services are delivered, introducing innovative new ideas and doing things that existing public servants lack the capacity to do. Nevertheless, at the more threatening end of the continuum, there is evidence to suggest that elements within the consultant industry see the State as a means of extracting rents (as per Lethbridge's analysis). Furthermore, there appears to be a somewhat uncritical appetite on the part of policymakers and decision makers in the public sector for the intervention of management consultants as bearers of the sort of tools that will assist them in making their desired changes.

Ultimately, managerialism has become well established in the public sector, either as an ideological agenda or through ever increasing private sector involvement in the delivery of public services. Although it would be naive to seek any nostalgic or misremembered conceptualisation of benign paternalistic bureaucracy and although some have scorned public administrators' attempts to imitate the apparently enterprising heroics of their counterparts in the private sector (*see* Wright, 2009), the impact, both already felt and potential, of managerialism in the public sector is to be taken seriously. More than ever before, the climate and structure of the public sector would appear to provide an appropriate fit for a potent and distinct managerial agenda.

Paradoxes and prospects

Paradoxes

At the start of this book we argued that public sector employment relations were distinct from employment relations in the private sector and thus merited separate study. Is this distinctiveness likely to continue? There are countervailing and paradoxical trends. On the one hand, as we have shown, private sector managerialist discourses are now commonly heard in the public sector, with words like customer focus, business plans, benchmarks and incentivisation often being used, reinforced by the rhetoric of leadership and the use of management consultants; (*see* McGurk, Chapter 9, in this volume and Graham, Chapter 11, in this volume for a fuller discussion). At the same time, as previously noted, there has been a trend to privatisation and outsourcing resulting in some public services being delivered by the private sector. In short, from this perspective the boundaries between the public and private sectors have become blurred and workers previously in the public sector have found that, although continuing to work for the state, they now have a private sector employer.

On the other hand, employment relations in respect of those still working in the public sector are increasingly different from those of their counterparts in the private sector. For instance White, (Chapter 5, in this volume) showed that pay in the private sector was commonly determined by management unilaterally, while in the public sector the most common pay determination methods were collective bargaining and pay review bodies. Similarly, public sector workers, unlike their private sector counterparts, tended to enjoy defined benefit occupational pension schemes and service-related incremental pay scales. Symon (Chapter 10, in this volume) showed how union density was significantly higher in the public sector, compared to the private sector, while Corby (Chapter 6, in this volume) found that the public sector equality duties were not reflected, even in an eviscerated form, in the private sector.

These paradoxical trends, that is, increasing separation versus convergence, seem set to continue with more privatisation and outsourcing and the intensification of managerialism on the one hand and with controls on top pay in the public sector, but not the private sector on the other hand (Hutton, 2010b).

Prospects

As to prospects for the future, only the foolhardy would make firm predictions. Accordingly, we merely indicate some signposts. In the face of austerity measures, it is difficult to envisage anything other than a rather pessimistic view of the fate of the public sector and its workforce. Reforming elites insist that there is no alternative to change: that the public expenditure levels of recent years are unsustainable and that the global economy requires public sector institutions to be responsive to the apparently legitimate expectations of the 'consumer' in our post-Fordist society. This reforming agenda has been brought into sharp focus at the time of writing by the Coalition Government's austerity measures and its programme of reform and re-engineering of the State and its institutions (e.g. Free Schools and the reforms of the NHS in England published in January 2011). Even if seen as responses to the financial/fiscal crisis, the planned reforms to the public sector only serve to demonstrate how the State acts as an appurtenance to the prevailing model of accumulation (Hay, 2007; Shaoul, Chapter 3, in this volume).

In terms of the workforce of the public sector, they face challenges that arguably are the most serious yet and which, according to some accounts, threaten the very notion of state-administered public welfare and, which at the same time, undermine public sector union density (see Symon, Chapter 10, in this volume). However, the imperative that the unions establish support for their resistance of potentially damaging reform has been established.

Since 1919, the public sector has to a greater or lesser extent consciously sought to espouse the ideals of the model employer and to set an example to the private sector, a project that was never fully realised but has come under severe strain in the past three decades (see Corby Chapter 6, in this volume and Symon, Chapter 10, in this volume). Nevertheless, despite the pressures experienced in that time public sector employers continued to display many laudable examples of best practice. For example, Corby (Chapter 6, in this volume) discusses how the equality agenda had always been more coherent and better upheld in the public sector than the private sector; but she explains how this practice is coming under threat, a threat that is likely to intensify in the near future. Similarly, Bach (Chapter 7, in this volume) discussed the role of assistants to public service professionals and the part they have played in shaping the modernisation agenda. Although he expresses reservations about their impact on the wider delivery of services and the work of the professionals (for example, nurses, teachers) that they support, it seems that they have been a force for the good. However, he explains that they face an uncertain future in the wake of the austerity measures with training budgets cut and recruitment frozen. They risk the prospect of much less rewarding experiences of work as a result.

The ultimate question is: has a Rubicon been crossed in the metamorphosis of the public sector and the way in which it employs and deploys its workforce? It seems that the case for reform has been established and legitimated, which could undermine the institutions of public service provision, either retrenching/abolishing them or allowing the increased involvement of the private sector. Either way, there are potentially grave consequences for workers; the next few years will be crucial ones for those working for the State.

References

Burrows, R. and Loader, B. (eds) (1994) *Towards a Post-Fordist Welfare State?* (London: Routledge).

Clarke, J. and Newman, J. (1997) *The Managerial State* (London: Sage).

Dibben, P., James, P., Roper I., and Wood, G. (eds) (2007) *Modernising Work in Public Services: Redefining Roles and Relationships in Britain's Changing Workplace* (Basingstoke: Palgrave Macmillan).

Du Gay, P. (2000) *In Praise of Bureaucracy: Weber, Organisation, Ethics,* (London: Sage).

Habermas, J. (1975) *Legitimation Crisis* (London: Heinemann).

Harkin, J. (2008) *Big Ideas: The Essential Guide to the Latest Thinking* (London: Atlantic Books).

Harvey, D. (2007) *Spaces of Global Capitalism: Towards and Theory of Uneven Geographical Development* (London: Verso).

Hay, C. (2005) 'Globalization's impact on states', in J. Ravenhill (ed.) *Global Political Economy* (Oxford: Oxford University Press).

Hoggett, P. (1996) 'New modes of control in the public service', *Public Administration,* 74:1; 9–32.

Hood, C. (1991) 'A public management for all seasons', *Public Administration,* 68:1; 3–19.

Hutton, W. (2010a) *Them and Us: Changing Britain: Why We Need a Fair Society* (London: Little Brown).

Hutton, W. (2010b) *Hutton Review of Fair Pay in the Public Sector: Interim Report.* *December* (London: HM Treasury), Online at http://www.hm-treasury.gov.uk/d/ hutton_interim_report.pdf [accessed 20 December 2010].

Hunt, T. (2004) *Building Jerusalem: The Rise and Fall of the Victorian City* (London: Weidenfield & Nicolson).

Kersley, B., Alpin C., Forth, J., Bryson, A., Bewley, H., Dix G. and Oxenbridge, S. (2006), *Inside the Workplace: Findings from the 2004 Workplace Employment Relations Survey* (London: Routledge).

Kirkpatrick, I. (2006) 'Post-Fordism and organizational change in state administration', in L. Enrique-Alonso and M. Martinez Lucio (eds) *Employment Relations in a Changing Society: Assessing the Post-Fordist Paradigm* (Basingstoke: Palgrave Macmillan).

Le Grand, J. (2003) *Motivation, Agency and Public Policy: of Knights and Knaves, Pawns and Queens* (Oxford: Oxford University Press).

Marsh, D. and Rhodes, R. (eds) (1992) *Implementing Thatcherite Policies: Audit of an Era* (Buckingham: Open University Press).

Putnam, R. (2000) *Bowling Alone: The Collapse and Revival of American Community,* (New York: Simon and Schuster).

Symon, G. and Crawshaw, J. (2009) 'Urban labour, voice and legitimacy: economic development and the emergence of community unionism', *Industrial Relations Journal,* 40:2; 140–155.

Thompson, P. and McHugh, D. (2009) *Work Organisations: A Critical Approach,* 4th edn (Basingstoke: Palgrave Macmillan).

Wood, G., and James, P. (eds) (2006) *Institutions, Production and Working Life* (Oxford: Oxford University Press).

Wright, P. (2009) *A Journey Through Ruins: The Last Days of London* (Oxford: Oxford University Press).

Index

ACAS, 95
Accenture, 214–15
accountability, 71, 76, 77
Action Zones, 197
administrative structure, 33
advisers, private sector, 74–5
affordability, 16, 94, 133
Afghanistan, 63
age, 89, 108, 111, 112, 119, *see also* pensions
Agenda for Change, 95, 115, 139
armed forces, 4, 90, 116–17
Assistant Practitioners (APs), 133
assistants
  consequences for, 138–9
  crafting of assistant roles, 136–7
  evolution of the assistant workforce, 134–5
  impact on professionals and service users, 139–41
  role, 129–30, 141–3, 236
  role and profile of the workforce, 132–4
Attlee, Clement, 191
audit, 151, 154, 155–6, 162
austerity
  age of, 17, 142–3, 147, 153–4, 184
  measures, 43, 63, 231, 235–6
Australia, 15, 60, 171

banks
  bailout, 60–2, 97
  nationalisation, 62
  public sector, 3
bargaining groups, 89, 94
Beamten, 31, 34
benefits
  private sector employment, 87, 89, 100, 104
  public sector employment, 87, 89, 100, 104–5, 234
  voluntary sector, 159
  welfare, 44, 45, 46, 51, 63, 191

Best Value, 14, 57
Beveridge, 8, 10
Bichard, Sir Michael, 73
'Big Society', 48, 147, 162
Blair, Tony, 190
bonus systems, 89, 99, 115
Bradford & Bingley, 61
British Airways, 10
British Rail, 181, 195
British Telecom, 10
Brown, Gordon, 199
Building Schools for the Future (BSF), 58
bureaucracy
  civil service, 7
  commercialised, 167, 177, 181–3
  decentralisation, 26
  ideal type, 27–8, 233
  professional, 167, 177, 179–81
  traditional public sector, 167, 177–9
  Weberian, 6–7, 27
bureaucratic behaviour, 71
Burnham Committee, 7–8
Business Process Reengineering (BPR), 212, 219

Cabinet Office, 11
Cameron, David, 75
Care Commission, 156
care services, 72, 151
career structures
  assistants, 133, 135, 138, 141, 142
  career development, 89, 138, 141, 204
  consultants, 218
  employment relations, 27
  equal opportunity strategies, 133
  NHS, 100, 133, 139
  promotion criteria, 32
  US health sector, 139
cars, 92, 100
central government

consultants, 59–60, 210
decentralisation, 76–7
employee attitudes, 102
equality policies, 120–1
Europe, 28–9 (Table 2.1), 30, 35, 36, 39
expenditure, 45, 48, 59–60
motivation levels, 102
private sector organisations, 3
special employment status, 28–9 (Table 2.1)
target setting, 199
trade unions, 7, 191
Changing Children's Services fund, 153
charities, 73, 149, 230
chief executives, 12, 103–4, 173
childcare, 13, 101
Children Schools and Families, PFI/PPP, 58
choice, individual, 12, 15
Citizen's Charter, 12
civic culture, 32
civil servants, 67–8
civil service
  benchmarking exercise, 11
  bureaucracy, 6–7
  chief executives, 12
  equality policies, 110, 111, 114, 117, 120–1
  executive agencies, 11
  feminisation of workforce, 8
  number employed, 23
  pay decentralisation, 96
  pay negotiations, 92
  pay ratios, 104
  pay review body, 90
  privatisation, 10
  redundancy arrangements, 16
  reforms to reward systems, 105
  values, 73, 80
classroom assistants, *see* teaching assistants
Clegg, Professor Hugh, 89
coal, 8, 10, 109
Coalition Government
  assistants policy, 142–3

austerity measures, 231, 235–6
bank bailout policy, 63
consultants, 220–1
cuts, 8, 43, 63, 102, 205, 206
equality policies, 109, 118–20, 121
free schools, 79–80, 120, 230
localism agenda, 120, 122, 199
payment by results, 77–8
public sector pay policy, 98–9, 103–4
public sector pensions policy, 103
public sector policies, 16–17, 63–4, 74–80
shrinking the size of the state, 74–7
Spending Review, 43–4, 67, 75, 230
Total Place initiative, 78–9
trade union issues, 190, 206
voluntary sector policies, 162–3
COIN database, 213–14
collective agreements, 8, 29, 34, 95, 157, 195, 205
collective bargaining, 7, 29, 95–6 (Table 5.1), 197–8, 231
Commission for Racial Equality (CRE), 116
competitive tender, 10, 48, 210
Comprehensive Spending Review, *see* Spending Review
compulsory competitive tendering (CCT), 10, 23, 50, 57, 198
conditions of service, 89, 100, 104–5
Confederation of British Industry (CBI), 91
Conservative governments (1979–97)
  competitive tendering, 10, 14
  equality policies, 110–11, 121
  individualisation, 199
  marketisation, 12
  neoliberalism, 4, 229
  outsourcing public services, 147, 148, 150, 198
  public expenditure, 51, 230
  public sector pay policy, 88, 91–3, 104
  public sector reforms, 10–13, 23, 104, 195, 229
  target setting and monitoring, 15
  trade union policies, 11